ABOUT ISLAND PRESS

Island Press, a nonprofit organization, publishes, markets, and distributes the most advanced thinking on the conservation of our natural resources—books about soil, land, water, forests, wildlife, and hazardous and toxic wastes. These books are practical tools used by public officials, business and industry leaders, natural resoruce managers, and concerned citizens working to solve both local and global resource problems.

Founded in 1978, Island Press reorganized in 1984 to meet the increasing demand for substantive books on all resource-related issues. Island Press publishes and distributes under its own imprint and offers these services to other nonprofit organizations.

Support for Island Press is provided by The Geraldine R. Dodge Foundation, The Energy Foundation, The Charles Engelhard Foundation, The Ford Foundation, Glen Eagles Foundation, The George Gund Foundation, William and Flora Hewlett Foundation, The James Irvine Foundation, The John D. and Catherine T. MacArthur Foundation, The Andrew W. Mellon Foundation, The Joyce Mertz-Gilmore Foundation, The New-Land Foundation, The Pew Charitable Trusts, The Rockefeller Brothers Fund, The Tides Foundation, and individual donors.

ABOUT THE CENTER FOR INTERNATIONAL ENVIRONMENTAL LAW

The Center for International Environmental Law (CIEL) was founded in Washington, D.C. in 1989 to bring the energy and experience of the public interest environmental law movement in the United States to the critical task of strengthening and developing international and comparative environmental law, policy, and management throughout the world. CIEL's goals are to incorporate fundamental principles of ecology and democracy into international law, to strengthen national environmental law systems and public interest movements throughout the world, to educate and train public-interest-minded environmental lawyers, and to improve the effectiveness of law in solving environmental problems. CIEL provides legal assistance in both international and comparative environmental law, including independent research, advice and advocacy, and education and training.

CIEL's Trade and Environment Program focuses on providing greater public participation, accountability, and transparency in domestic and international trade decision making. CIEL also provides legal counsel and policy support to other nongovernmental organizations, national, state, and local governments, congressional members and their staffs, and international organizations as they attempt to understand and address the interplay of trade and the environment. Financial support for CIEL's Trade and Environment Program is provided by The Pew Charitable Trusts, the Jessie Smith Noyes Foundation, The Moriah Fund, The Max and Anna Levinson Foundation, the W. Alton Jones Foundation, the Organization for Economic Cooperation and Development, the United Nations Environment Programme, and the U.S. Environmental Protection Agency.

TRADE AND
THE ENVIRONMENT

TRADE AND
THE ENVIRONMENT
LAW, ECONOMICS,
AND POLICY

Edited by
**Durwood Zaelke, Paul Orbuch,
and Robert F. Housman**

CENTER FOR INTERNATIONAL ENVIRONMENTAL LAW

ISLAND PRESS

Washington, D.C. o *Covelo, California*

ISLAND PRESS is a trademark of The Center for Resource Economics.

Library of Congress Cataloging-in-Publication Data

Trade and the environment : law, economics, and policy / edited by
    Durwood Zaelke, Paul Orbuch, and Robert F. Housman.
        p.   cm.
    Includes bibliographical references and index.
    ISBN 1-55963-267-4 (cloth : acid-free paper) :   -- ISBN
1-55963-268-2 (pbk. : acid-free paper) :
        1. International trade--Environmental aspects. 2. Sustainable
development. 3. Commercial policy. 4. Environmental policy.
I. Zaelke, Durwood. II. Orbuch, Paul. III. Housman, Robert F.
HF1379.T72   1993
363.7--dc20   93-37811
                                                            CIP

Printed on recycled, acid-free paper

Manufactured in the United States of America

10 9 8 7 6 5 4 3 2 1

Contents

Acknowledgments   xv

Introduction   xi
   Durwood Zaelke, Paul Orbuch, Robert F. Housman

PART I
TRADE AND ENVIRONMENT BACKGROUND

1. A Guide to Trade and the Environment   3
    Tom Wathen

2. The Trade and Environment Nexus: What is New Since '72?   23
    Charles S. Pearson

3. The International Trade Regime and the Municipal
    Law of Federal States: How Close a Fit?   33
    David A. Wirth

4. Integrating Trade and Environment Policy Making:
    First Steps in the North American Free Trade Agreement   45
    Daniel C. Esty

5. Managing Through Prices, Managing Despite Prices   57
    Hal Kane

PART II
GLOBAL AND REGIONAL PERSPECTIVES

6. An Action Agenda for Trade Policy Reform to Support
    Sustainable Development: A United Nations Conference
    on Environment and Development Follow-Up   71
    Charles Arden-Clarke

Contents

7. The Organization for Economic Cooperation and
    Development and the Re-emergence of the
    Trade and Environment Debate   83
    Candice Stevens

8. A European Perspective on Trade and the Environment   93
    Konrad von Moltke

9. Free Trade and Environmental Enhancement:
    Are They Compatible in the Americas?   109
    Ambler H. Moss, Jr.

10. A Business Perspective on Trade and the Environment   121
    Robert J. Morris

11. Foreign Direct Investment and Environmental
    Protection in the Third World   133
    Norman A. Bailey

PART III
TRADE AND ENVIRONMENT CONFLICTS

12. Problems with Free Trade:
    Neoclassical and Steady-State Perspectives   147
    Herman E. Daly

13. Trade and the Environment: The False Conflict?   159
    Jagdish Bhagwati

14. Why Environmentalists Are Angry about the
    North American Free Trade Agreement   191
    John Audley

15. The United States Government, Public Participation,
    and Trade and Environment   203
    Jan C. McAlpine and Pat LeDonne

Contents

PART IV
RECONCILING TRADE AND THE ENVIRONMENT

16. World Trade Rules and Environmental Policies:
    Congruence or Conflict?   219
    John H. Jackson

17. Complementarities between Trade and
    Environment Policies   237
    Robert Repetto

18. Environmental Strategies for Agricultural Trade   247
    Justin R. Ward

19. Environmental Policy and Trade Agreements:
    The New Nexus   257
    Senator Max Baucus

20. Environmental Harmonization and Trade Policy   267
    Steve Charnovitz

Afterword   287
    Ambassador Michael Smith

Selected Sources and References   295

Index   299

Contributors   313

Acknowledgments

The editors would like to sincerely thank the W. Alton Jones Foundation, who made this book possible with their generous grant, and Island Press for publishing *Trade and the Environment* on an expedited schedule. We would like to thank Tom Louderback, who took on the onerous task of overseeing the entire editing and manuscript production process with unwavering enthusiasm, often in the face of adversity. David Hunter joined the project toward the end, but his advice made the book immeasurably better. Of course, we would not have this book without the contributing authors. We appreciate their work, patience, and good humor throughout the publication process.

A number of other people worked extensively on the book whose names do not appear on the spine or the list of authors. Theresa Peters, Katherine Ray, and Jessica Seacor put in countless hours reviewing and editing chapters with little thanks beyond our praises. Tad Ferris, Mary Coleman Ragsdale, Catlan Thorne, Keith Brown, Michelle Ratcliff, and Eric Gould also contributed their efforts. We also send a heartfelt thanks to Hal Kane, whose expertise and advice were invaluable. Without the tireless assistance of these individuals, it is unlikely that you would have this book before you now. Though many assisted us in our efforts to make a perfect manuscript, any errors are ultimately the fault of the editors.

August 1, 1993
Washington, D.C.
D.Z.
P.O.
R.H.

Introduction

In roughly 1990, trade and environment sprung with little warning to the forefront of public policy debate. Denmark incensed Germany with its bottle law, Mexico outraged U.S. citizens with its challenge to one of America's most revered environmental laws, and Germany upset almost every other nation with its packaging law. It seemed that virtually everyone, free traders and environmentalists alike, was mad at something having to do with trade and environment. The trade and environment debate became the hot issue, and legions of experts set about the reconciliation of these two vital spheres of public policy.

Unfortunately, as this book goes to press little has changed. Business continues to fret over a host of new waste reduction and packaging laws, like those of Germany and Denmark, and U.S. unilateral environmental protections still raise hackles around the world. Worse yet, we still are without answers to the most basic issues. For instance, when can a country restrict trade for an environmental end without breaking its trade obligations? Nearly three years into the trade and environment debate, our list of issues is still growing, but our list of answers remains wanting. Paraphrasing Einstein, as our circle of light has expanded, so to has our circle of darkness around it.

If any bright spot of progress exists, it is at the regional level. Although the North American Free Trade Agreement (NAFTA) and its side environmental agreement are not without environmental flaws, the NAFTA package does move several steps forward in the trade and environment area. For example, despite its significant limitations, the Commission for Environmental Cooperation being formed under the NAFTA side environmental agreement is the first serious step ever taken toward dealing with the environmental impacts of trade at the international level. Even with this and other gains, NAFTA is not by any stretch of the imagination a model for reconciling all trade and environment issues. For example, NAFTA's dispute resolution processes, the processes by which environmental, health, and safety protections will be judged, fall far short of providing the public with an effective means of participating in trade challenges to environmental, health, and safety standards.

That NAFTA does not successfully reconcile all our trade and environment problems, even at the regional level, should not be a surprise. The trade and environment debate is a complex one. Both trade and environmental policies are vital to our societies. Trade is widely viewed as a tool of both prosperity and security. Trade has played a major role in world progress, bringing pasta to Italy, silk to France, Columbus to the Americas, polio vaccine to the world, and Ben & Jerry's ice cream to Moscow. Trade has also changed over time. The word *trade* now encompasses a host of things that never saw the hold of a Dutch East Indies Company ship—intellectual property and antitrust protections to name but two.

On the other hand, we recognize that environmental, health, and safety protections also secure our prosperity and security. Environmental, health, and safety laws ensure that the water we drink is clean, the food we eat is pure, and the air we breathe is safe. They also ensure the continued viabil-ity of our environment. This means that there will be rainforests and wetlands for our grandchildren and their progeny. It also means that the natural resources upon which economic activities are ultimately dependent, will continue to be available for our beneficial use—it would after all be difficult to trade in oak tables if we had harvested the last oak tree. Like the terms of trade, environmental protections are also evolving. Today, environmentalism addresses not just what comes out of a factory's smokestack, it encompasses all facets of a product's manufacture, use, and disposal.

The trade and environment debate is further complicated because there are few absolutes. At times, barriers to trade may serve the goal of environmental protection—for example, a ban on trade in endangered species—at other times they undercut environmental goals—for example, subsidies for chemical intensive, single crop agricultural production.

Despite the complexities of the interrelationship between trade and environment, our continuing failure to define the terms of that interrelationship is cause for concern. The trade and environment debate is our first real opportunity to implement environmentally sound and sustainable development. Through procrastination and trepidation we have yet to realize the benefits that stand to be gained through the successful reconciliation of these two policy spheres. As Henry Kissinger once said, "competing pressures tempt one to believe that an issue deferred is a problem avoided; more often it is a crisis invented."

The potential for crisis here is real from both a trade and an environmental perspective. Far from a level playing field, the widely divergent systems of environmental laws, rules, and regulations around the globe can create an unnavigable obstacle course for trade. Without some degree of mutually acceptable discipline, haphazard environmental protections are ripe for protectionist picking.

From an environmental perspective, trade institutions remain in many instances aloof, if not openly hostile, to environmentalists and environmental issues. For example, within the General Agreement on Tariffs and Trade (GATT), debate continues over whether the 117 member countries of the Montreal Protocol on Substances that Deplete the Ozone Layer, a membership larger than that of GATT, acted contrary to their trade obligations when they agreed to the use of trade sanctions. Because trade is one of the very few means of affecting the behavior of countries, it can be a powerful tool for environmental ends. However, if a country's environmental protection is found to be an unjustifiable trade barrier by GATT's terms, than the force of trade suasion can be a real threat to the environmental standard.

The crisis is nearer than most would prefer. The list of trade challenges to environmental protections continues to grow, as does the list of potential environmental trade barriers.

Bearing Mr. Kissinger's advice in mind, this book attempts to tackle trade and environment issues head on. First, it clarifies and defines the terms and history of the debate. Then it provides insights as to how trade and environment issues may be reconciled.

The chapters were selected by the Center for International Environmental Law because each and every one represents a critical aspect in the trade and environment debate. The authors were similarly selected because they are all leading authorities with unique perspectives and insights into these critical issues. The editors are confident that this book will play a vital role in the reconciliation of trade and environment.

The Editors

PART I

Trade and Environment Background

1

A Guide to
Trade and the Environment

Tom Wathen[1]

INTRODUCTION

When trade representatives from ninety nations gathered in Punta del Este, Uruguay, in 1986 to renegotiate the General Agreement on Tariffs and Trade (GATT), only a few individuals understood how important these talks would become for environmental protection in the United States and around the world. The connection became apparent five years later. On August 16, 1991 a three-member panel of GATT trade arbitrators ruled that the embargo provisions of the U.S. Marine Mammal Protection Act (MMPA) are an unfair trade barrier. MMPA bans the sale of tuna in the United States from countries like Mexico, whose fishermen kill more dolphins than U.S. standards allow.

The tuna-dolphin ruling illustrates how the growing movement to promote free trade can clash with environmental preservation. In an attempt to remove all possible barriers to free trade, free trade advocates want to "harmonize" environmental regulations to international standards. They also want to remove trade sanctions from environmental laws and treaties, such as the Montreal Protocol on Substances that Deplete the Ozone Layer (Montreal Protocol).

The ensuing struggle will invade all policy areas of domestic and international environmental protection. New changes in GATT and the formation of the North American Free Trade Agreement (NAFTA) could dictate U.S. environmental regulation of forest harvesting, wildlife trading, marine fishing, agriculture, pesticides, energy use, hazardous waste shipments, toxic chemicals, recycling, biotechnology, and food safety.

3

The nexus between free trade and environmental protection is complicated, involving a rich interplay between international and national law, national sovereignty, market economics, and sustainable development. In fact, trade policy is becoming the forum for deciding whether the global economy will be based on the ethics of sustainable development or on laissez-faire market principles.

This chapter provides a basic overview of international trade, explains how environmental protection is related to trade, and describes the proposals made in the current GATT trade talks that could weaken U.S. environmental laws.

DIFFERING NATIONAL APPROACHES TO INTERNATIONAL TRADE

International trade refers to the buying and selling of goods across national borders. As with other border issues, like immigration, rules for international trade are set by each national government. There are three broad approaches to international trade: protectionism, free trade, and managed trade.

PROTECTIONISM

The goal of protectionism is to protect domestic industries from foreign competition. Protectionism was the dominant trade policy in the United States and the rest of the world until the 1930s. Congress restricted imports by imposing tariff surcharges averaging 60 percent of the cost of the product, so that foreign goods would be more expensive than comparable domestic products. High tariffs are still used for some goods, but overall tariffs are currently much lower, averaging 5 percent. Protectionism can also take the form of quotas on the amount of imported goods, such as most countries have set for textiles. It may also take the form of outright bans on certain imports, such as the Japanese ban on rice imports. It also may take the form of a request for voluntary import restraints, which the United States has made for Japanese cars.

Restricting foreign imports protects domestic industries, but it may cause other countries to retaliate. Because most products, like textiles, are not unique, a country that chooses protectionism risks losing access to foreign markets. A protectionist country may still be able to export goods that are scarce or unique, but overall it may be confined to a self-contained, domestic economy. For example, the fiercely protectionist former Soviet Union was able to export diamonds, even as the rest of its economy remained isolated. Moreover, protectionist policies raise the costs of goods to domestic consumers by limiting price competition.

FREE TRADE

Free trade means the unlimited exchange of commerce between buyers and sellers across national borders. Although free trade is often associated with deregulation, it does not necessarily require the elimination of product standards, worker protection rules, or environmental regulations. Instead, free trade seeks to assure that a country's worker, consumer, and environmental regulations are not administered in a way that unfairly discriminates against foreign companies.

The heart of the free trade concept is an economic principle known as comparative advantage. The principle of comparative advantage suggests that a country should specialize in those goods it produces most efficiently and trade with other countries for the goods they produce the most efficiently, even if both countries can produce comparable goods at home. This specialization theoretically enhances the overall level of economic activity in all trading nations. Free trade, based on comparative advantage, thus makes all countries ultimately stronger than they would be if their economies were isolated.

Beyond its economic advantages, free trade has been promoted as a way to achieve international political stability by fostering cooperation and interdependence among nations. Proponents claim that interdependence lessens the likelihood of war by promoting intercultural understanding and by increasing the potential economic loss from conflict. The European Common Market, for example, was forged in part to solidify relations among the warring nations of Western Europe.

MANAGED TRADE

If protectionism and free trade are opposite ideals, then managed trade is somewhere in between. Governments that employ this practice allow extensive international trade, but seek to intervene through tariffs, subsidies, and other policies to make domestic products more attractive at home, to nurture new industries, and to stimulate domestic research and development. Managed trade describes U.S. efforts to set numerical targets for Japanese imports of designated U.S. goods like super computers and automobile parts.

INTERNATIONAL TRADING AGREEMENTS AND INSTITUTIONS

While the rules of international trade are determined by each country, they are often set within the parameters of international agreements. Currently, the international trading system is governed by a patchwork of multilateral, regional, and bilateral trade agreements. Additionally, a number of international institutions have important roles in coordinating trade policies among groups of nations.

GENERAL AGREEMENT ON TARIFFS AND TRADE

GATT is the major multilateral agreement on trade rules, providing a framework for international trade policy and a forum for trade disputes. Currently, over one hundred countries have signed the agreement, including former and current communist countries. Another thirty countries, mostly developing countries, abide by the rules but are not formal Contracting Parties.

GATT primarily seeks to encourage lower tariffs on raw materials and manufactured goods. Since the agreement was first struck in 1948, Contracting Parties have negotiated the average tariff down from 40 to 5 percent. However, a large amount of world trade is exempted from GATT's provisions. For example, agricultural commodities and services like banking and insurance are excluded. The current round of GATT negotiations, known as the Uruguay Round, has focused on expanding GATT to cover more goods, as well as services, and to tackle more non-tariff barriers to trade.

ORGANIZATION FOR ECONOMIC COOPERATION AND DEVELOPMENT

The Organization for Economic Cooperation and Development (OECD) is a forum for industrialized countries to coordinate monetary, trade, and economic development policies for themselves and the rest of the world.

Formed in 1960, OECD has twenty-four member countries, including most of Western Europe, the United States, Japan, Australia, Canada, Turkey, and Iceland. OECD establishes joint economic policies that the world's most powerful trading nations bring to the table in GATT negotiations. Finance ministers attend OECD meetings, while trade representatives attend GATT meetings.

OECD has recently turned its attention to trade and environment issues. In 1989 OECD ministers declared that members should consider environmental issues when formulating trade policies. In 1991 OECD issued a report that outlined the need to understand further the relationship between trade and the environment. OECD is continuing to develop principles in this area.

UNITED NATIONS CONFERENCE ON TRADE AND DEVELOPMENT

The United Nations Conference on Trade and Development (UNCTAD) is an official body of the United Nations (UN) that was formed in 1964 at the insistence of developing countries seeking an alternative to GATT. UNCTAD became a permanent organ of the UN in 1974, but lost much of its impetus when GATT subsequently embraced special provisions for developing countries. UNCTAD has no formal power over trade. Rather, UNCTAD convenes a conference every four years to exchange views on trade between countries that have different levels of development or different economic systems. In keeping with its developing country orientation, UNCTAD focuses on policies providing trade preferences for developing countries and on commodity agreements.

EUROPEAN COMMUNITY

The European Community (EC) is the largest and most advanced regional trade zone in the world. The EC is made up of twelve countries: France, Germany, England, Italy, Spain, Portugal, Belgium, Ireland, the Netherlands, Luxembourg, Greece, and Denmark. Some other European and Scandinavian countries and dozens of former European colonies enjoy special status with the EC. The economic integration of the EC is based on free trade in many goods and services and may eventually lead to a common currency. A number of government functions have also been integrated and some policy areas are closely coordinated by the members.

NORTH AMERICAN FREE TRADE AGREEMENT

To pressure other countries to renegotiate GATT, and in response to the challenge posed by an economically integrated EC, the Reagan, Bush, and now Clinton administrations have pursued free trade agreements with Canada and Mexico. A free trade agreement with Canada, known as the U.S.-Canada Free Trade Agreement, went into effect in 1989. In 1990 the United States and Mexico began talks on a similar agreement.

In 1991 these talks metamorphosed into a three-way negotiation among the United States, Canada, and Mexico. NAFTA does not aim for the level of political and economic integration found in the EC. Rather, NAFTA would be limited to a free exchange of products, commodities, services, and investments—along the lines of the proposals the United States has made to expand world trade through a more powerful GATT.

ENTERPRISE FOR THE AMERICAS INITIATIVE

In 1990 President Bush formally announced the goal of establishing "a hemispheric free trade zone from Alaska to Argentina." To this end, President Bush announced his Enterprise for the Americas Initiative, through which the United States offers market access, financial and technical resources, and debt reduction opportunities to Latin American and Caribbean nations. In return, these countries promise to liberalize their trade and investment regimes, to maintain economic policies conducive to investment and competition, and to manage their international debt obligations. As of mid-1993, framework agreements in both the trade and investment area and in debt reduction have been negotiated with Bolivia, Chile, and Jamaica. Numerous other nations of the region have reached agreement with the United States in one of these areas or have begun preliminary negotiations.

OTHER REGIONAL AGREEMENTS

Throughout the world there are regional agreements that serve as fora for cooperation, but fall short of the integration envisioned by either the EC or NAFTA. In all, there are nearly sixty regional free trade zones, common custom unions, or regional trade pacts. Examples include the Association of Southeast Asian Nations (ASEAN), a forum for the emerging economies of Southeast Asia, and the MERCOSUR, a pact among Argentina, Brazil, Paraguay, and Uruguay.

U.S. BILATERAL AGREEMENTS

Although multilateral and regional trade agreements have increased in influence, the vast majority of trade is still governed by agreements between two countries. A myriad of tariffs,[2] unilateral quotas, and other agreements control trade between the United States and every other country. Sometimes, as with Israel, Canada, and Mexico, a broad free trade agreement is negotiated that aims to phase out these controls. More often, a narrower agreement is struck, freeing certain goods from import controls.

In general, bilateral trade agreements either cover trade that does not fall under GATT, or are designed to evade GATT provisions. For example, even though Japan is a member of GATT, the United States asked the Japanese to limit automobile imports into the U.S. market "voluntarily." This "voluntary export restraint" allows the United States to sidestep GATT rules on quotas.

The principles of free trade, and agreements that embody them, often conflict with international and domestic efforts to protect the environment. This chapter will now explore these conflicts, especially with respect to GATT, and examine the possibilities for reconciling these disparate fields.

CONFLICTS BETWEEN TRADE AND THE ENVIRONMENT

In the past, neither environmental regulation nor international trade policies was sufficiently developed worldwide to cause many direct clashes. As recently as January 1991, for example, OECD published a report on trade and the environment that could not identify any significant distortions in trade caused by current environmental policies. Nonetheless, rapid developments in both areas are bringing the two issues into collision.

WHY FREE TRADE ADVOCATES FEAR ENVIRONMENTAL REGULATION

Free trade advocates fear that stronger measures to protect the environment will stifle open business competition between nations. For example, companies from developing countries may not have the technology or expertise to meet advanced environmental standards in developed countries and may lose access to those markets. Moreover, free trade advocates maintain that environmental protection standards are often designed or administered in a way that protects domestic industries. State laws restricting the export of raw logs from the U.S. Pacific Northwest illustrate this point. The restrictions are deliberately formulated to ensure that trees from these forests are processed by U.S. mills.

Such concerns have led free trade partisans to advocate the harmonization of local, state, and national environmental regulations throughout the world. If all countries have the same environmental regulations, they argue, then foreign companies will not be at a disadvantage when competing with domestic companies. In theory, the degree of environmental regulation is not important, so long as there is a "level playing field."

In practice, however, a titanic struggle will be waged to determine the stringency of harmonized international standards. The same legions of corporate lobbyists who advocate minimal environmental regulation within the United States can be expected to lobby aggressively for low international environmental standards. Developing countries will also be lobbying for low environmental standards. If the standards are set too high, developing companies may be unable to afford appropriate technology and be permanently excluded from markets, even in their own countries. Lower standards, on the other hand, may unacceptably reduce environmental protection.

WHY ENVIRONMENTALISTS FEAR FREE TRADE

Before learning about GATT, environmentalists only thought of trade when pushing for import restrictions against environmentally damaging products or for sanctions to enforce international environmental agreements. Now, environmental and citizen groups worry that a deregulated, free trade system will undercut existing environmental protection laws. As companies seek to reduce production costs, many industries may shift production to countries with weak environmental laws or lax enforcement.

The flight of U.S. industries to the U.S.-Mexico border illustrates this danger. Under a U.S.-Mexico agreement, American-owned factories operating just within the Mexican border, so-called *maquiladoras*, can import U.S. components duty-free into Mexico, then export the finished products back to the United States with a tariff imposed only on the value added through the assembly in Mexico. The flight of U.S. companies south of the border has been exacerbated by differences in the two nations' systems of environmental protection. Many U.S. companies have moved to Mexico, in part, to avoid the costs of U.S. regulations on the use, transportation, and disposal of toxic waste.

Furthermore, the free trade principle of comparative advantage pushes an economy toward specialization. Environmentalists fear that increased specialization will cause developing countries to base their economies on export commodities, like timber, or on certain agricultural crops, like bananas or coffee, which can be environmentally damaging. Moreover, some environmentalists believe that intensive specialization undermines efforts to promote diversified, community-based economies that are less resource-intensive and more in harmony with local ecological constraints.

AN INTRODUCTION TO GATT

Of all the multilateral and bilateral trade agreements now being negotiated, the Uruguay Round negotiations to expand GATT will have the greatest impact on environmental protection. Not only will GATT affect trade among its signatories, it could also compel each Contracting Party to make sweeping changes in their own environmental protection laws. To understand the complexities of the Uruguay Round, it is useful to examine GATT in depth.

GATT PROVISIONS

GATT contains thirty-eight separate articles, covering everything from tariffs to customs duties to state-owned enterprises. The breadth of the agreement reflects the core GATT principle that international trade should be conducted through multilateral, rather than bilateral, rules. Despite its complexity, GATT can be reduced to three basic elements: tariff reduction, non-discrimination, and disclosure of non-tariff barriers.

GATT members agree to binding maximum tariff schedules for each import product or raw commodity category. Then, countries may agree to lower the schedules in a reciprocal fashion. For example, if the United States lowers tariffs for a category of Japanese products, then the Japanese must lower tariffs on an equivalent amount of U.S. products. It is hoped that this reciprocal arrangement will drive tariffs down over time. Maximum tariff schedules are renegotiated, and often lowered, during each round of GATT negotiations.

A country signing GATT grants other Contracting Parties most-favored-nation status and agrees not to discriminate, favorably or unfavorably, among countries in controlling imports and exports. GATT also requires its member countries to treat foreign goods from GATT Contracting Parties in the same way they treat domestic goods, once those goods have entered the country. This is known as affording the foreign goods "national treatment," and it applies to taxes and product regulations.

GATT also requires all "non-tariff" barriers to be made "transparent" enough so that trading partners can readily differentiate between actions that meet legitimate national concerns and actions that are merely protectionist. Non-trade barriers include many government efforts to discourage imports—for example, import quotas, complicated customs regulations, discrimination against foreign products when setting domestic taxes, or restrictions on the purchase of foreign goods in government procurement programs. Non-trade barriers also may include a country's use of subsidies to assist industries at home or to stimulate their exports.

ENFORCEMENT OF GATT

There are two ways GATT is enforced. If a domestic company believes that a foreign company is violating GATT in the domestic market, then the company can ask the home government to impose trade sanctions on goods entering the home market. If a domestic company believes that its foreign sales are being reduced because of GATT violations, the company can ask its government to lodge a formal complaint with the GATT Secretariat. GATT's formal complaint process follows a distinct procedure.

First, the two disputing countries conduct diplomatic negotiations to attempt to resolve the dispute. If they cannot resolve the matter, a "dispute panel" is appointed to conduct a hearing. The dispute panel's ruling is important, but it has no legal force. Instead, the panel ruling is a recommendation to the full GATT membership. The membership must agree by consensus to uphold the ruling, meaning that the country that lost the ruling can veto the decision. Despite such weak enforcement provisions, GATT panel rulings are frequently upheld. Mutual dependency provides a powerful incentive to comply.

DEVELOPMENT OF THE URUGUAY ROUND

The current Uruguay Round is motivated by two paradoxical impulses— fear of retreat and thirst for expansion. Free trade advocates fear that GATT is being undermined by increasingly bold efforts by governments to manage trade. Articles in business magazines and journals routinely speculate about whether GATT can be saved. *The Economist*, for one, believes that if the Uruguay Round fails, then GATT is dead and only managed trade remains. While many fear GATT's demise, Uruguay Round negotiators are striving to expand greatly the agreement's coverage and authority. The talks aim to bring all goods and services under the purview of GATT, remove barriers to foreign investment, protect intellectual property rights, and set up a more powerful enforcement mechanism. Perhaps because of the underlying paradox, the Uruguay Round is stalled and the negotiators have become impatient for positive action.

Although the first GATT agreement required no congressional approval, subsequent rounds have required revisions in U.S. laws to conform to new provisions. In 1974 Congress adopted a procedure for approving trade legislation known as "fast track," which means that Congress agrees to vote on legislation submitted by the president within sixty days, with no amendments allowed.

On March 1, 1991 the Bush administration notified Congress of its intention to keep GATT on the fast track for another two years. The administration also included NAFTA in the fast track notification. In the end, Congress narrowly agreed to renew fast track authorization until June 1, 1993. In June 1993 Congress approved fast track reauthorization for the Uruguay Round until December 15, 1993.

ENVIRONMENTAL IMPACT OF GATT AFTER THE URUGUAY ROUND

Historically, GATT has viewed environmental protection only in terms of barriers to trade. Written in 1948, GATT does not mention the word *environment* anywhere in its text. Nonetheless, GATT allows a country to restrict imports if it is "necessary to protect human, animal or plant life or health" or relates to "the conservation of exhaustible resources." However, restrictions are not allowed if they constitute "unjustifiable" discrimination against foreign competitors or are not done in conjunction with similar restrictions on domestic production and consumption.

Despite this language, GATT negotiators have resisted the idea that trade policy should be fashioned to promote environmental protection. When Sweden, Switzerland, and Austria proposed amending GATT during the Uruguay Round to attempt to protect the environment, developing countries generally opposed the amendment.

Formulated under the leadership of the former Director General of GATT, Arthur Dunkel, the latest Uruguay Round draft agreement of GATT is known as the Dunkel draft. Among other things, the Dunkel draft aims to control environmental regulation in GATT member countries by bringing domestic and international environmental regulation in line with GATT trading principles.

This effort is based on three broad principles. The two GATT principles that already have the greatest impact on environmental regulation are the following:

Multilateralism - Actions affecting trade between countries must be taken under widely accepted international rules.

Non-discrimination - All trading partners should be treated equally and foreign companies should have the same rights as domestic concerns.

The Uruguay Round would add a third principle to environmental regulation:

Harmonization - In order to follow the principles of multilateralism and non-discrimination, domestic business regulations should not exceed international standards.

The Uruguay Round negotiators are also considering a new Multilateral Trade Organization (MTO) to take the place of the current GATT agreement. This expansion of power could allow the MTO to challenge American environmental laws in U.S. courts. The MTO may also be able to change international trade rules affecting the environment more easily than is allowed by the current process for negotiating changes to GATT.

Reducing Controls on Environmentally Damaging Imports and Exports

As noted, the 1992 GATT tuna-dolphin panel interpreted the current GATT agreement to prohibit the United States from applying the MMPA to Mexican tuna fishing boats operating outside of U.S. territory. The panel stated that "extraterritorial" enforcement is not legitimate under GATT's principle of multilateralism. The ruling also held that laws regulating the process by which a product is harvested or produced are harmful to free trade because they can be used to discriminate against foreign companies.

In its report on trade and the environment, the GATT Secretariat indicated that GATT would have to change to accommodate laws like the MMPA. The Dunkel draft, however, does not make any such change. Instead, the draft has retained the language that the tuna-dolphin panel relied on in rendering its decision. The logic of the tuna-dolphin ruling could also easily compromise the Endangered Species Act, the African Elephant Conservation Act, the Migratory Bird Act, and a host of other U.S. environmental laws that control imports.

The existing GATT also limits restrictions on exports destined for the territory of any other GATT member country. Exceptions can be made for preserving natural resources, but only if domestic companies are also denied access to these resources. To the degree that the Uruguay Round successfully increases the authority of GATT, this provision could begin undermining efforts to conserve energy-producing resources and to stop exports of raw logs and hazardous waste.

Harmonizing Environmental Regulation of Business

The proposed changes in GATT, as proposed in the Dunkel draft, also mandate the use of international standards for regulating industrial and agricultural products where such international standards exist or are imminent. Where such standards do not exist, the Dunkel draft calls for developing them.

The Dunkel draft classifies environmental standards as "Technical Barriers to Trade." These can include standards on the product itself or on the process by which a product is grown, harvested, manufactured, or shipped. "Product" standards include such regulations as airbags in automobiles, child-proof drug packaging, and asbestos-free hair dryers. "Process" standards include a wide range of environmental, worker safety, and human rights regulations such as waste water discharge standards or child labor laws.

Under the terms of the Dunkel draft, all governmental and nongovernmental bodies that set standards will be required to abide by the "Code of Good Practice for the Preparation, Adoption and Application of Standards," which states that national standards must be based on international norms. An exception is made where the international standards will be "ineffective" or "inappropriate," or where the national standards are used to pursue "protection of human health or safety, animal or plant life or health, or the environment."

However, any exceptions to international standards must be the least trade-restrictive standard possible and must be supported by "available scientific and technical information." The terms scientific and technical are not defined, but some environmentalists fear that this language will be used to stop innovative or precautionary domestic environmental standards.

RISK ASSESSMENT CRITERIA

Additionally, the Dunkel draft seeks to establish universal risk assessment criteria in setting pesticide residue levels and other health standards found in environmental laws. The proposed criteria would require that when setting standards, the risks to human health be offset by balancing the economic benefits of the harmful activity. Such a balancing is already found in the Federal Insecticide, Fungicide, and Rodenticide Act (FIFRA), the U.S. pesticide law that has long been criticized by environmentalists for being too weak.

Although it is used in FIFRA, this balancing approach differs from the approach taken in other U.S. laws, which base their standards primarily on human health effects. The Delaney Clause of the Food and Drug Act, for example, requires the Food and Drug Administration to prohibit food additives and pesticide residue levels that pose any risk of cancer.

OVERRULING STATE AND LOCAL ENVIRONMENTAL LAWS

The proposed changes to GATT require each country to bring the laws of their sub-national governments into line with international standards. This could be read as requiring the U.S. government to pass legislation overriding any state or local law that is more severe than international standards. However, because of constitutional and political concerns, it is more likely that this GATT language will compel Congress to insert specific preemption clauses into a vast array of environmental statutes that now allow state and local governments to exceed federal standards.

OVERRULING INTERNATIONAL ENVIRONMENTAL AGREEMENTS

Increasingly, international environmental treaties, like the Montreal Protocol and the Convention on International Trade in Endangered Species of Wild Fauna and Flora (CITES), are using trade sanctions as a means of ensuring compliance. Uruguay Round negotiators seek to subject any environmental regulation that impacts on trade to the approval of the GATT Council, a sub-body of GATT's Contracting Parties. At least twenty-four international environmental agreements could then require waivers from a majority of the world's trade ministers to ensure the validity of their trade sanction provisions.

PROHIBITING GOVERNMENT SUBSIDIES IN ENVIRONMENTAL PROGRAMS

Currently, the subsidy restriction under GATT is sweeping. If a government program provides funds for cleaning up pollution or preserving natural resources, those funds can be challenged under GATT as an unfair trade subsidy if the program benefits the exports of domestic companies that then cause "injury" to the domestic industry in the importing country. The Dunkel draft makes no attempt to exempt environmental programs from GATT subsidy restrictions. On the other hand, strict application of the prohibition on subsidies will also eliminate many environmentally damaging subsidies.

RECONCILING ENVIRONMENT AND TRADE

Environmentalists and free trade advocates alike are discovering the intricate connections between international trade rules and environmental protection. Reconciliation of environmental protection and trade policy will require considerable efforts on many policy fronts. Before these efforts can be successful, however, advancements must be made in three underlying areas, outlined below.

IDENTIFYING CONDITIONS WHEN INCREASED TRADE IS GOOD FOR THE ENVIRONMENT

Free trade advocates contend that increased trade will enhance global economic development sufficiently to fund improved environmental protection in developing countries. For example, a country's new wealth might be used to pay for sewage treatment or smokestack scrubbers. Proponents of free trade also claim that open markets will lead to more efficient use of natural resources by utilizing economies of scale, penalizing overproduction, and eliminating subsidies. They point to subsidized agriculture in the United States and Europe that leads to overproduction, which increases soil erosion and pesticide pollution.

Despite the efficiency claims, environmentalists remain unconvinced that free trade will somehow naturally result in greater environmental protection. On many levels, free trade without sound sustainable development policies can hurt the environment. A 1991 report commissioned by the Austrian government—one of the few studies to address the impact of free trade on the environment—found that increased trade will harm the environment if it increases consumption of goods made from nonrenewable resources or increases manufacturing processes that pollute. Moreover, increased transportation of goods across long distances will mean more oil consumption and more pollution. Even free trade advocates acknowledge that the environmental benefits of free trade will be realized only if environmental costs are "internalized" in the price of products through process standards, pollution taxes, or pollution permit schemes. If trade advocates are to be successful in softening environmental critics, they must develop clearer policies on internalizing environmental costs and more tangible demonstrations of free trade's benefits to environmental protection.

HARMONIZING INTERNATIONAL AND
NATIONAL ENVIRONMENTAL REGULATIONS

As noted earlier, the move toward harmonized standards is one of the major challenges by GATT to environmental protection. Traditionally, international environmental agreements have been seen as supplements to domestic environmental protection efforts. In this way, these agreements constitute something of an international "floor" for environmental regulation. The interplay between CITES and the U.S. Endangered Species Act illustrates this point. CITES requires each country to restrict the imports and exports of endangered species. The U.S. has gone further, by requiring that the habitat of endangered species also be protected.

The "harmonization" principle embraced in the Dunkel draft is seen by environmentalists as flipping the international environmental regulations upside down—turning them from a floor to a ceiling. The Dunkel draft would require each country to adopt international environmental standards as their own, precluding more stringent domestic regulations.

Other approaches are possible. For example, the European Free Trade Association (EFTA), led by Austria, has urged GATT to adopt an environmental code that would serve as a floor rather than a ceiling. In their draft report, the Austrian researchers maintained that countries with high environmental production standards should be allowed to charge compensatory fees on imports from countries with low standards. Harmonization, they argue, should mean setting minimum standards. Subsidies that are fairly applied for specific domestic environmental and conservation objectives should be free from GATT challenge. Finally, the researchers contend that GATT should defer to national laws and international agreements that protect wildlife, natural forests, and marine fisheries.

At the core of this issue is how efforts to harmonize standards can be tailored to leave room for national and sub-national governments to adopt policies reflecting local ecological conditions and local value preferences. Resolving this issue will take innovative and flexible approaches to harmonization policies.

INCREASING INTERNATIONAL COOPERATION
AND PUBLIC PARTICIPATION IN FREE TRADE NEGOTIATIONS

The degree of international cooperation envisioned by free trade advocates is unprecedented. Governments at all levels are being asked to relinquish sovereignty over the regulation of business in environmental protection and a host of other areas. This centralization of authority poses the issue of what forum is most appropriate for making decisions about the balance between international, national, and local rules.

In the Uruguay Round, GATT negotiators are clearly making a bid to become that forum. GATT member nations are being asked to adopt international environmental standards selected in GATT negotiations and to ensure that their state, provincial, or local governments do the same. International environmental agreements with trade provisions, such as the Montreal Protocol, would require a waiver from the GATT Council in order for their trade provisions to be considered GATT consistent. But GATT is an organization with little or no expertise in environmental issues, and is oriented toward promoting international commerce. It is unclear whether the current GATT would provide waivers for international environmental agreements.

Moreover, like many international institutions, GATT deliberations remain closed to citizen involvement. All GATT proceedings, including negotiations, dispute proceedings, and committee deliberations, are held in secret sessions. Even the decisions of GATT dispute panels remain secret. All information on GATT must be transmitted through a country's official trade representative. This secrecy is rationalized by the need to insulate diplomacy from the pressures of domestic public opinion. Such secrecy may be warranted for certain diplomatic exchanges and for sensitive military matters, but environmental policy in the United States has traditionally been subject to and strengthened by extensive citizen participation. Internationally, the 1992 United Nations Conference on Environment and Development went out of its way to encourage the involvement of literally thousands of non-governmental organizations, setting a standard that GATT should follow.

CONCLUSION

In the last two decades, environmentalists have attempted to weave a safety net of local and national laws and international agreements to protect endangered habitats, species, and resources. Federal, state, and local governments have passed these laws and others that protect consumers from harmful food additives, pesticides, and unsafe products. To advocates of free trade, many of these laws seem like protectionist barriers to the uninterrupted flow of commerce. Conversely, to environmentalists, trade agreements such as GATT and NAFTA seem like threats to many of these environmental protections. Rather than debating whether protecting the environment or promoting free trade is better, we should look for methods to reconcile these two laudable policy goals and move toward sustainable development. The first step for such reconciliation is increasing the dialogue and understanding between the trade and environment camps.

NOTES

1. This article was adapted from Thomas A. Wathen, *A Guide to Trade and the Environment* (New York: Environmental Grantmakers Association, Consultative Group on Biological Diversity, 1992).

2. Although adjustments are made for individual products or countries, the United States sets tariffs according to these categories:

   Most Favored Nation (MFN) Tariffs - MFN tariffs are those that the United States has generally agreed to under GATT. These tariffs currently average 4 percent of the cost of the product and are the most favorable tariff accorded to any country by the United States.

   Non-MFN Tariffs - Non-MFN tariffs are those set under the Tariff Act of 1930 (Smoot-Hawley Act). They average 40 percent.

   Special Tariffs - Special tariffs are discounted or waived tariffs granted to specific countries for specific products. Special tariffs include those negotiated in free trade agreements and those granted to developing countries by U.S. programs such as the Generalized System of Preferences or the Caribbean Basin Initiative.

2

The Trade and Environment Nexus: What Is New Since '72?

Charles S. Pearson

INTRODUCTION

W e can start to answer our title question immediately. There *is* something new in the trade-environment issue as it has emerged in the 1990s. But there are also roots that can be traced to an active theoretical and policy debate in the early 1970s. Understanding these roots casts light on current discussions. While it is now commonplace to view the intersection of trade and environmental systems as a source of friction or conflict, a historical perspective suggests that the extent of conflict can be easily exaggerated.

To avoid confusion we need to sort out the various questions that arise when meshing trade and environmental policy. Virtually all current trade-environment issues fall within one of four categories:

- The trade effects of environmental regulation of production (the competitiveness issue);
- The trade effects of environmentally related product standards;
- The use of trade measures to secure international environmental objectives; and
- The environmental effects of trade and trade liberalization.

The first two sets of issues were recognized, analyzed, and subject to international policy as early as 1972. Nevertheless, the main analytical perspective at that time was from the viewpoint of the trade system, not identical to the environmental perspective. That is, the perspective was the trade community viewing environmental measures, rather than the environmental community viewing the trade system. In contrast, in the 1990s environmentalists are raising questions about the trade system. And, as we shall see, the discussion has been enriched since the 1970s by new empirical research, and by new developments in the trade and environmental areas. Finally, the second two issues listed above—using trade measures to attain environmental objectives and anticipating the environmental consequences of trade liberalization—received little attention in the 1970s, but have since blossomed into heated controversies. Thus we have something old and something new in the debate.

HISTORICAL ROOTS

Trade-environment issues first surfaced in the early 1970s, partly as a consequence of the first United Nations Conference on the Human Environment, held in 1972 in Stockholm. A principal concern at that time was that if one country moved vigorously to establish strong environmental protection through pollution taxes, effluent and emission standards, or otherwise, its international competitive position would suffer. This is known as the competitiveness effect. The emphasis of both national environmental legislation and trade-environment analysis was on industrial pollution control, not on environmental effects in natural resource sectors. Despite the subsequent empirical studies suggesting that, thus far, the aggregate trade effects from different pollution abatement regimes are minimal, the competitiveness issue that captured considerable attention in the early 1970s remains a concern today.

At the level of theory, the response to the competitive question was twofold. First, it was argued that under an extended notion of comparative advantage, which includes a country's endowment of environmental resources, some reallocation of world production and trade would be desirable. Under this theory, differences among countries in the supply of and the demand for environmental resources could be a source of gains from trade. This is not unlike differences among countries in labor supply and demand being the source of gains from trade. Second, the theory suggests that the overall competitive position of a country, measured by its trade balance, could be maintained by appropriate exchange rate changes, which would *improve* the competitive position of clean industries. For example, tightening restrictions on pollution intensive sectors such as pulp and paper would tend to depreciate the exchange rate, giving a boost to "clean" export industries and the services sector.

In the absence of transnational pollution, these arguments remain valid today. But the positive role that trade could play would not materialize if governments subsidize pollution abatement costs undertaken in the private sector and maintain the split between private and social production costs (the latter including environmental protection costs). Indeed, it is a fundamental principle of both sound trade policy and sound environmental policy that prices reflect all production costs, both private and environmental. For this reason, the Organization for Economic Cooperation and Development (OECD) developed the Polluter Pays Principle in 1972.

The Polluter Pays Principle has been much misunderstood. As elaborated by OECD, it is a cost allocation principle. Pollution abatement costs are kept in the private sector rather than being borne by governments. By closing the gap between market prices and social production costs, the principle minimizes trade distortions *and* is the basis for sound environmental policy. By "trade distortions" we simply mean the misallocation of resources domestically and internationally.

The term Polluter Pays Principle is misleading, however. As used by OECD, nothing in the principle prevents industry from passing on pollution abatement costs to consumers in the form of higher product prices. Nor does it require that victims be compensated for residual environmental damages, after the optimal level of pollution abatement is achieved. (In general, the theory concludes that zero pollution is uneconomic, as the marginal costs of abatement exceed marginal benefits.) Thus the Polluter Pays Principle is consistent with "payments" by consumers and victims, leading to some confusion. Incidentally, OECD's principle did contemplate some temporary government assistance to industry during the transition to stronger environmental protection. Today, it is desirable to extend the principle beyond OECD to the former centrally planned economies of Eastern Europe, the Soviet Union, and developing countries. By closing the gap between market prices and the real social costs of production, environmental resources are conserved *and* trade is less distorted. Nevertheless, there may well be a role for government assistance in cleaning up past pollution in Eastern Europe, the former Soviet Union, and the developing countries.

A second concern in the early 1970s was that environmentally related product standards—pesticide residue standards in food products, for example, or auto emission standards—might become non-tariff trade barriers. This concern posed no new conceptual problems. The trade system has long confronted nationally established health, sanitary, and safety standards as potential impediments to trade. The arguments for international harmonization of such standards are to minimize their use as covert trade barriers and to reduce the high costs of design, production, inventory, and information in selling to fragmented markets. The opposing argument is that countries differ in assimilative capacity, income levels, preference, and so on, and that an internationally uniform standard would be too high for some, while too low for others. This is the lowest common denominator issue.

The trade system has struggled with the harmonization of product standards issue for decades. That struggle has been played out in many fora, including the Codex Alimentarius Commission, an international organization that attempts to harmonize food standards globally, the General Agreement on Tariffs and Trade (GATT) Code on Technical Barriers to Trade, which disciplines a country's use of product standards as covert trade barriers, and efforts by the European Community (EC), which attempt to create a single market by establishing more uniform product standards among members. Nevertheless, it is fair to say the issue as it relates to environmentally related product standards has not been resolved and is a major point of contention in the Uruguay Round negotiations of GATT and in the North American Free Trade Agreement (NAFTA). At issue is whether the United States and other countries with strict standards will continue to have the right to set product standards as they deem appropriate.

The international response to the environmentally related product standards issue has been pragmatic. GATT recognizes the right of countries to establish such standards but tries to discipline their use, mainly through Article XX of the GATT, which allows exceptions to general GATT obligations. The interpretation of Article XX in environmental cases remains a contentious issue, and environmentalists are not happy with a number of GATT panel decisions. An especially vexing question is whether product regulations can or should reach back to the *process* through which the product was produced. The U.S.-EC *Beef Hormone* case and the U.S.-Mexico tuna-dolphin dispute are examples.

The 1972 OECD *Guiding Principles Concerning the International Economic Aspects of Environmental Policies* (OECD *Guiding Principles*), which contains the Polluter Pays Principle, also addressed the product standards issue. The OECD *Guiding Principles* require member governments to avoid the use of such standards as covert trade barriers, to provide national treatment and nondiscrimination to imports and, where feasible, to work toward international harmonization of standards. Interestingly, the procedures for consultation and discussion set up by OECD in 1972 to examine trade-environment disputes have not been used. This suggests that either intra-OECD conflicts have not been numerous, or there is little confidence in the OECD dispute settlement procedures. GATT also anticipated some friction and set up a trade-environment working group early in the 1970s, but that working group did not meet until 1991. This discrepancy may be interpreted as either a lack of serious problems or the casting of a blind eye toward growing friction.

Finally, in 1972 OECD considered what has become a highly topical question: Should countries have the right to use border adjustment (tariffs and export rebates) to offset international differences in environmental control costs? It gave a negative answer in its *Guiding Principles*. Presumably OECD felt that it would not be possible to distinguish between legitimate differences in standards and costs, the trade consequences of which are desirable, and artificial comparative advantage by countries following a "pollution haven" strategy. OECD may also have feared capture of such measures by protectionist interests, as well as unending friction among trade partners. The use of border adjustments to offset environmental cost differences has not been tested in GATT. If the cost difference arose because of a foreign financial subsidy to its firms for pollution abatement, it might be countervailable under normal GATT export and domestic subsidy provisions. But it is unlikely that a border adjustment for the purpose of offsetting cost differences from different standards would be found to be GATT consistent.

In summary, many of the current trade-environment issues were addressed two decades ago by OECD and, to a lesser extent, by GATT. What new developments keep them alive, and what new issues have emerged since then?

MORE RECENT DEVELOPMENTS

There are three fundamental reasons why the trade-environment nexus has reemerged in the 1990s as a major issue. They are:

- The increasing integration of national economies through trade and investment;

- The increasing attention to transboundary and global environmental threats; and
- The new umbrella of "sustainable development" that broadens environmental concerns from pollution abatement to conservation of natural resources.

THE INTEGRATION OF NATIONAL ECONOMIES

The decline of overt protection at the border and new efforts at regional economic integration (EC, the U.S.-Canada Free Trade Agreement, and NAFTA) focus attention on *domestic* policies that affect production costs (the competitiveness issue) and conditions of sale (the product standards issue). Actually, the question is much broader than environmental protection. Many ostensibly domestic policies, such as antitrust, social security, health, and minimum wage policies, affect production costs, and hence international competitive position. The issue, yet unresolved, is whether they should be subject to scrutiny by trade partners. One example of such mutual scrutiny is the Structural Impediments Initiative talks between the United States and Japan, in which each country's domestic policies that indirectly but strongly affect their international competitive position have become fair game for mutual discussions.

Regional economic integration itself increases the saliency of all four categories of trade-environment issues. With regional free trade and investment, environmental policies that affect production costs become more important. A major thrust of the EC is to create a unified single market that, strictly speaking, requires uniform product standards. Negotiating a free trade agreement, such as NAFTA, provides the *opportunity* to use trade as an inducement or sanction to change foreign environmental practices. And, finally, a regional free trade agreement changes the pattern and composition of production and consumption, the environmental consequences of which deserve identification and, perhaps, policy action.

Trade-environment questions have been addressed in quite different fashion in various regional integration efforts. As noted above, harmonizing product standards has been central to efforts within the EC, but the competitiveness issue has been muted. Despite strong supranational institutions, the EC has not been able to establish fully uniform product standards. Instead, the EC relies on the subsidiary principle (decisions are made at the lowest political level competent to deal with the problem) and the doctrine of mutual recognition (a product legally sold in one member country cannot be barred from sale in another member country).

Despite the importance of natural resource trade (energy, fish, agriculture), and despite a long history of border environmental problems, the U.S.-Canada Free Trade Agreement of 1989 paid little attention to questions of environmental protection or natural resource conservation. Canadian environmental groups did raise many of the same questions that were subsequently asked in NAFTA negotiations, but apparently with little effect. It was not until NAFTA negotiations that the trade-environment issues were fully joined. Perhaps this is not surprising. The disparity in labor costs between the United States and Mexico, the important role of foreign investment in Mexico, and the well-documented pollution problems of the *maquiladora* industries on the border, underscored the possibility that, if left unregulated, NAFTA would encourage a "pollution haven" strategy in Mexico. Because environmental groups were late in recognizing the environmental implications of trade liberalization, the Uruguay Round negotiations leading up to December 1991 did not address these concerns. Consequently, NAFTA became the first "green" trade agreement. Whether it is sufficiently green to satisfy environmentalists and the Congress remains an open question.

The Globalization of Environmental Problems

Transboundary and global environmental threats, with the corresponding trade implications, did not fully emerge on the public agenda until the late 1980s. It is true that transnational pollution—the physical movement of pollutants outside the territory of one state that damage the environment of other states or international common property resources such as the oceans—was recognized and analyzed in the 1970s. Indeed, the *Trail Smelter* case between the United States and Canada in the 1930s helped develop international law in this area. But the connection to trade was minimal. There had been a number of international environmental and resource conservation agreements (seventeen between 1933 and 1990) that involved trade measures, but, for the most part, they were confined to protection of fauna and flora and phytosanitary regulations. The 1973 Convention on International Trade in Endangered Species of Wild Fauna and Flora is the best known. But it was not until the Montreal Protocol on Substances that Deplete the Ozone Layer (Montreal Protocol) in 1987, which attempts to limit chlorofluorocarbon (CFC) damage to the ozone layer, that the use of trade measures to secure international environmental objectives began to take on major trade significance. Even then, the compatibility of the protocol's trade provisions with GATT was given little attention, which is a bit surprising. Not only does the protocol restrict trade in CFCs, and trade in products containing CFCs, but it contemplates trade restrictions on products whose production uses CFCs. If this last measure comes into effect, the impact would be felt on many industrial and consumer products entering international trade.

The core of the trade-transnational pollution problem can be stated in the following way. Because there is no supranational environmental protection agency, and because the incidence of abatement costs and benefits is not congruent with national borders, international environmental agreements that address transboundary and global problems must either rely on side payments or compensation to induce compliance, or must use more coercive measures. The system of international payments is rudimentary at best, although the recently established Global Environmental Facility is a start. The most obvious coercive measures lie in the trade field. Hence the temptation is to secure compliance with international environmental protection agreements and discourage "free riders" by using trade restrictions.

This question *is* clearly new since '72. There is no guiding principle that reconciles the objective of liberal trade (which implies a sparing use of trade measures for noncommercial foreign policy objectives) and the goal of effective regulation of international environmental externalities. Criteria for such a principle are being actively discussed in OECD and GATT. Presumably such criteria will make a distinction between unilateral use of trade measures (which raises the "eco-imperialism" issue) and multilateral environmental agreements with trade provisions.

THE EMERGENCE OF THE CONCEPT OF SUSTAINABLE DEVELOPMENT

A final reason for the resurgence of attention to the trade-environment intersection is an increase in interest in sustainable development, which broadens environmental concerns from industrial pollution to natural resource conservation. Sustainable development was popularized in the mid 1980s, mainly through the publication by the United Nations of the Brundtland Commission report, *Our Common Future*, which, in turn, led rather directly to the June 1992 United Nations Conference on Environment and Development in Rio.

The concept of sustainable development itself has roots in the 1970s. One strand can be traced to the 1972 United Nations Conference on the Human Environment in Stockholm, which redefined environmental degradation from a narrow emphasis on pollution to include the conditions of poverty—unsanitary water supplies, endemic disease transmitted by environmental media, urban slums, and squalor. This redefinition brought developing countries squarely into the environmental *problematique*. Another strand was the publication of *Limits to Growth* by the Club of Rome at about the time of the 1972 oil price shock. *Limits to Growth*, although much criticized for its primitive use of price and market economics, directed attention to the interaction between economic activity and the natural and environmental resource matrix in which all economic activity is embedded. The recognition of these links is central to the concept of sustainable development.

There are many connections between international trade and sustainable development that are just now being explored. Clearly, trade liberalization in the absence of adequate domestic environmental protection policies can add environmental stress. It does not necessarily follow, however, that trade restrictions improve environmental quality. Indeed, some studies show that economies that are relatively closed to trade and investment are burdened with higher pollution levels than countries well-integrated into the trade system. Also, policies that protect agriculture in the EC and elsewhere may result in excessive use of agricultural chemicals and environmental degradation. In that case it is trade restriction, not trade liberalization, that causes environmental stress.

Environmental and resource protection costs are not being internalized in product prices in many natural resource sectors. This is true for the United States (water and grazing rights are two examples) as well as for other developed and developing countries. This lack of internalization creates a trade distortion and, in this sense, trade contributes to the misallocation or misuse of natural and environmental resources. The overuse of natural and environmental resources is a prime example of unsustainable development. The early emphasis in the 1970s on industrial pollution control failed to recognize this, and we therefore have another reason to reexamine the trade-environment nexus. But again, it does not necessarily follow that trade restrictions are the best way to deal with unaccounted-for costs in production. An export or import tax on tropical timber, for example, may or may not contribute to sustainable forest management practices, depending on local consumption in the timber producing country, the terms of log concessions, and other factors. The better solution is likely to include changing property rights and increasing timber royalties.

CONCLUSION

There are few inherent conflicts between liberal trade and environmental protection. Many of the apparent conflicts arise either because countries have failed to take appropriate domestic environmental protection measures, in which case trade can be the agent but not the root cause of environmental degradation, or because the persistence of import barriers and subsidies themselves misallocates the use of environmental and natural resources. Environmentally motivated trade restrictions will not solve these conflicts.

In the early analysis of trade-environment connections, the emphasis was on the trade-competitiveness impact of differences in environmental control regimes, and on environmentally related product standards. The use of trade measures to secure environmental objectives, and the environmental effects of trade liberalization, were given little attention. Policies developed in the early 1970s, especially the OECD *Guiding Principles,* have proved not to be incorrect, but to be incomplete. A new principle, dealing with the appropriate use of trade measures to secure international environmental objectives, is badly needed. Also needed are research and improved models that link trade to the national and environmental resource base, not for the purpose of restricting trade, but to anticipate and manage demands on environmental resources.

3

The International Trade Regime and the Municipal Law of Federal States: How Close a Fit?

David A. Wirth[1]

INTRODUCTION

Within the past few years, international trade agreements have come under close scrutiny by concerned observers who have discovered that the existing international trade regime, as well as anticipated modifications to trade pacts that have yet to be implemented in final form, may have adverse environmental impacts. Moreover, little has been made of clear opportunities in both theory and practice to utilize trade agreements as affirmative vehicles to promote environmental conservation and enhancement. A workable solution has not yet been found for the potential conflict between liberalized trade and environmental protection—both goals that are ultimately intended to improve human welfare.

Some commentators have sought to address international trade and environmental conflicts by analogy to similar efforts within federal or federalizing systems like the United States and the European Community (EC). While law and practice in federal or federalizing systems may provide informative and helpful perspectives about the international legal system, recent developments have suggested a need to be extremely careful not to overextend the comparison. In the absence of a wholesale transformation of international law into a supranational world government, the international trade regime will continue to be dramatically different from the legal structure in place in federal states. This chapter compares criti- ical elements of the international trade system with the institutions and procedures found in U.S. and EC federalist systems. The chapter concludes with a review of the Polluter Pays Principle, which offers one of the more promising avenues for addressing disparities between countries within the international trade system.

INTERNATIONAL AND FEDERALIST APPROACHES

The international system contains no rule-making authority with sovereign powers analogous to the U.S. Congress or the Council of the European Communities. Instead, the principal "legislative" process, the negotiation of multilateral treaties like the General Agreement on Tariffs and Trade (GATT) and international environmental agreements, proceeds according to the related principles of consensus and consent. The GATT Uruguay Round and the Framework Convention on Climate Change opened for signature in June 1992 at the United Nations Conference on Environment and Development (UNCED) have demonstrated that a single powerful nation like the United States can in some cases dictate the terms of a multilateral agreement or prevent its adoption altogether. When multiplied by the number of participating states, this dynamic can produce least common denominator results—pulling higher standards down to the level of the lowest nation—that are not responsive to real-world problems like excessive trade barriers or threats from environmental externalities. In other cases, as demonstrated by the decision of the United States not to immediately sign the UNCED Convention on Biological Diversity, states need not accept the obligations even in supposedly universal instruments. Other states, although signing a multilateral treaty, may encounter political obstacles at home that prevent acceptance of the international obligations. The necessity for signature and, especially, ratification can delay or, in extreme cases, preclude the entry into force of a multilateral agreement.

Most often, delays come in the form of minimum signatory requirements. For example, thanks to the reluctance of some powerful states, including the United States, to accept the obligations in the 1982 United Nations Convention on the Law of the Sea, that instrument has yet to enter into force. In the United States, the necessity of adopting implementing legislation can create delays for most trade and certain environmental agreements. The Convention on the Regulation of Antarctic Mineral Resource Activities will probably never become effective because of domestic environmental opposition in a number of states, including France and Australia, which are necessary for the convention's entry into force.

Moreover, ratification of a treaty does not guarantee compliance, and international enforcement mechanisms are of limited availability and efficacy. Professor John Jackson has suggested that GATT dispute settlement has "developed into a remarkably full procedure that has been largely, but not totally, effective." Unfortunately, the same cannot be said of mechanisms to enforce international environmental obligations. Reservations about the efficacy of dispute settlement in trade agreements have been magnified many times in the environmental field. In short—although we do not often admit it—the international system as currently structured invites the proliferation of holdouts, free riders, laggards, scofflaws, and defectors.

This situation is not necessarily good or bad, right or wrong. It is, however, a practical reality that creates dynamics that are totally different from those in a federal system like that of the United States, or a federalizing system such as the EC. For example, there is no precedent within federal systems for the use of countervailing duties to offset disparities in national production processes in sub-national bodies such as the states of the United States. The reason for this is obvious. In a federal system, there are effective law-making and law-enforcement mechanisms that provide alternatives to unilateral measures enacted by subsidiary governmental units that disrupt trade flows. Indeed, federal systems like the United States and the EC can and do invalidate rules adopted by their constituent components that impede trade.

This phenomenon, however, reveals relatively little about the appropriate use of trade measures in an international system in which the mechanisms for defining and implementing law to address such issues as environmental externalities are considerably less effective and less responsive than in a federal system. In a smoothly functioning federal system, there is little or no need for self-help. But at the international level, as GATT and other international trade agreements at least implicitly recognize, at-the-border adjustments and countervailing duties may be the only remedy available. The question then becomes not *whether* unilateral trade measures are appropriate, but *under what circumstances* they are warranted.

INTERNATIONAL TRADE AND
INTERNATIONAL ENVIRONMENTAL POLICY

The international trade system, whatever its flaws, is a considerably more mature regime than the totality or any part of international environmental law. GATT came into existence soon after World War II. By contrast, the first binding, substantive, and potentially universal multilateral agreements on such pressing environmental problems as exports of hazardous wastes and depletion of the stratospheric ozone layer have been concluded only in the last five years or so. Negotiations on the only international legal norms designed to safeguard the integrity of the Earth's climate and the first comprehensive attempt to provide protection for the planet's biological diversity concluded only with the opening of new multilateral conventions for signature at UNCED in 1992.

GATT is effectively an international organization with a secretariat housed in Geneva that potentially has jurisdiction over the entire range of trade-related issues. The ongoing Uruguay Round is the eighth in a more or less linear sequence of international attempts to overcome impediments to free trade in a unified fashion by establishing a reasonably well-developed set of norms in a setting of considerable organizational continuity. These rules govern an increasingly wide array of substantive issues, including, in the proposed Uruguay Round, not only food safety laws but also intellectual property rights. As noted above, GATT's dispute settlement provisions, while perhaps not as effective as they might be, are generally more efficacious than in other areas of international law. Bilateral or regional trade agreements, like the proposed North American Free Trade Agreement (NAFTA), generally rely on fundamental GATT principles and are consciously structured to be consistent with the global trade regime.

In the environmental arena, there is no similar central focal point. The United Nations Environment Programme (UNEP) headquartered in Nairobi, the International Maritime Organization in London, the Economic Commission for Europe in Geneva, the Organization for Economic Co-operation and Development (OECD) in Paris, and the United Nations Food and Agriculture Organization in Rome, all play major roles in environmental issues. Each of these organizations has negotiated multilateral environmental agreements and protocols, each employing the organization's own staff, processes, and structure. The negotiation of the recently adopted climate change convention was entrusted to another, new body, the Intergovernmental Negotiating Committee. The Intergovernmental Negotiating Committee's work is built on that of yet another specially created institution, the Intergovernmental Panel on Climate Change, a cooperative undertaking of UNEP and still another international organization, the World Meteorological Organization. By comparison with GATT, international environmental agreements are largely unconnected and uncoordinated attempts to deal with discrete problems like protection of the stratospheric ozone layer, conservation of endangered species, and environmental harm from international shipments of hazardous wastes.

Just as environmental measures may be subject to the constraints established by a trade regime, environmental standards may govern trade in commodities such as CFCs, endangered species, hazardous wastes, industrial chemicals, and pesticides. However, the enforcement mechanisms in most environmental agreements are thin, and there is nothing comparable to the GATT dispute settlement process to encourage compliance with those agreements' standards on a more or less routine basis. While most international environmental agreements do not provide for binding third party dispute resolution, there have recently been attempts to craft informal, multilateral processes to encourage implementation and compliance that are somewhat analogous to the GATT panel procedures. The climate change convention establishes a subsidiary body to supervise implementation by participating states and contains a provision stating that the parties to the agreement intend to consider a multilateral consultative process to resolve conflicts arising from the convention. Generally, however, environmental measures are considerably more likely to be subjected to discipline from a trade agreement than the other way around. And, from an environmental point of view, the trade dispute settlement process provides only one remedy: a conclusion that the offending environmental measure should be eliminated for the singular goal of liberalizing trade.

One effect of this disparity has been a gradual but persistent tightening of the trade constraints on unilateral, or even multilateral, environmentally motivated trade measures to fill the gaps in global regimes that do not necessarily respond with sufficient quickness or effectiveness in addressing environmental externalities. For example, GATT Article XX(b) provides an explicit exemption for measures designed to protect human, animal, or plant life or health, so long as those measures are "necessary." The 1991 GATT tuna-dolphin panel report interpreted "necessary" to imply a requirement that a state "exhaust[] all options reasonably available . . . through measures consistent with the General Agreement." GATT Article XX(g) contains a second exemption that applies to exhaustible natural resources "if such measures are made effective in conjunction with restrictions on domestic production or consumption." One GATT panel examining Canadian measures affecting exports of unprocessed herring and salmon interpreted this provision as requiring a demonstration that the measures in question were "primarily aimed at the conservation of an exhaustible natural resource." A panel convened under the auspices of the U.S.-Canada Free Trade Agreement, which incorporates GATT Article XX by reference, suggested in addition that a trade measure would have to satisfy a cost-benefit test to qualify for the exemption. Moreover, both exceptions are interpreted narrowly. Not surprisingly, barely a single trade measure whose validity turns on the application of one or the other of these exemptions has ever been held to be consistent with GATT.

The tuna-dolphin panel report concluded that trade measures to protect resources outside the jurisdiction of a contracting party are not permissible.[2] This conclusion is clearly new law. The rule has obvious and significant implications for the Montreal Protocol on Substances that Deplete the Ozone Layer (Montreal Protocol), which restricts trade in ozone-depleting chlorofluorocarbons (CFCs), certain products containing those chemicals, and, potentially, products that need CFCs to be manufactured, with states not party to the agreement. During the negotiation of the Montreal Protocol, the U.S. Trade Representative issued an opinion on the agreement's anticipated trade measures that endorsed the use of trade measures to protect the ozone layer, described the natural resources exception as "broad," ignored the "extraterritorial" question on which the GATT panel's conclusion rested, failed to address the desirability or necessity of a GATT waiver, and ultimately gave a clean bill of health to trade measures of the sort contemplated for that agreement. Representatives of the GATT Secretariat attended at least some of the negotiating sessions leading up to the Montreal Protocol. As a practical matter, it would have been inconceivable for the agreement to be adopted in its current form if the GATT Secretariat had objected.

If an analogy to the United States and the EC is appropriate, one might be tempted to conclude that a free trade regime ought to have primacy in the international system and that the current GATT text should be sufficiently flexible to provide a basis for a needed transition to a system that more effectively accommodates environmental values. But whether the international trade regime can be rendered environment-friendly or not, it is unrealistic to expect this to occur without a thorough reevaluation of the current system.

ENFORCING ENVIRONMENTAL STANDARDS

In contrast to federal systems like the United States and the EC, GATT dispute panels do not have the power to compel performance of relevant standards, environmental or otherwise. The GATT dispute settlement process results only in a conclusion that a particular action is or is not consistent with the regime. From a trade point of view this makes perfect sense. Impediments to trade result from affirmative governmental measures, like tariffs, and the principal goal of a free trade regime is to eliminate those governmental measures. By contrast, international obligations with respect to the environment—and many other areas as well—anticipate and require the implementation of affirmative governmental actions intended to address particular problems. From an environmental point of view, the international trade regime as currently structured is a no-win proposition: There are no mechanisms for assuring the implementation of minimum governmental measures, and once those policies that do exist are subjected to trade-based scrutiny, nothing more than maintenance of the status quo can be expected to result even in the best possible case. Interestingly, the GATT Uruguay Round would mobilize the international trade regime to require governments to adopt and enforce minimum intellectual property protections, including a patent term of at least twenty years. A similar approach, however, has yet to be adopted for minimum, internationally agreed-upon environmental standards.

Trade measures that further the purposes of multilateral regimes for protecting resources of the global commons, like Antarctica and the high seas, appear to have the best prospects for acceptance within the framework of international trade agreements. The tuna-dolphin case provides an interesting gloss on this perspective. As a partial solution to the tuna-dolphin dispute, a new federal statute would lift the ban on imports of tuna products from Mexico if that nation were to enter into a bilateral commitment to, and in fact implement, immediate reductions in dolphin mortality, culminating in a five-year moratorium on setting nets on dolphin beginning in March 1994. As of this writing, Mexico has not made any commitment of the sort contemplated by the new statute. As the tuna-dolphin panel pointed out, unilateral measures invite a crazy quilt of inconsistent and often ineffective national approaches that may impede trade. On the other hand, national trade measures like the U.S. import ban can provide some minimal protection for resources beyond the jurisdiction of any state that might otherwise be victims of the tragedy of the commons. Moreover, as in the tuna-dolphin case and countless others, unilateral regulation can galvanize bilateral and multilateral processes by increasing the incentives for effective international responses such as the commitments by foreign governments anticipated by the new statute.

THE POLLUTER PAYS PRINCIPLE

Fortunately, there is growing recognition and acceptance of a principle, the Polluter Pays Principle, that could enable greater international enforcement of environmental standards throughout the trade system. A 1972 OECD recommendation was one of the first efforts to articulate the Polluter Pays Principle. The principle provides an informative framework for analyzing the international significance of disparities in domestic environmental policies. As the title suggests, the recommendation states that those that create environmental externalities ought to bear the associated costs. The instrument also includes a substantive standard of cost internalization as a test of the adequacy of domestic environmental policy. Reflecting the views of environmental economists, the recommendation states that:

> [w]hen the cost of [environmental] deterioration is not adequately taken into account in the price system, the market fails to reflect the scarcity of such resources both at the national and international levels. Public measures are thus necessary to reduce pollution and to reach a better allocation of resources by ensuring that prices of goods depending on the quality and/or quantity of environmental resources reflect more closely their relative scarcity and that those concerned react accordingly.[3]

Further, "the cost of [pollution control measures] should be reflected in the cost of goods and services which cause pollution in production and/ or consumption." For present purposes, the most interesting portion of the recommendation is a passage that states that one of the purposes of the

Polluter Pays Principle is "to avoid distortions in international trade," a goal apparently motivated as much by concerns about competitiveness as by the desire to conserve environmental amenities.

Although GATT permits application of the Polluter Pays Principle as a domestic environmental measure, the international trade regime generally does not authorize the enforcement of that standard with respect to imported goods through at-the-border measures like fees or duties to offset the costs to domestic industries of pollution control measures. The 1972 OECD recommendation does not suggest a change in the resulting GATT distinction, as reiterated in the tuna-dolphin panel report, between products and processes. Instead, the instrument states that "[e]ffective implementation of the guiding principles set forth herewith will make it unnecessary and undesirable to resort to at-the-border adjustments like countervailing duties to equalize disparities in national environmental policies."

The Polluter Pays Principle has been accepted, in principle, in the EC since the 1972 OECD recommendation, and an allusion to it is now included in the Treaty of Rome. Principle 16 of the Rio Declaration, adopted at UNCED in June 1992, affirms the Polluter Pays Principle at an unprecedented level of generality and universality. Principle 16 does not mention trade implications except to note that the principle ought to be applied "without distorting international trade and investment." Since the principle is intended to *prevent* trade distortions, this caveat is quite curious, if not downright incoherent.

Presumably, the reasoning in the 1972 OECD recommendation proceeds from the assumption that cost internalization is a minimum standard of good practice that should be adopted by all countries. Those that do not do so obtain unfair trade advantages, the elimination of which is a principle purpose of the international trade regime. The 1972 OECD recommendation consequently elevates environmental policies that otherwise would be purely domestic matters to the international level, which explains the justification of the principle as a mechanism "to avoid distortions in international trade." Similarly, the failure to adopt a minimum standard of internalization is analogous to an export subsidy—a "pollution subsidy"—that creates unfair trade advantages for industries in those states with environmental policies below the international minimum standard.

Some have suggested that the calculation of external costs, particularly in a foreign context and most especially in developing countries, would not be easy. But the principle of cost internalization is a central and familiar one in environmental economics. If this is a mortal defect in a trade context, it should be no less fatal in a variety of others. Some have questioned the wisdom of so-called environmental countervailing duties to encourage countries to follow the Polluter Pays Principle. Whatever the merits of those arguments, there is no reason in principle to draw the line at measures to protect the global commons adopted through multilateral processes.

CONCLUSION

We can set our sights somewhat higher than mere peaceful coexistence between trade and the environment. When more than one hundred heads of state gathered at UNCED for the largest summit meeting ever, the notion that there are no internationally accepted environmental minimum standards was no longer consonant with current realities. Indeed, cost internalization and the Polluter Pays Principle have emerged from Rio as precisely such international standards. For some time trade agreements like GATT have targeted certain export subsidies, and, based on news reports, it sounds as if further trade disciplines for agricultural subsidies are an essential precondition to the conclusion of the Uruguay Round. Although the task is not necessarily easy and will require leadership and political will, there is no reason in principle why an international trade regime could not move in the direction of imposing a similar discipline on de facto pollution subsidies provided by those countries with substandard environmental policies.

NOTES

1. This work was supported by a grant from the Cresswell Foundation and originally appeared in the *Washington & Lee Law Review*, vol. 49, p. 1389 (1992).

2. This conclusion is not necessarily immune from criticism as a matter of treaty interpretation. An equally, if not more, plausible interpretation of Article XX would apply to cases in which there might be effects on human, animal, or plant life or health or natural resources within a state's jurisdiction even if the

activities that give rise to the trade restrictions take place outside that jurisdiction. Such effects are accepted in international law as a basis of jurisdiction to prescribe, which goes well beyond the sovereign authority to establish at-the-border trade measures. See *Restatement (Third) of the Foreign Relations Law of the United States*, vol. 1, § 402(c) (St. Paul, Minnesota: American Law Institute, 1987).

3. Organization for Economic Cooperation and Development, *Guiding Principles Concerning International Economic Aspects of Environmental Policies*, OECD Doc. C(72)128, Annex, para. 2 (May 26, 1972).

4

Integrating Trade and Environment Policy Making: First Steps in the North American Free Trade Agreement

Daniel C. Esty

INTRODUCTION

U ntil very recently, trade and environmental policy making have been pursued on separate tracks. The General Agreement on Tariffs and Trade (GATT), which embodies the central principles guiding the international trading system, does not even mention the word *environment*. And little consideration has been given to the trade implications of the broad array of environmental laws, regulations, and programs that have been developed in the United States.

Today, these parallel tracks are increasingly intersecting. The environmental disasters uncovered in Eastern Europe and the former republics of the Soviet Union—cities blackened with soot, abandoned waste pits teeming with hazardous chemicals, water not only unfit to drink but also so corrosive it is unusable in industrial processes—have made clear the price that is paid in reduced life expectancy, increased cancer rates, and other public health and ecological effects for the blind pursuit of economic goals without environmental safeguards. The United Nations Conference on the Environment and Development (UNCED) in June 1992 helped drive home the point that economic growth (including expanded trade) must be pursued "sustainably"—that is, in a manner that does not degrade the environment on which our quality of life and future economic growth depend.

Both trade and environmental officials have begun to see direct connections between their policy realms. For example, trade officials have looked on nervously as international environmental agreements, such as the Montreal Protocol on Substances that Deplete the Ozone Layer (Montreal Protocol), the Basel Convention on the Control of Transboundary Movements of Hazardous Wastes and their Disposal (Basel Convention), and the Convention on International Trade in Endangered Species of Wild Fauna and Flora (CITES), have incorporated trade sanctions to encourage broad participation and to discipline countries that choose not to participate or fail to abide by the agreed upon environmental standards. From a trade perspective, these agreements pose a risk to worldwide efforts to reduce non-tariff barriers to trade by potentially creating a basis for trade protectionism in the guise of environmentalism.

This wolf-in-sheep's-clothing fear is even more pronounced in cases in which countries have acted on their own to restrict trade in the pursuit of environmental goals without the benefit of an international agreement. The most widely discussed case of such unilateral action is the U.S. ban on Mexican tuna imports undertaken in response to Mexican fishing practices that failed to meet the dolphin protection standards of the U.S. Marine Mammal Protection Act. In this case, a GATT dispute panel concluded that the U.S. action was not a legitimate environmental or conservation measure qualifying as an exception under GATT, but rather a GATT-illegal burden on trade.

Environmentalists around the world viewed this decision as a "smoking gun," proving the environmental insensitivity of the trade world in general and GATT in particular. On the other hand, trade officials—particularly those outside the United States—saw the decision as an important rebuff to U.S. efforts to impose unilaterally its policy preferences extraterritorially outside the United States. While the tuna-dolphin case has achieved unparalleled notoriety, many other countries have taken various unilateral environmental actions, including some with extraterritorial application, making it difficult to blame the United States alone for seeking to advance environmental policies through trade mechanisms. Indeed, there is growing support for the proposition that trade should be undertaken in an environmentally sustainable fashion and that significant environmental goals may appropriately be reinforced through trade restrictions, just as we use the international trading system to promote other important societal values such as the protection of intellectual property rights and the prohibition on trade in goods produced by prison labor.

While environmentalists have recently come to appreciate the positive face of trade—the potential use of trade restrictions to promote and enforce environmental policies or agreements—they have also begun to focus on the negative face—the prospect of liberalized trade spurring increased industrial activity and generating new sources of pollution without appropriate environmental review and protection. Indeed, fear of "unsustainable development" and a deteriorating environment in the context of expanded trade under a North American Free Trade Agreement (NAFTA) among the United States, Canada, and Mexico has done much to bring the trade and environment connection into sharp relief.

THE EMERGING CLASH OF CULTURES

Prior to the NAFTA debate, environmentalists had not perceived themselves as having much of a role in trade policy making. Similarly, the trade community had seen little threat from environmental programs and had developed little expertise in environmental matters. Thus, the emergence of NAFTA-related environmental issues during the "fast track" debate in the spring of 1991 touched off a clash of cultures as the U.S. Trade Representative (USTR) and others in the trade world scrambled to address the new environmental issues, and the environmental community entered the unfamiliar territory of international trade.

Each of these worlds has distinct traditions, procedures, and even language. Trade negotiators are generally seen as *outcome*-oriented (focused on concluding trade agreements and promoting free trade) and secretive (a necessity to some degree during negotiations). The environmental community has frequently been characterized as *process*-oriented (concerned about public participation in policy making) and committed to open (transparent) decision making. Substantively, the trade community pursues a holy grail of higher incomes through expanded trade; the environmental world traditionally has feared that economic development is a false deity, and that monetary prosperity will be achieved only at a price of ecological degradation.

Differences in vocabulary exacerbate the cultural divide. For instance, to a trade aficionado, "dumping" means selling exports below home market prices. To an environmentalist, it connotes waste being put into rivers, oceans, or soil. Bridging this stylistic and substantive divide has proven to be no small task. But the process has begun.

NAFTA: FIRST STEPS

The NAFTA environmental debate brought forth a range of issues including:

- Fears of pollution spilling over into the United States from increased Mexican industrial activity;
- Concerns that the high standards of environmental protection achieved in the United States after many hard fought legislative and legal battles would be compromised in the NAFTA negotiations and harmonized down to a lowest common denominator;
- Distress over the perceived lack of opportunities for the environmental community to shape the trade policy development process; and
- Questions about the rigor of Mexico's environmental standards and enforcement program with fears of a "pollution haven" emerging south of the Rio Grande.

While the responses to these concerns have not fully reconciled competing trade and environmental goals, they have provided some important first steps toward the establishment of mutually reinforcing trade and environmental policies. The evolution in policy can be broken down into procedural and substantive advances.

PROCEDURAL ADVANCES

Concerns about the need to provide opportunities for environmental issues to be raised and debated have been met with a variety of responses. USTR created a seat on its Advisory Committee on Trade Policy and Negotiations for a leading environmentalist [former U.S. Environmental Protection Agency (EPA) Administrator and Chairman of the World Wildlife Fund Russell Train) and placed other environmentalists (Peter Berle of the Audubon Society, John Adams of the Natural Resources Defense Council, John Sawhill of the Nature Conservancy, and Jay Hair of the National Wildlife Federation] on its other advisory committees. These officials, all forceful and outspoken advocates for environmental sensitivity, provided—and continue to provide—clear reminders that the environment must not be taken for granted in trade policy development.

To ensure that the learning process went both ways, the EPA set up a Trade and Environment Committee under its National Advisory Committee on Environmental Policy and Technology. Drawing on distinguished trade professionals (including former Deputy Trade Representative Michael Smith, GATT expert John Jackson, and former National Association of Manufacturers head Sandy Trowbridge) as well as leading environmentalists (including Mike McClosky of the Sierra Club, Stewart Hudson of the National Wildlife Federation, and Konrad von Moltke of Dartmouth College), the Committee analyzed the challenges presented in integrating trade and environmental policy making and produced a series of recommendations for EPA Administrator William Reilly.

USTR also coordinated, with the assistance of EPA and other agencies, a comprehensive environmental review of the prospective NAFTA. This unprecedented analysis addressed the full spectrum of possible environmental effects of closer trade relations and helped to sharpen the focus of the U.S. negotiators on the environmental challenges and opportunities they faced. In addition, because the review was launched at the outset of the negotiations and completed while the process was in midstream, the U.S. negotiators were made aware of environmental sensitivities at an early enough stage in the process to reflect them in the U.S. negotiating position.

The review, produced in draft in the fall of 1991, was made widely available for public comment and sparked considerable debate at six public hearings. A final review and recommendations, subject to being reopened if the negotiations took an unexpected turn, was released in February 1992. Both Canada and Mexico undertook their own NAFTA environmental reviews, further expanding the public dialogue.

To address the "pollution spillover" concern, EPA and its Mexican counterpart, the Social Development Secretariat (SEDESOL), produced an *Integrated Border Environmental Plan.* This document looks comprehensively for the first time at the spectrum of environmental matters at issue along the two thousand mile U.S.-Mexico border and stands as a blueprint for how the two countries will address these issues. Debate over the draft border plan drew standing-room-only crowds at a series of seventeen public hearings on both the U.S. and Mexican sides of the border during September 1991. The openness of the process and the participation by the Mexican public were unprecedented. The final border plan, released in February 1992, identifies a range of activities and projects to address air, water, and waste issues along the shared border, creates priorities, and sets a timetable for their accomplishment.

While funding for the program of work identified in the border plan has not been adequate, EPA and SEDESOL have established six workgroups—covering the areas of air, water, waste, chemical emergencies, pollution prevention, and environmental enforcement—to ensure ongoing border cooperation and follow-through on the border plan. Whether resources adequate to meet the considerable needs identified will be forthcoming remains an open question.

Another important procedural development that strengthened the environmental sensitivity of NAFTA was the central role EPA officials played in the actual negotiations. EPA co-chaired the NAFTA negotiating teams on technical environmental standards (covering, among other things, pesticide registration and the regulation of industrial chemicals) and sanitary and phytosanitary measures (regulating food additives and contaminants). EPA actively participated in a number of other negotiating groups covering such areas as dispute settlement, investment, services, surface transportation, and automobiles. Thus, the U.S. NAFTA negotiating team incorporated a broader degree of environmental expertise than had been at the negotiating table for any prior trade agreement.

In addition to the public outreach on the NAFTA environmental review and the border plan, USTR and EPA engaged in a broad program of consultations about NAFTA environmental issues with key senators and congressmen, congressional staffers, business officials, environmental group representatives, think tank and policy center researchers, state and local officials, and the general public. Through these meetings, both formal and informal, the trade community began to understand the desires and concerns of environmentalists—and the environmental community began to appreciate the goals and approaches of free traders.

SUBSTANTIVE ADVANCES

By all accounts, NAFTA is the "greenest" trade agreement ever negotiated. This does not mean that all of the sticky trade and environment issues have been resolved, but the agreement does reflect progress in a number of areas.

First, the preamble to NAFTA establishes a context of sensitivity to environmental concerns. It calls on the parties to pursue their programs of trade liberalization so as to promote "sustainable development" and to "strengthen the development and enforcement of environmental laws and regulations." It further declares that all of the trade goals enunciated in the preamble should be pursued "in a manner consistent with environmental protection and conservation." In establishing this platform of environmental concern, the preambular language advances the goal of integrating environmental and trade aspirations—and provides a concrete example of the systematic coordination of economic growth and environmental protection efforts called for at UNCED.

A second substantive environmental advance in NAFTA can be seen in the treatment of international environmental agreements. NAFTA parties agreed that international environmental agreements with trade provisions (Montreal Protocol, Basel Convention, and CITES) should be given precedence if there is any conflict between a party's obligations under the environmental agreement and NAFTA. The parties also agreed that the list of "protected" international environmental agreements may be expanded by simple written agreement of the parties, thus anticipating the likely future growth in the number of international environmental agreements. The protection granted under NAFTA for international environmental agreements provides a potentially useful model for the international community to consider as the same potential clash between trade provisions of environmental agreements and GATT obligations occurs.

Recognizing that protectionist abuses are possible, even within the scope of efforts to uphold an international environmental agreement, NAFTA negotiators called upon the parties to exercise the "environmental obligations first" provision so that "where a party has a choice among equally effective and reasonably available means of complying with such obligations, the party chooses the alternative that is the least inconsistent with other [i.e., trade] provisions" of NAFTA. This constraint on the "environmental obligations first" language should ensure that parties implement environmental agreements in ways that permit achievement of the environmental goal while minimizing the impacts on trade. It also provides an interesting direction to pursue in the search for alternatives to the "necessary" test that has emerged in the application of the key environmental exception to GATT trade obligations, found in GATT Article XX.

Under current GATT practice, a country claiming an environmentally based right to violate GATT trade obligations must demonstrate, when challenged, that the violation is "necessary"—that there existed no other less-GATT-inconsistent means of achieving its stated environmental objective than the action it took. The stringency of this hurdle has led the environmental community to reject the "necessary" test as currently applied as another element of GATT's structural bias against the environment. The NAFTA language, limiting a party's obligation to search for less trade intrusive policies to those alternatives that are "equally effective" and "reasonably available," reduces the burden of searching for "less inconsistent" policy tools and strengthens the hand of those seeking to use trade measures to support environmental goals.

There nevertheless remain a number of issues that must be resolved in applying the "environmental obligations first" provision in practice or in a broader GATT context. For example, how many countries must sign on to an environmental agreement for it to count and to be given precedence over trade obligations? How does the precedence rule apply vis-à-vis non-parties to the environmental agreement? Who decides if a country is properly carrying out its obligations under an environmental agreement, GATT panels or parties to the environmental agreement?

Another substantive advance in integrating environmental concerns into trade policy can be found in the NAFTA sanitary and phytosanitary provisions that make clear that each country retains the unrestricted right to set and maintain standards to achieve its chosen level of protection. The right to exceed international standards is explicitly affirmed, as are the rights of political subdivisions (states and local communities) to set their own standards. Sanitary and phytosanitary measures must be based upon scientific principles, not maintained in the absence of any scientific basis, and must be derived from a risk assessment appropriate to the circumstances. These disciplines do not apply to the development of technical standards.

With respect to both technical standards and sanitary and phytosanitary measures, the GATT concept of "least trade restrictive" has been removed. NAFTA provides only that technical standards must not create "unnecessary obstacles to trade," and these are deemed not to be created if the country can show that the purpose of its measure is to achieve a legitimate objective, defined to include, among other things, environmental protection and sustainable development. Sanitary and phytosanitary measures are subject to the discipline that they be applied only as necessary to achieve the jurisdiction's subjectively determined level of protection.

NAFTA provides that parties may provisionally adopt technical regulations based on the best information available and may take further action as they obtain sufficient information to perform a full risk assessment. It also promotes upward harmonization of standards, calling explicitly for parties to work jointly to enhance standards, and establishes two committees to promote coordination of standards.

Mention of the environment in the investment chapter of NAFTA marks another break with the past. In the "Environmental Measures" article of this chapter, NAFTA Parties make clear that each country remains free to adopt and enforce any environmental measure it deems necessary to ensure that new investments within its territory do not degrade the environment, so long as these measures apply equally to domestic and foreign investment. In addition, the parties confront the "pollution haven" concern with a provision that declares it "inappropriate" to encourage or seek to retain investment by relaxing environmental standards or enforcement.

There has been considerable debate over this "pollution haven" provision because the remedy provided to a party that believes another has induced investment through a reduction in the rigor of its environmental regime is consultations and not binding dispute resolution. The consultations are to be undertaken "with a view to avoiding any such encouragement," but there is no threat of "snap back" tariffs or other trade penalties if consultations do not resolve the issue. Environmental critics of NAFTA argue that this provision has no bite and will not deter derogation from basic standards of environmental protection. The most ardent free traders and some members of the business community express a contrary fear that this provision opens a protectionist point of attack on NAFTA and will result in a flood of complaints, many of which will be against the United States. They see any further movement toward permitting formal dispute resolution over claims of environmental shortcomings as leading to intractable practical problems. Specifically, what standard must be met? Should it be a country's own standard, the U.S. standard, or an undefined world standard? And what is the starting level against which a derogation should be measured? They argue that such a provision, while aimed at perceived low Mexican standards and inadequate enforcement, might well boomerang on the United States and result in hundreds of cases against U.S. producers.

The drafters of this "pollution haven" language sought to establish a provision sufficiently rigorous to deter parties from using environmental degradation as a point of comparative advantage and yet not so easily invoked as a means of inflicting costs on competitors that it undermines the basic free trade thrust of NAFTA. They concluded that none of the NAFTA Parties could withstand the public pressure likely to be generated by awareness of any environmental performance lapse revealed in consultations, particularly in light of the active environmental communities in each country. Whether mechanisms will be established to ensure that the glare of publicity will be sufficiently bright to shame the NAFTA Parties into reforming any practice that is called into question under this provision remains an open issue—and one that bears ongoing scrutiny as NAFTA implementation goes forward.

NAFTA's dispute resolution provisions offer another example in which a new course of greater environmental sensitivity has been charted. In GATT, parties violating trade obligations for environmental reasons must justify their actions by reference to the exceptions provided in GATT Article XX. This puts the burden of proof on the party defending its environmental program. In contrast, NAFTA, at least with regard to sanitary and phytosanitary standards, shifts the burden of proof onto the party with the trade interest at stake, forcing the party challenging an environmental standard to demonstrate that the measure in question is inconsistent with NAFTA trade obligations and outside the protections provided for environmental actions.

Moreover, when disputes involving environmental issues arise, NAFTA expands the dispute panel's access to advice from scientific or technical experts. This creates an opportunity for environmental experts, not trade lawyers, to evaluate questions of environmental benefits and values.

When a country's environmental standards are called into question as a potential obstacle to free trade or when a party's use of trade measures to fulfill its obligations under international environmental agreements is challenged, the party defending its environmental program may demand that the dispute be heard by a NAFTA panel. This "anti-circumvention" provision makes certain that parties defending environmental interests will have available the environmental advances of NAFTA enumerated above. This is in contrast to the usual NAFTA rule, which is that an aggrieved party may take its case to either a NAFTA or a GATT panel.

UNRESOLVED ISSUES

While NAFTA advances environmental protection in the trade context, there remain a number of important environmental concerns that it does not address or resolve. For instance, the idea of greater "transparency" or openness in the dispute resolution process is not developed. Nor does NAFTA clarify when a party may take action *unilaterally* or with *extra-territorial* impacts in defense of its environmental policies. Thus, NAFTA fails to resolve the issues raised by the infamous tuna-dolphin case. In addition, there remain significant competitiveness issues relating to how a country should respond to competition in the marketplace from a company that is achieving a cost advantage by failing to meet environmental standards.

Some environmental concerns (perhaps those relating to competitiveness) may best be dealt with through programs of environmental cooperation rather than confrontation. For example, Mexico's capacity to develop and enforce environmental regulations appears more likely to be advanced rapidly by U.S. technology transfers and technical training than by the threat of environmental countervailing duties. Nevertheless, one element of a program designed to reduce competitiveness considerations driven by environmental factors might be an effort to converge differing standards at a high level of protection. Where countries cooperate, they are often willing to do more to protect the environment jointly than any single country would have been willing to do alone. For instance, the Montreal Protocol and later amendments have resulted in far more aggressive worldwide action to reduce the emissions of chemicals harming the ozone layer than any country was willing to undertake on its own.

Work undoubtedly needs to continue on the integration of trade and environmental policy making toward a goal of mutually reinforcing efforts that provide both trade-driven economic growth and environmental advances that enhance the quality of life on our planet. NAFTA offers some hopeful first steps in this direction, but many more remain to be taken.

5

Managing Through Prices, Managing Despite Prices

Hal Kane

O nly two hundred years ago, most of the earth's land lay either wild or under the domain of tribal peoples.[1] Hence, the dominant forms of environmental and economic management were traditional ones: rituals, religions, mythologies, and ancestral knowledge. And even in those few societies that had joined in the industrial revolution, traditions and religions continued to play major roles in industrial decisions, production, and trade.

But those ritualistic economic tools have lost much of their influence. Few cattle ranchers decide how many steers to butcher based on an ancient story about a failed marriage between a woman and a buffalo, as the American Indians did for centuries with great success. Few bankers consider the biblical morality of being neither a lender nor a borrower. Although pharmaceutical companies rely on some species long used in traditional rituals and in healing, they are not often led to the species by tribal beliefs.

The age-old methods of managing economic production have given way to a new set of economic tools; and these are a particularly arcane set, not understood by most members of the public even in the most educated societies, relegated to one or two departments at universities, and governed by small groups of individuals. These new tools are exchange rates, interest rates, the amount of money printed by national treasuries, the laws that block or allow trade, and a few other related measures.

Not many more odd groups of choices have ever directed society. (Or maybe they have, depending on which myths and traditions you like to read about.) A falling exchange rate may find coverage only in the less popular sections of the newspaper, but it can stimulate the exports of all the shoes, silverware, telephones, and timber that a country can produce by making them less expensive internationally. Falling interest rates make money cheaper to borrow, which, in turn, encourages investment, such as the opening of new dry cleaners, computer software firms, and multinational operations, and hence creates more jobs. These are powerful tools, ones that can be manipulated more swiftly than any myth, which would have had to be passed down through generations, and more swiftly than any religious law, which would have had to vie with a body of scholarly interpretation and discussion.

Economic decisions made centrally by a government now have across-the-board effects on every industry and household and on the natural environment. Cultures, too, are affected, as well as industries, households, and the natural environment of other countries. It is no wonder that people try to influence these government decisions by lobbying politicians and bureaucrats. In fact, it is quite surprising that so few speak out about the effects, for better or for worse, of monetary and trade policy. Their small numbers may be a testament to how obscure those subjects really are in modern society.

Quite rightly, however, a discussion has begun to revolve around the effect of monetary and trade policies on the environment. Though they lay dormant and unaddressed in academic and public circles for many years, the interactions between economic decisions over exchange rates, interest rates, and trade legislation and the environment are some of the most dynamic and fundamental of all current trends. When we refer to trade, we mean taking products made by using the environment, or taking the environment itself, and sending it off to other countries. And when we decide what to do with our trade policies, or interest rates, we also decide how, and how much, we will use the environment.

The relationships are exceedingly complex. What will a trade barrier mean for soil erosion, or acid rain, in a country that puts up that barrier? Only the broad, general outline of an answer would be available even to people who studied the situation carefully, and those people still could be easily surprised by the eventual results. What makes these complex relationships so much more difficult to grasp is that the links between economics and environment cannot be categorized solely as good or bad, as people have a tendency to want to do. Each provides many services for the other; each causes some harms.

Discussions of monetary and trade policies and the environment have focussed primarily on two kinds of economic decisions, and are beginning to focus on a third. The first includes the projects of the World Bank and other international development banks that fund hydroelectric dams, the building of new roads, the promotion of fisheries, and many other development schemes. The World Bank uses economic analyses to select its projects—but many of the projects touch heavily on the environment, and environmental analyses often have shown the projects to be costly in many ways that economic models did not discover.

The second debate began recently, only becoming prominent in the early nineties. This debate is over the effects of international trade on the environment. Like the debate over development bank projects, it stems largely from the idea that ordinary economic analysis fails to recognize many of the results of economic decisions, such as the results for the environment. According to environmental thinking, trade institutions like the General Agreement on Tariffs and Trade, the North American Free Trade Agreement, and others all make decisions about how we will use the environment—something which was rarely considered by the nations that are parties to those agreements.

Finally, in 1992 the first detailed studies of the environmental impacts of a type of economic planning called "structural adjustment" were offered. Structural adjustment has historically been the domain of the International Monetary Fund, but now the World Bank also implements such programs. Structural adjustment means changing, among other things, an indebted country's exchange rate, interest rates, wages, trade policies like tariffs and quotas, and fiscal policies like subsidies for energy and food. Structural adjustment is designed to improve the financial health of a country's economy, enable the repayment of debts, avoid dramatic inflation, and permit future economic growth. But these policies put a heavy burden on the poor, whose wages often fall and whose access to previously subsidized food, energy, and health care can also be curtailed. Moreover, as has only recently been shown, structural adjustment affects the environment and therefore a country's long-term potential.

Just as the environment was once an important part of the myths, religions, and customs that historically governed people's activity, it is now becoming an important part of our economics and economic institutions. Yet many questions remain about how environment and economics will come together.

PAYING FOR A TREE

Much of the significance of the environment's place in economic policies like trade, stems from the failure of markets to properly value the services that the environment provides. The prices of common objects like furniture, cars, and houses settle at the point where the amount one person will pay for them equals the amount another person will accept. But with the environment, that system does not always work—much of the environment is used for free, even though its value is greater than zero; much of it is owned by one person, even though other people still rely on it; and many times, environmental goods are sold for what they are worth in the short run, without measuring their longer-term value when they remain part of an ecosystem.

Take the case of a tree. It can be used to illustrate how the environment is likely to be priced below the real value that it gives to society while the tree remains standing. For example, consider the difference between a living tree and a dead one: the ecological functions of a living tree are not tradable. They cannot be moved, and international trade is inherently about moving things. A living tree must be cut and killed in order to be moved to another location, or, even if at major expense it is kept alive when transferred, its connected role in the ecosystem is lost.

The dollar amount ascribed to a living tree often is set equal to the price at which a dead piece of timber can be sold in a market. The myriad of functions of a living tree in ecosystem maintenance, watershed protection, habitat provision, soil stabilization, forest crops, aesthetics, and recreation all fail to be included in that price. For a proper pricing to take place, the cumulative values of each function would somehow have to be totalled. For example, if one person receives fifty cents worth of benefit from taking nuts or fruit from an individual tree, a different person takes eighty cents of benefit from not having his or her land flooded nearby, and a third person just likes to look at the tree, all three can lose if a fourth person will pay one dollar to cut it and remove it, even though the combined worth to the three people is well above a dollar. Barring some cooperative mechanism among the three losers, the marketplace will have functioned in a way that did not optimally serve its people.

The valuations, of course, are random, and it would not be easy to put more objective prices on environmental functions. The purchase of wood for timber can be valued easily because it equals the going rate that a log sells for in a lumber yard. But it is less possible to know the value of not having one's ecology disrupted, even though agriculture, supplies of drinking and industrial water, conservation of species, climate moderation, rainfall patterns, and recreation could suffer.

Hence, the ballot box steps in. Politics and culture take up roles. Governments set aside national parks; they protect endangered species; they pay farmers not to farm the most erodible soil; they prohibit the dumping of chemicals into rivers; they require scrubbers on smoke stacks. All of these are attempts to reassert the multiple values of the environment into a system that often values the environment singularly. And in international trade, for better or for worse, barriers are set up to maintain the environment when the functioning of the free market might dictate that it not be maintained: tuna caught with nets that also kill dolphins is banned from import while other tuna is allowed. Human priorities and judgements have found a way to inject themselves into the international trading system.

Even though much of our environmental protection does not stem from a desire to conserve economic well-being, it nevertheless often promotes sound long-term economics by maintaining the health of the ecosystems that will maintain our economies well down the road. Membership in environmental advocacy organizations may be driven by human, cultural, or family priorities, but it also can pay off in future economic health. In fact, before the advent of the modern economy, such cultural methods were a normal part of the guidance of the long-term development of local and regional economies.

Today, the scope of the corrections that social or cultural beliefs can inject into economic practices is larger than ever. Not only can trees be undervalued easily, but they can be cut and traded on a mass scale. And similarly, the oil, coal, and natural gas that fuel today's economies release billions of tons of carbon into the atmosphere every year, as if no costs or losses will be felt in the future as a result. Hence, the services of the atmosphere may be undervalued. Likewise, pollution of water and land is widespread, and much of it is carried out for free or at discount rates. Furthermore, potential improvements, like technologies or procedures for using energy or scarce water more efficiently, are underfunded—receiving less support in the marketplace than their value would call for in the eyes of public opinion.

PAYING FOR PEOPLE

Much as the plight of a tree, in an economic system that only values part of its worth, can illustrate the situations that drive trade and environment, so can the circumstances that human beings find themselves in. The way that we account for the value of the tree and the value of a person are treated with a similar lack of comprehensiveness.

Markets already are not left to themselves when it comes to many human priorities, like health care. Markets could be left alone to determine how much medical attention people will receive by letting markets set prices and supplies. People would pay for as much as they found worthwhile or could afford and would not receive what they did not pay for. But many people find this unacceptable. For moral reasons, they believe that people have a right to health care; and public and private organizations, like insurance companies, step in with plans to restructure medical payments to protect people.

But health care is valuable for more than just its morality. It is also valuable for what it contributes to economic well-being by enabling people to function productively in full health, to take care of their families properly, and not to miss time at work routinely. Most academic economic models do not incorporate the health of populations into their calculations, but it has a major effect. In countries where health tends to be good, there will not be too much of a block to a sound economy; but in countries with massive malnutrition, inadequate immunization programs, and unsanitary conditions, poor health blocks development.

To undervalue the economic significance of health, as an entirely price-based system could do, is to distort economic decisions that then might be made with priorities different from those that society holds most important. And likewise, to undervalue the cultural development of society, or to undervalue education or good affordable housing, is to contribute to a decision-making process that sometimes will not accomplish the goals that are held to be most important.

If, because of the ease with which goods can be traded internationally, corporations locate or relocate in regions where they will not have to pay for the health care costs of their workers or even for safe places for them to work, then the trading system may have functioned in a way that did not best take care of the people it was meant to serve. And it also may not have best taken care of its own economic health, because sick workers are not productive. Even if one company is able to make profits under such a system, it will have done so without contributing to the well-being of the region, and hence without building an area where other companies will find productive human resources in the future.

So societies rally against economic decisions made by economic pricing that has not kept society's human values at heart. People lament the *maquiladora* region on Mexico's border with the United States, where they say that liberal trade policies have led to, besides pollution, abominable living and working conditions for impoverished Mexicans. They regret the relocation of industries from traditional regions to ones with cheaper labor or more lax environmental laws. They point out the immorality of shipments of hazardous wastes to regions that did not produce them and do not have proper means to dispose of them.

Environmental issues are proving effective examples for illustrating the sub-optimality of economic decisions that exclude such "noneconomic" effects. Social and cultural issues will follow, as the sub-optimality of economic strategies that impose so heavy a burden on people that development is curtailed becomes increasingly clear. If timber is bought by one country at prices that do not reflect the full worth of the forest that was sacrificed in another country through trade, then the timber will be overconsumed. The prices that would normally rise so high that consumption of the timber would fall will not rise that high because they are decoupled from the forest's value by prices that do not count such value. If poverty rises because of an economic situation only designed to maximize short-run profit, then the poverty will mean illiteracy, hunger, and illness that will slow long-term development. Planners who are learning to take environmental values into consideration will also learn to take human ones into account.

Of course, extensive benefits from trade exist, and often they take care of peoples needs and desires and enable them to live more productive lives. Competition from foreign firms because of trade spurs innovation and efficiency. Medicines made in one country become available in others; solar electrical equipment made in industrial countries empowers developing countries; books from one culture educate another. The challenge is to set up a trading system that reflects the value of its products, cutting its abuses without impairing its benefits. The current trading system has some distance to go before it attains that success.

One reason is that today's trading system only recognizes the products that are themselves traded, but fails to recognize the many effects of extensive production that went into those products. In a 1937 address to the

U.S. Congress, President Franklin Delano Roosevelt said, "Goods produced under conditions that do not meet a rudimentary standard of decency should be regarded as contraband and not allowed to pollute the channels of international commerce." What one person will pay and another will accept decides the price of a product. Whether the product was made with clean processes, or with ones that make a product cheaper by putting carbon, sulfur, chlorine, and other materials into the air or water is not counted. Whether a product was made by well-trained workers in a safe environment, or by underpaid labor of unhealthy children carries no weight, and even misrepresents societal preferences by making the less-appropriately produced item less expensive.

Even though prices partially determine how products will flow around the world, and even though that flow partially determines how and where people work and live, prices do not carry social judgements about "standards of decency" or about long-term health of people or ecosystems. In those respects, the price system of trade, when left solely to itself, is not one that is capable of managing society.

Of course, the other side of the coin is that when governments decide what decency is and take morality into their own hands, they often make decisions even worse than those of the marketplace. Prices determined entirely by supply and demand are (usually) not racist, sexist, or otherwise prejudiced. Governments still can be. Politics is not known for morality any more than markets are.

With trade and environment, the idea has come up that products made with undesirable processes could be barred from entering a country, or required to bear unusually high tariffs. The famous U.S. ban of tuna caught with nets that also trapped dolphins illustrates that thinking. Many people have described it as an inherent "conflict" between free trade and the environment. More deeply, however, it is a failure of market prices to include the values of more desirable or less desirable production *processes*. If the price of the tuna included the dolphins that were killed alongside, then the price would rise drastically, going above the price of other tuna, and no one would buy the dolphin-threatening food. If production processes were more fully internalized, the price system itself would favor the dolphin-safe products.

But this is rarely the case. "Internalizing" externalities is difficult at the best of times and impossible otherwise. So the problem continues, or faces government regulation. Up until now, internalization of a wider range of values has been done through societal priorities and government action. Child labor is illegal in many places, as is prison labor. But international trade can undermine those priorities. Products made in a country with more lax laws can be sent into a country with stiffer laws, and hence the products are still sold. So even where society has sorted out its values through regulation or tacit agreement, trade can break in. A mechanism for making trade conform to cultural values by adjusting prices accordingly does not exist.

For the people who make them, and for the environment, products are more significant for how they are produced than they are for their own sake. The methods of production determine how much energy will be used, and whether it will be heavily polluting coal, or non-polluting solar power. They determine what materials will be used, whether benign or toxic. Finally, the methods of production dictate who will be hired, what they will spend their time doing, what conditions they will work in. And the result—a door knob, or a window, or a shirt—will usually play a minor role in someone's life, or occasionally an important role. But it will rarely approach the importance to a person of his or her time, health, and work.

Included in a product, but invisible in it, are the impacts of extraction of materials from the earth, their processing, transport, packaging, marketing, retailing, consumption, disposal, and all the people associated with those operations. A trading system that recognizes the object produced but does not fully recognize the inputs that created it will not successfully put market forces to work to meet societal or cultural or environmental goals. The true job carried out by the trading system is not only to determine supply and demand of products but also to determine supply and demand of their inputs: the raw materials, the energy for processing, the transportation, labor, and all other contributors.

PROTECTIONISM FROM ENVIRONMENTAL COSTS

On a practical level, many people wonder whether public actions to protect the environment or social issues will hurt businesses by making them pay higher costs. The assumption is usually that businesses will be hurt. A different answer, however, can be found by adapting the existing literature about international trade. Even though that literature rarely deals with environment, its concept of protectionism fits the way that companies have traditionally used the environment for free.

When firms do business, the environment and society bear some of the costs of that work through degradation or pollution in water, air, and soil, and through the results of that pollution on public health. If firms do not pay the full costs of the repercussions of their work, then they are being "protected" from those costs. They are allowed to use for free resources that in reality are not free. To stimulate business, they are being protected from the costs, much as domestic business sometimes is "protected" from foreign competition.

Protection from environmental costs, like protection from foreign competition, can be called protectionism—and its effects will be the same. The ordinary functioning of the marketplace to spur continuing improvements and innovations in products will be slowed, because firms will have less reason to do so. They do not react to competition by improving their products if they are not faced with competition; they will not maximize their efficiency and cut down on waste if they can use environmental resources without paying for them. It is only when money can be saved and competitiveness can be stoked by using energy and materials more effectively that the full incentive to do so is present. Protectionism from environmental costs is the opposite of the trade policies that most countries desire—policies that will make their firms more competitive and more environmentally sound.

It is no coincidence that the countries that have protected their firms the least from environmental costs are also the countries whose products are the most competitive in international markets. Where energy prices are high, as in Japan and Western Europe, energy efficiency is high and competitiveness is strong. Where air, water, and soil pollution are carefully regulated, pollution is minimized because firms have designed processes that use fewer hazardous materials, and therefore neither pay for as many materials nor dispose of as many. In fact, they sell their cleaner processes abroad in environmental technology markets, which are among the fastest growing of all global markets.

But at the same time, there are limits to how many environmental and social costs firms can bear, and to the improvements that would be caused by such an internalization. Making those firms collapse would not serve people's needs. To a point, internalization of costs will rationalize production. Past that point, however, it will no longer do so. Finding the point, of course, will be no easy matter, and it will differ according to every individual circumstance. Ultimately, the goal is sustainability, both for the environment and for the businesses that use it. If either collapses, the other will suffer.

How would the world trading system have to change to become sustainable? This is an open question, and there are many possible answers. One is that it would have to focus more on production processes instead of exclusively on products. But would it also have to meet the needs of people in the poorest countries much better than it has done so far? Poverty, instability, and disease reign in many countries that have few or no products that they can sell competitively on international markets. To be sustainable, should trade become more of a tool to address those problems? Should it continue to encourage efficiency among producers through competition, as it has been doing? Should it internalize more environmental costs? Should it be used as a diplomatic tool for foreign relations?

Many people argue that trade should not have other priorities or goals attached to it, beyond the single goal of its own expansion. They say that those other priorities would inhibit trade's proper functioning, and they say that trade is not well suited to meeting other goals. But trade is one tool among the variety of foreign policy and domestic policy options that governments have. Like any of them, it can be given the task of accomplishing other goals. It does not have a sacred wall around it, holding other needs away.

Where governments and people find trade policy a useful mechanism for attaining a desired end, they will use it. The larger goals of societies sometimes will hold trade and all of economics subservient. So in the future, international trade agreements are likely to be adapted for environmental purposes, or for social purposes. And those adaptations are likely to have some of the most powerful and fundamental effects of all the attempts that have been made to secure environmental quality and social needs. Not all of the effects will be for the better, as actions taken for one reason sometimes will cause harm in other areas. But they will be done nonetheless. Thus, trade is not likely to enjoy protection from environmental costs and values, and perhaps social values, in the future as much as it has in the past.

NOTES

1. *See* Alan Thein Durning, *Guardians of the Land: Indigenous Peoples and the Health of the Earth,* Worldwatch Paper 112 (Washington, D.C.: Worldwatch Institute, 1992).

PART II

Global and Regional Perspectives

6

An Action Agenda for Trade Policy Reform to Support Sustainable Development: A United Nations Conference on Environment and Development Follow-up

Charles Arden-Clarke

INTRODUCTION

Restructuring international trade in the world's natural and techno-logical resources, and redirecting financial flows associated with trade, is one of the keys to securing sustainable development. This is made explicit in Chapter 2 of Agenda 21, signed by 156 countries at the United Nations Conference on Environment and Development (UNCED) in June 1992. Signatories to Agenda 21 committed themselves to making trade and environment policies "mutually supportive." Unfortunately, Agenda 21 fails to set out a specific, action-oriented program for achieving this objective. The document also shies away from trade policy reforms that are essential to achieving sustainable development.

The weakness of the Agenda 21 text on trade is not an accident; governments shied away from the task of integrating trade and environment policies throughout the UNCED negotiations. There was an unspoken agreement that decisions taken at UNCED must not interfere with any other multilateral negotiating processes, in particular the Uruguay Round of the General Agreement on Tariffs and Trade (GATT) negotiations.

Why was this the case? Multilateral trade negotiations, such as those in GATT, are protracted and difficult even when they focus exclusively on

trade issues. Trade delegates and trade ministries seem loathe to compli-
cate the task by properly integrating environmental concerns. Nor have
many accepted that trade is only a means to an end, and not an end in itself.
Many politicians have yet to accept that given the ultimate objective of
sustainable development, free trade can only take place within the social
and environmental limits prescribed by this objective.

Adjusting trade flows in accordance with sustainable development
objectives and making trade and environment policies mutually supportive is undoubtedly a politically and technically complex multilateral task.
However, it is a task that cannot be avoided if trade policies and agreements
are to support rather than undercut national and local policies aimed at
sustainable development. Without trade reforms, economic forces generated through the world market will drive national and global economies
down unsustainable paths. Conversely, appropriate trade reforms will
reinforce sustainable national policies, and the world market will send the
signals necessary to secure sustainable economies throughout the world.

Trade and trade policies also have an enormous—and largely un-
tapped—potential to direct financial and technological resources to solving environmental problems wherever they occur. The international financial flows associated with trade dwarf those associated with debt and aid.
World trade in goods alone currently stands at $3.5 trillion per annum. If
trade in commercial services is included, the figure rises to $4.3 trillion.
This compares with official aid flows of $55 billion, and developing
country annual debt service requirements of $130 billion. A mere $2
billion new and additional funding was committed at UNCED for implementation of Agenda 21 and the other agreements. In contrast, diversion
of a mere 1 percent of the proceeds of world trade toward achieving
sustainable development would raise $43 billion annually.

These figures, combined with the best available estimate of the costs of
implementing the UNCED agreements—$600 billion annually—indicate
the importance of harnessing the enormous financial flows associated with
trade for sustainable development. Furthermore, there seems to be a
general agreement among developed and developing countries that more
diverse and fairer trade is preferable to more aid.

For all these reasons, implementing policies that integrate trade and
environmental objectives must be a priority in UNCED follow-up. Ironi-
cally, the flaws in the Agenda 21 text on trade can provide the starting point
for developing these policies. An action agenda can then be elaborated in
two parts: reform existing trade policies and agreements, and develop

wholly new trade and policy agreements with a sharp focus on environmental objectives.

A CRITIQUE OF AGENDA 21'S TEXT ON TRADE

Chapter 2 of Agenda 21 fails to identify, let alone initiate, the policy actions necessary to achieve the stated overall objective of making "trade and environment [policies] mutually supportive." The trade section is weak on action, long on words, and contains major inconsistencies. In particular, the text fails to identify two prerequisites for sustainable trade patterns.

First, the price of all traded goods (not just commodities) must incorporate or internalize the full social, environmental, and resource costs. Second, GATT rules must be reformed to discourage externalization of environmental costs. At present these rules encourage externalization of environmental costs and endorse it as a legitimate way to gain a competitive advantage. This runs directly counter to the Polluter Pays Principle.

The Agenda 21 text also ignores the fact that the Uruguay Round negotiations have more or less completely ignored the environmental implications of trade liberalization under current GATT rules. Notwithstanding the Uruguay Round's failings in this regard, the Agenda 21 text endorses the round as a key to sustainable development. Such a judgement cannot be made without assessing the impact of the consequent trade liberalization on the environment and natural resource base.

The Agenda 21 text is in accordance throughout with the line adopted by the GATT Secretariat in its report on trade and the environment—that is, that trade liberalization should take precedence as a policy objective, and that the economic growth based on free trade will then deliver the wealth for sustainable development by trickling down. This discredited classical economic theory ignores environmental lessons that have been learned the hard way. No automatic mechanism guarantees that money from trickle down economies reaches the environment. The UNCED accords also ignore the fact that environmental damage is cheaper to prevent than cure, and in some cases the damage is irreversible.

The Agenda 21 text on trade omits any reference to the need for internalizing environmental costs to reach sustainable development when discussing "sound economic policies and management." Internalization is also not mentioned as the mechanism necessary to link and contribute to securing the five goals outlined in Paragraph 2.3 of Agenda 21. The five goals are to:

- Promote sustainable development through trade liberalization;
- Make trade and environment mutually supportive;
- Provide adequate financial resources to developing countries;
- Encourage macroeconomic policies conducive to environment and development; and
- Deal with international debt.

Without internalization of costs, the multilateral trading system also will not allocate resources efficiently, another primary goal of Agenda 21.

The Agenda 21 text also calls for compatibility of environmental trade measures with "international obligations," presumably meaning GATT rules. This is extraordinary in a text purporting to deliver sustainable development. On the contrary, what is required is the compatibility of these "international obligations" with environmental necessities.

It is instructive to note that the following paragraph was deleted from the penultimate draft of the trade text at the final contact group meeting negotiating the text during the Fourth UNCED Preparatory Committee in New York: "Improve the multilateral framework to identify and address circumstances when environment-related trade measures could be the most effective policy option for promoting the environmental goal, while avoiding unnecessary trade restrictions."

The multilateral framework must presumably be taken to mean GATT. This was a crucial reference, acknowledging the deficiencies and the need for reform or reinterpretation of GATT, and the potentially important role of trade measures in the pursuit of sustainable development. By deleting this paragraph, the UNCED negotiators shied away from policy reforms that are central to the integration of trade and environment policies.

SECURING MUTUALLY SUPPORTIVE TRADE AND ENVIRONMENT POLICIES

Agenda 21 understates the importance of having a multilateral framework for trade that is wholly supportive of national and multilateral environmental policies. Trade regulations, and/or economic pressures that those regulations put on the world markets, can hamper the adoption of sound environmental policies. The sheer volume and economic value of trade make it inconceivable that most countries, particularly developing countries, can resist such pressures when they bear down on the environment.

Unless these trade-related problems are identified and addressed, it will not be possible to make trade and environment policies mutually supportive.

Adopting the appropriate perspective on trade, environment, and sustainable development is crucial to the policy reform process. Trade is a means to an end—namely environmental security and sustainable development—and not an end in itself. In particular, "free trade" is an ideal—not a reality. Unless it contributes to internalization of costs, it will not secure sustainable development. Sound environmental policies cannot, therefore, be surrendered solely to secure the objective of trade liberalization.

Integrating this perspective into the existing multilateral trade system requires the reform of trade policy. Some of these reforms can be achieved at a national level, but others will require reform or renegotiation of existing multilateral trade agreements or creation of new ones. In some cases it will be necessary to link financial and technology transfers to trade reforms to secure environment and development objectives. The implications of such reforms for social and economic equity must also be considered. An integrated approach is required to ensure that actions in one policy sector do not contradict or override actions in another. National and multilateral policies will therefore have to be coordinated to the same end.

REFORM OF GATT

The more than one hundred Contracting Parties to GATT currently account for more than 90 percent of the world trade in goods, and more countries are due to join soon. The Uruguay Round negotiations are set to extend the scope of GATT rules to include other important trade sectors, such as financial services, investment, and intellectual property rights. At present, GATT is the most important trade agreement, and the only one that is truly global rather than regional.

Incorporated into the Uruguay Round is a proposal to create a new Multilateral Trade Organization (MTO) that will supersede GATT. The MTO will integrate and implement the series of agreements that make up the current GATT with those that will stem from the Uruguay Round. If the round ends in agreement, trade rules developed under the auspices of GATT will then apply to trade valued annually at approximately $6 trillion. GATT and its potential successor, the MTO, will be considered the global regulatory framework for trade. In the wake of a Uruguay Round agreement, this framework of rules for world markets would be broader and more enforceable than those currently in force. However, this framework will undermine, rather than support, efforts to achieve sustainable development.

Current GATT rules discourage internalization of environmental costs. Indeed, the restrictive interpretation of GATT rules derived in a recent GATT dispute confirms externalization of environmental costs as a legitimate source of competitive advantage. If this interpretation is endorsed by GATT Contracting Parties and carried forward to the MTO, then the multilateral trading system will continue on its unsustainable path.

Trade measures, in the form of import tariffs or pollution control subsidies, can have a crucial role in maintaining the competitive position of countries that choose to internalize environmental costs. If denied the use of such interim measures, the countries will simply have to bear the short-term economic cost that accompanies the loss of competitiveness. These countries, and in many cases the global environment, will ultimately bear the long-term economic and environmental cost if these pressures force a relaxation of environmental standards. Accordingly, GATT rules tend to perpetuate current environmentally damaging production processes, and in some cases may reverse the trend toward adoption of sustainable production methods.

If they are to address this problem, the GATT Contracting Parties must consider amending or reinterpreting two elements of the recent tuna-dolphin dispute. The most important of these is that Contracting Parties cannot "discriminate between like products on the basis of the method of the production." The implication is that the Contracting Parties cannot apply trade measures that discriminate between the same product derived from a polluting as opposed to a pollution-free process.

The second element of the ruling provides that the GATT Contracting Parties cannot take trade measures to protect the environment or natural resources outside their legal jurisdiction. A subsequent GATT Secretariat publication elaborates on this point by stating that when the environmental impacts stemming from production of goods are strictly domestic, the choice of whether or not to externalize these costs is also strictly domestic. This interpretation implies that a country taking trade measures to maintain the competitiveness of an industry that has internalized its costs is trying to impose its environmental judgement on another country. This imposition would have an extrajurisdictional effect, and therefore be contrary to GATT. The ruling also prevents individual countries from employing trade measures to conserve the global commons (such as the high seas, Antarctica, and the upper atmosphere).

If GATT is to allow countries to address the problem of competitiveness and the environment, it is necessary, in the context of internalization of environmental costs, to reject the principle of nondiscrimination on the basis of production method. On the extrajurisdictional issue, a more flexible interpretation of GATT rules is required, which recognizes that economic linkages created by trade can force countries to relax environmental policies and damage their own or the global environment. In other words, GATT must recognize the intrajurisdictional effects of goods imported at a price below their environmental cost. The GATT Contracting Parties must retain the ability to use trade measures to deal with this problem.

Governments and multilateral fora should also develop clear guidelines to enable the use of trade measures to protect the global commons. The relationship between GATT and international environmental agreements that incorporate trade measures must also be clarified. This clarification should in no way increase the potential for signatories or nonsignatories to environmental agreements, so called free riders, to benefit from such an agreement without incurring any of the costs.

NATIONAL AND MULTILATERAL SOLUTIONS

Multilateral solutions demand the constructive participation of all the GATT Contracting Parties. The existing GATT working group on Environmental Measures and International Trade should refocus its agenda on this issue. The work of the Organization for Economic Cooperation and Development's Joint Session on Trade and Environment is more advanced on these issues, but would benefit from greater cooperation and consultation with developing countries. A third multilateral forum with a primarily environmental perspective on these issues would help to balance the trade bias of GATT. The United Nations Environment Programme or the United Nations Commission on Sustainable Development are possible hosts for such a forum.

At a national level, close cooperation is required between trade and environment ministries in the resolution of these problems. The perception of trade ministries, that GATT is their exclusive preserve, must be broken down. Establishing a balance between the trade and environment ministries, and their respective objectives, is a key to making their policies mutually supportive.

The overall objective of all these initiatives should be to identify and address circumstances where environmentally related trade measures are the best or only option for promoting environmental objectives. Provisions will have to be made to make these decisions on a case-by-case basis. A specifically designed trade and environment dispute settlement mechanism is needed, and should be based on the principles of transparency, equity, and democratic accountability. It must be equitable between nations in its application and enforcement and provide for open consultation with people directly affected by trade and environment disputes. Environmental objectives must be given at least equal the weight given trade objectives, and sustainable development should be the overarching priority.

COMPLETION OF THE URUGUAY ROUND

The Uruguay Round negotiations have barely considered the far-reaching environmental implications of this trade liberalization process. Environmental considerations were omitted from their original mandate. Since then, expansion in the scope of these trade negotiations, and the acknowledged need to integrate trade and environment policies, urgently require a remedy for this omission. Any trade liberalization measures and any new world trade body emerging from the Uruguay Round must support, rather than undermine or obstruct, sustainable development.

Shifts in trade flows that stem from the Uruguay Round should be reviewed for their impact on environmental and natural resource management. The legislative implications of the round for existing and proposed environmental policies and agreements should also be examined. This review process should be initiated during the multilateral negotiations. At the conclusion of the round, the GATT Contracting Parties should commit themselves to extend this review to the national level, during implementation of the agreement. The review process would play a crucial role in directing implementation toward the goal of sustainable development and further identifying and addressing trade and environment linkages.

The proposal to create the MTO, currently incorporated in the Uruguay Round, should be the subject of a separate negotiation process. This process should be accompanied and informed by the fullest possible public participation and consultation. The text of the proposal should be revised to ensure that the MTO will enhance the prospects for sustainable development. In particular, the MTO must contain four elements. First, the agreement must make a legal commitment to sustainable development in the main body of the text. Second, the proposal must include a free-standing article on the environment, enabling review of the agreements making up the MTO, as well as any revision necessary to support sustainable development. Third, one element of the organization must be a standing committee on trade and environment. Finally, the agreement must contain provisions securing greater transparency and democratic accountability in the MTO than currently exist in GATT.

The creation of the MTO represents the first major opportunity for governments to give substance to Agenda 21's commitment to making trade and environment policies mutually supportive. Regular reports from the MTO to the United Nations Commission on Sustainable Development would facilitate this process. These amendments to the MTO text would turn it into the overarching multilateral agreement necessary to achieve integration of trade and environment policies. The MTO will enable GATT reform, as well as the coordination, integration, and redirection of the Uruguay Round package toward the goal of sustainable development. Conversely, failure to amend the MTO will tend to exacerbate conflicts between trade and environment policies.

COMPLEMENTARY TRADE AGREEMENTS
AND POLICY REFORMS

Potentially important avenues for the integration of trade and environment policies exist beyond GATT and the Uruguay Round processes. In particular, measures that secure more equitable terms of trade between developed and developing countries could make important contributions to environmental protection and sustainable development. These initiatives can be pursued on a bilateral or a limited multilateral basis, and should provide for further evolution during the implementation process. Linkages between these initiatives and national and multilateral policies can then be exploited fully. Agenda 21 identified the commodities trade sector as a priority area for action. The text called for developing countries to internalize the environmental, social, and resource costs in the price of their commodities. However, after the 50 percent fall in non-fuel commodity prices during the 1980s, the scope for internalizing these costs has been dramatically reduced. This internalization process will require bilateral and multilateral cooperation between producing and consuming countries. Without cooperation, any government unilaterally raising the price of a commodity will simply price itself out of the market.

Negotiated trade measures could be used to circumvent this problem. If designed in accordance with the Polluter Pays Principle, such measures would encourage both internalization of these costs and direct financial investment toward sustainable production methods. This could be achieved bilaterally by the repatriation to producer countries of tariffs levied on imports whose price does not incorporate their full environmental cost. It could be achieved multilaterally through commodity agreements, that incorporate an "environment fund" jointly administered by the parties to the agreement.

A number of studies have investigated the practicality and potential rewards of such agreements. Governments should accelerate the negotiation and implementation of model arrangements, as this appears to be the best option for confronting problems and constructing functional agreements.

Securing greater equity in North-South trade in other ways can also contribute to sustainable development. The establishment of commodity processing industries in producer countries, and diversification of their economies away from dependence on exploitation of commodities could merge these objectives. Developed countries' trade barriers to processed commodities should be removed so that, for example, the widespread practice of maintaining tariffs that escalate with the degree of processing of a product is halted.

Conversely, developing countries should be allowed to retain trade measures that "protect" processing industries during their establishment phase. These measures should only be applied where they do not conflict with the objective of internalizing environmental costs. Subsidies or other measures that lead to the overexploitation of natural resources should be removed. Agricultural subsidies in developed countries are a prime target in this respect. However, the reform or removal of these subsidies must be carefully integrated with environmental policy objectives.

Governments should also investigate the combination of trade measures and financial and technology transfer mechanisms that could be used to raise environmental standards around the world. Countries that take the lead in raising costs should not be penalized on world markets for reflecting a higher proportion of a product's environmental cost in the price. Environmental leaders must be able to take trade measures that "level the playing field" between environmentally sound and unsound goods.

However, levelling the playing field will not in itself provide developing countries with the financial and technological resources necessary to raise domestic standards. Developed and developing countries should cooperate in the search for trade-related measures to secure both these goals. Financial resources will be generated from import tariffs levied on goods produced under low environmental standards. Some portion of these tariffs should be repatriated to the exporting country to be invested in raising environmental standards. Countries should also explore linking technical cooperation and the sale or transfer of technology on favorable terms to trade measures that protect the competitiveness of industries with higher environmental standards.

International cooperation will be the key to successfully integrating trade and environment policies. However, lack of progress at a broad multilateral level is not an excuse for inaction. If the political will exists, there are many opportunities that trading partners can explore, in pairs or in groups, to address trade-related environmental problems. Action-oriented cooperation holds out the best prospect for early and successful solutions to trade and environment conflicts.

7

The Organization for Economic Cooperation and Development and the Re-emergence of the Trade and Environment Debate

Candice Stevens

INTRODUCTION

rade and environment issues are being intensely discussed and debated at the Organization for Economic Cooperation and Development (OECD) in Paris, just as they were some twenty years ago. OECD was set up under a convention signed in December 1960 to further the coordination of the economic policies of its twenty-four member countries, which include the United States, Canada, Australia, New Zealand, Japan, and the Western European countries. The range of concerns at the OECD includes policies related to environment, trade, agriculture, industry, science and technology, employment, education, and other areas.

In the early 1970s, OECD held trade and environment discussions that led to what is still the only international accord addressing the general trade aspects of environmental policies—the OECD Council recommendation on *Guiding Principles Concerning the International Economic Aspects of Environmental Policies* (OECD *Guiding Principles*) adopted on May 26, 1972. The most famous of the OECD *Guiding Principles* is the Polluter Pays Principle; there are also other tenets pertaining to harmonization, national treatment and nondiscrimination, and compensating import levies and export rebates. The trade and environment discussions now being held at OECD are expected to lead to a set of trade and environment guidelines for increasing the mutual compatibility of these two policy areas in the current era. These discussions will include a review of the original OECD *Guiding Principles*. To this end, a joint working group was set up in early 1991 composed of representatives of the trade and environment ministries of the twenty-four OECD countries. Together, trade and environment delegates are trying to develop general recommendations for heading off potential conflicts before they arise.

Trade and environment issues are being reviewed not just at OECD, but in numerous other international fora, including the General Agreement on Tariffs and Trade (GATT), the International Bank for Reconstruction and Development (World Bank), and the United Nations Conference on Trade and Development. What has caused this renewed interest in trade and environment issues? What has led to such intense activity at the national, regional, and international levels to reconcile trade and environment interests? Put simply, there have been three significant and fundamental areas of change since the original OECD *Guiding Principles* were developed in 1972. In the intervening twenty years, changes have occurred in the following areas: the nature of environmental problems, the direction of environmental policies, and the direction of trade policies. The juxtaposition of trends in these three areas has led to the current trade and environment debate.

THE CHANGING NATURE
OF ENVIRONMENTAL PROBLEMS

In the early 1970s, when the original OECD *Guiding Principles* were formulated, global and transboundary environmental problems were not widely recognized. The issues were more narrowly framed and the debate focused on the effects of environmental policies, particularly those relating to pollution abatement and the trade competitiveness of industry. Environmental problems and policies were otherwise believed to be confined generally within a country's national borders. The introduction to the OECD *Guiding Principles* states specifically that they do not address issues relating to what was then called "transfrontier pollution."

Today, global and transboundary environmental problems have emerged as the main environmental challenge confronting policymakers. Global warming, ozone depletion, and biodiversity loss are at the forefront of environmental issues for all countries. These issues, along with acid rain, pollution of shared water bodies, and cross-border air pollution are environmental problems that need to be addressed by countries acting together. Commerce in hazardous wastes, dangerous chemicals, and endangered plant and animal species demonstrates how trade between countries can itself contribute directly to environmental degradation. Globalization of environmental problems has paralleled globalization of the world's economy; it is just as difficult to place national labels on environmental problems as on merchandise and multinational corporations.

Increasingly, the global and transboundary environmental actions and behaviors of one country have extrajurisdictional effects on environmental assets shared with other countries. In general, global environmental problems are those relating to the protection of the global commons and those resources that are necessary to the continued functioning of the globe as an environmental unit. Transboundary environmental problems are those in which pollution, hazardous substances, migratory species, and other environmentally sensitive features cross national borders or have transborder effects.

An increasing environmental consciousness at the grassroots level combined with the perception of a real threat to one's own environment and health have led to increased public pressures to combat transboundary ecological menaces. Countries have sought to use extrajurisdictional trade measures as part of the policy arsenal to redress global and transboundary environmental problems. Through the use of import restrictions, countries can try to influence the environmental behavior of their trading partners and attempt to correct ecologically damaging policies or actions that are degrading their shared environments.

Use of these extrajurisdictional trade measures to address environmental actions with extrajurisdictional effects are legitimized when they are within the context of regional and international environmental agreements. There is a wide range of opinion about the nature, severity, and political responsibility for global and transboundary environmental problems. Compromises and solutions are best reached through negotiations among all the countries concerned. Countries recognize implicitly that there are some forms of environmental degradation that need concerted action, and that more than one country has jurisdiction over shared environments. They can then decide collectively whether trade actions are needed, in addition to other policy instruments, to address the issue at hand.

There are currently about twenty international environmental agreements that include trade provisions. Among the more well-known are the Montreal Protocol on Substances that Deplete the Ozone Layer (Montreal Protocol), the United Nations Convention on International Trade in Endangered Species of Wild Fauna and Flora (CITES), and the Basel Convention on the Control of Transboundary Movements of Hazardous Wastes, as well as the London Guidelines for the Exchange of Information on Chemicals in International Trade. In the future, trade provisions may be included in international agreements to address global ecological concerns relating to climate change, biodiversity, desertification, deforestation, and other problems. However, such trade provisions, particularly those that discriminate against nonsignatories to the international environmental agreement, may be incompatible with the more general trade rules found in GATT. Current trade and environment discussions at OECD and GATT are partly directed at finding means of accommodating this trend toward the use of trade provisions in environmental agreements without undue distortions to the international trading system.

Another facet of ongoing trade and environment discussions concerns the legitimate scope for the use of extrajurisdictional trade measures by individual countries seeking to influence the environmental behavior of other countries. Some countries want the ability to impose restrictions on imports or exports in the interest of protecting the global environment. Trade restrictions on imports of tuna to protect dolphins or on tropical timber to protect rainforests are examples. Environmentalists are advocating more flexibility in the use of unilateral measures to encourage environmentally friendly foreign behavior, particularly when there exists a clear danger to global or shared ecological assets and when such measures would provide an incentive for cooperating through an international agreement. In the past, countries have unilaterally restricted imports of ozone-depleting substances (prior to their regulation by the Montreal Protocol) and of endangered species (prior to their listing by CITES). The practical difficulty is in designing criteria to ensure that such trade measures are not disguised restrictions on trade and do not give undue advantages to domestic industries. The changing nature of environmental problems—from national to international in character— has been instrumental in prompting the current trade and environment debate.

THE CHANGING DIRECTION OF
ENVIRONMENTAL POLICIES

One of the OECD *Guiding Principles* advocated the harmonization of environmental policies when no good reasons for differences exist and where such differences may give rise to trade problems. This principle reflected the concern, which still exists today, that differing national environmental product standards could pose non-tariff barriers to trade and could, in some instances, constitute disguised restrictions on trade. For this reason, countries should attempt to harmonize their environmental, safety, and health standards to the greatest extent possible. Great progress has been made in increasing the compatibility of national environmental standards and reducing their potential to become trade barriers—through the GATT Agreement on Technical Barriers to Trade, through the adoption of mutual recognition and equivalency systems to facilitate cross-border trade, and through harmonization efforts such as those of the United Nations Food and Agriculture Organization and the OECD Chemicals Program.

But new challenges have arisen to both the trading system and to these harmonization initiatives as environmental policies have tended toward life-cycle management approaches. More and more, policy initiatives are attempting to characterize products according to the environmental manner by which they are produced and disposed of—in terms of their entire life cycle. As environmental policy increasingly becomes oriented toward the life cycle of products, it is coming into conflict with GATT's system of rules oriented toward the products themselves—specifically, the transfer of products from producers to consumers. Life-cycle policies can be enforced when products stay within one country, but are difficult to implement when products are traded across national borders.

The opportunities for clashes between environmental and trade policies are increasing with the trend toward life-cycle concepts. Eco-labeling schemes, eco-packaging rules, and recycling programs are no longer fads, but specific examples of the implementation of life-cycle concepts. They are widespread in OECD countries and even in some non-OECD countries. Many schemes are voluntary, but more and more are government sponsored. Current trade rules, however, do not allow trade discrimination against a product based on how it is produced, and regulations on the disposal or recycling of a product are often seen as potential trade barriers.

Eco-labeling schemes, for example, indicate to the consumer which product deserves to be purchased on environmental grounds. Eco-labels are usually granted on the basis of criteria relating to the ecological impacts of a product throughout its life cycle. There are now labels identifying biodegradable detergents, recycled paper products, environmentally safe batteries, dolphin-safe tuna, and a myriad of other goods. But countries may have completely different criteria for granting eco-labels, which can cause consumer confusion with regard to domestically produced and imported products. Countries may not have provisions for granting their own eco-labels to imported products or may not have the means to ensure that imported products meet their eco-labeling criteria. The trade community fears that eco-labeling may be used as a means to discriminate against products based on the environmental soundness of their method of production and to impose the environmental standards of one country on another.

Eco-packaging approaches are also examples of the trend to life-cycle management in environmental policies. New government programs and regulations to promote the return, recycling, or safe disposal of packages and containers are being announced daily. In the effort to cut down on mounting waste and to deal with waste disposal problems, some countries are demanding that all goods, both domestic and imported, be encased in recyclable packaging. Other countries are enacting deposit-refund schemes for bottles and containers or proposing a tax on products depending on the recyclability or environmental friendliness of its packaging. These are innovative and valuable approaches to coping with waste problems, but they can pose problems for imported products. Products that travel long distances may of necessity be packaged in greater amounts of more durable materials with fewer options for recycling. In addition, imported products may not have access to recycling facilities or deposit-return distribution networks in their countries of destination. There is also the real possibility that the structure and vertical integration of local recycling networks may act to shut imports out of domestic recycling markets.

Recycling programs can apply to more of a product than just its packaging. For example, greater attention is now being paid to the life-cycle management of automobiles. Companies are developing and advertising cars with recyclable components. But questions arise regarding the practicality of international recycling programs for automobiles, which are one of the most widely traded products. Requirements regarding the life-cycle characteristics of transport vehicles could pose problems for the trading system. Proposals are now being made for the international eco-labeling of automobiles, based on the recyclability of their parts as well as on their carbon emissions and fuel consumption.

Greater harmonization of eco-labeling, eco-packaging, and recycling approaches at the international level is being called for to prevent interference with trade. But such harmonization, particularly in the case of eco-labeling, would imply a significant degree of agreement among countries on the environmental criteria underlying these programs—a wholesale harmonization of environmental policies that will not be easy to achieve.

Above all, these environmental life-cycle approaches bring into question the concept of "like product" under international trade rules. Currently, products are considered "like" if their physical characteristics are alike; imported products "like" a domestic counterpart cannot be subject to trade discrimination. How competing products are produced is not considered relevant under current trade rules since it is the exporting nation, not the importing nation, that will be polluted in the process. How products are disposed of is now considered more of a problem for the importing nation, which should not impose undue burdens on exporting nations. The movement to define "like products" according to their life-cycle characteristics, rather than just the physical traits embodied in the product, raises new and difficult questions for the trading system. It is one of the best examples of how the current trade and environment debate differs from that of the 1970s and constitutes one of the main policy challenges for the trade and environment experts at OECD.

THE CHANGING DIRECTION OF TRADE POLICIES

The OECD *Guiding Principles*, like most of the analysis conducted on the trade and environment interface, were addressed toward minimizing the potential negative effects of environmental policies on trade. While looking at trade and environment interactions is not new, this analysis has always been done from the perspective of the trade impacts of environmental policies—the impacts on costs and competitiveness, their potential as trade barriers, the effects on foreign investment, etc. Now it is recognized that international trade can have environmental impacts. This recognition was prompted by the current trend in trade policies toward trade liberalization—through regional free trade and common market agreements and through the multilateral trade negotiations sponsored by GATT. The liberalization of the trading system has been proceeding rapidly but without much attention to its ecological dimensions. For example, the possibility that trade policies could have implications for the achievement of environmental goals was not considered when the OECD *Guiding Principles* were formulated.

Environmentalists are concerned that trade liberalization, with its focus on freeing up trade, could jeopardize environmental standards, could lead to more pollution and a more rapid draw-down of resources, and could change the global pattern of output with ecologically damaging results. Liberalizing trade in a context of nonexistent or inappropriate environmental policies can lead to all types of ecological impacts about which little is known. Trade liberalization initiatives have been generally carried out without attention to environmental effects because this type of trade and environment link has rarely been considered—either by trade policy makers or by environmentalists. Now attempts are being made to understand the positive and negative impacts of trade and trade liberalization and to develop means for accentuating the positive impacts and mitigating the negative effects.

For the most part, environmental degradation is due to market failures (when the prices of goods and services do not reflect their full environmental costs) and intervention failures (when government policies fail to correct market failures, or worsen them). Trade can be ecologically positive in helping to generate income to correct these failures. However, trade can also contribute to environmental problems by worsening existing market and intervention failures under certain conditions. OECD is attempting to develop an analytical framework for examining the environmental effects of trade and trade policies in terms of regulatory effects, product effects, scale effects, and structural effects.

Trade liberalization may have implications for national environmental rules and standards or regulatory effects that should be considered. Care must be taken to ensure that provisions regarding standards in trade agreements do not prevent governments from setting environmental standards appropriate to their national ecological conditions and preferences and do not compromise the achievement of a high level of environmental protection. Other regulatory effects pertain to the implications of trade policies for national laws and practices relating to environmental subsidies, environmentally related import and export measures, and commitments taken under international environmental agreements.

Trade liberalization can have positive product effects in facilitating the international diffusion of environmental technologies and services to address ecological problems. In a recent study, OECD has estimated that the market for environmental equipment and services is about \$200 billion worldwide and growing at a rate of 5.5 percent per year. On the other hand, trade and trade liberalization can have negative product effects in facilitating the international movement and exchange of goods that harm ecosystems, such as hazardous wastes, dangerous chemicals, and endangered species.

Trade liberalization can lead to positive scale effects in augmenting growth and the financial resources that can be used to tackle environmental problems. Trade acts to raise incomes so that there is more interest in and more funds to spend on environmental protection. However, if new environmental costs exceed the income gained through trade, the net outcome may be a debit rather than a credit. In addition, certain negative scale effects may stem from the pollution externalities associated with the expansion of economic activity and greater movement of goods. There is a potential for increased environmental damage to sensitive regions, border areas, and transport zones. Free trade and economic development are not an instant antidote to environmental degradation. Trade may expand opportunities for economic growth, but must be accompanied by appropriate environmental policies to lead to sustainable development.

Trade liberalization should have positive structural effects in promoting the more efficient use of resources and removing subsidies and trade barriers that can lead to both trade and environmental distortions. However, the expansion of trade in the presence of market and intervention failures might also worsen the distribution and intensity of some economic activities from the environmental standpoint. Because environmental values are generally not reflected in prices and markets, trade can locate production and consumption in geographic areas unsuited to the nature and intensity of the activity. Trade liberalization may thus exacerbate some ecological problems when environmental costs are not internalized and appropriate environmental policies are lacking. Only together can trade liberalization and environmental protection point the way to sustainable development. The sensitization of trade policies to environmental considerations and impacts is an important part of the current trade and environment integration effort.

INTEGRATING TRADE
AND ENVIRONMENTAL POLICIES

As environmental policies have focused on the life cycle of products, and as trade liberalization has progressed at the regional and multilateral levels, the trade and environment debate has re-emerged and has taken on new dimensions as environmental problems have become more global in scope. The OECD *Guiding Principles* are still relevant, but may not be sufficient to address the more complicated problems and conflicts at the current nexus of trade and environment. The thorniest problems relate to the direct use of trade measures at the national and international levels to achieve environmental goals, the life-cycle management of traded products, and the "greening" of trade policies and trade agreements.

To a greater extent than the trade and environment debate of the early 1970s, today's discussions at OECD are directed at improving the integration of trade and environmental policy making. Policy adjustments in both the trade and environment areas are necessary to head off potential conflicts. Trade objectives and principles—such as nondiscrimination, national treatment, and legitimacy—must be more fully taken into account by environmental policy makers. Environmental objectives and principles—such as sustainable development, the precautionary principle, and the Polluter Pays Principle—must be more fully taken into account by trade policy makers. The improved integration of trade and environmental policy making will help promote their mutual compatibility in the long term and contribute to the balanced resolution of conflicts that do arise. Through its joint trade and environment work, OECD hopes to make its contribution to this mutual sensitization and integration process.

8

A European Perspective on Trade and the Environment

Konrad von Moltke

INTRODUCTION

In many ways, Europe has been engaged in continuous free trade negotiations for the past forty years. The move toward integration in the European Community (EC) has been a long, continuous process marked by several major way stations: the European Coal and Steel Community in 1951; the EC and Euratom in 1957; the French veto of British membership and the Luxembourg Compromise in 1964; accession of Britain, Denmark, and Ireland (and a decision by Norway not to accede) in 1972; Greek accession in 1979; Spanish and Portuguese accession in 1985; the Single European Act in 1986; European Economic Zone with the European Free Trade Association (EFTA) in 1991; Maastricht in 1991; and the Danish and Swiss votes drawing into question the inevitability of integration. Next to the EC, the creation of the Nordic Council and EFTA pale in significance, but by comparison with developments elsewhere, both events would still be worth discussing. All of this was capped by the fall of socialist regimes across Central and Eastern Europe and the sudden elimination of long-established trade barriers between Western and Eastern Europe, leading to the incipient creation of a *maquiladora* industry along the eastern frontier of Germany and Austria.

If ever there was a region where evidence of the linkages between trade and environment can be expected to be found, Europe is it. Highly industrialized, heavily polluted, densely populated, economically integrated, Europe must be the fulcrum on which the trade and environment agenda emerges. How did the trade and environment agenda emerge in

93

Europe? What is its current shape? What lessons can be drawn? And what are the prospects for future developments?

HOW DID THE TRADE AND ENVIRONMENT AGENDA EMERGE IN EUROPE?

The environmental agenda did not emerge easily anywhere in Europe. Governments did not take to environmental action without strong public pressure. The environment has no constituency motivated by self-interest, the basis of interest group politics in modern democracies. Other well-organized economic interests, thinking they benefitted from the pollution they caused society at large, were entrenched and closer to the government's ear. Indeed, this remains true in most countries. Environmental management was not the priority of those in power, and allying oneself with environmental interests was considered a shortcut to political irrelevance. From the start, public pressure has been the bedrock of environmental action.

International policy making is generally more shielded from public pressure than domestic decision making. To begin with, much of the action takes place in remote locations rather than close to voting constituents. It is conducted in foreign languages by diplomats—that is, persons who do not speak for themselves but, like a lawyer, represent an absent client, their government. By all accounts, diplomats are part of a privileged class in any society that is capable of shielding itself from the most unpleasant realities of pollution and scarcity. If most governments were uninterested in environmental affairs, their diplomatic corps were downright hostile toward them.

By contrast, the position of trade liberalization has long been secure on a national scale of international priorities. Although not always popular domestically in all countries, the advantages of trade liberalization have not needed to be argued to international policy makers. Quite apart from its presumed economic advantages, trade liberalization has fit well with the general priorities of international relations. Closer economic links, represented by trade liberalization, could further political detente and thus contribute to a lessening of tensions and increased international stability. Indeed, the original concept of European integration—peace through economic cooperation—was the ultimate reflection of this world view and underlay the treaties that created the EC.

The inclusion of nuclear energy in the grand design for European unity was a logical extension of this view. Coal, steel, and energy were considered the very foundations of economic development, and what could be a more potent symbol of the will to create a peaceful family of nations from the ruins of world war than harnessing the destructive powers of the atom for the cause of peace. Unfortunately, coal, steel, and energy—most emphatically nuclear energy—were the engines of pollution and the symbols of environmental hazards in the developed world so that the fond vision of ever greater, ever more integrated economic unity leading to political integration ran directly afoul of basic environmental realities.

The strangely citizenless and undemocratic practices that the EC has long represented exacerbated the problem. Public accountability for decisions by the Council of Ministers had not developed; ministers met in secret, voted in secret, and wrote secret minutes that could materially affect the interpretation of published, legally binding instruments. Sporadic efforts to create a "Europe of Citizens" never eliminated the basic abuses of power these practices still represent.

At the same time, falling economic barriers between countries revealed the importance of related "noneconomic" policies such as environmental management or social and health policy as factors of international competitiveness. In particular, countries with strong measures in these areas sought to use the instruments of international cooperation to induce other countries to follow their lead. They were convinced that this represented sound social and environmental policy, and it helped avoid any distortions of competition that might arise through the imposition of environmental controls. Over the years, fears of such distortions have generally far outstripped any proof that they actually occur.

By the early 1970s, a perceptive observer could discern that the future of European integration depended vitally on developments in the private sector. Governments can drive the process of integration only a certain distance. It requires direct and active involvement of private parties, individuals, corporations, and other institutions, to make integration a reality. Environmental policy, based on citizen activism and clearly requiring international cooperation to achieve its goals, became one of the few areas of European policy that enjoyed widespread public attention and support. In this manner the needs of trade liberalization, of political integration, and of environmental management all converged to produce significant, sometimes surprising political consensus in favor of European action on the environment.

WHAT IS THE CURRENT SHAPE OF THE TRADE AND ENVIRONMENT AGENDA IN EUROPE?

The EC, representing Europe's largest and most comprehensive trade agreement, has the distinction of initiating some of the most far-reaching trade and environment ramifications for Europe and the world. The non-EC nations of Europe have also been active on this agenda, often on a regional or bilateral level, but to a lesser degree than the EC.

THE EUROPEAN COMMUNITY

The initial response of the EC to the environmental challenge was not particularly auspicious. At the 1972 Paris summit of EC heads of state and government (the forerunner of the "European Council"), a decision was taken to have the EC launch a program of environmental activities. This decision reflected a political response to growing public concern, highlighted by the United Nations Conference on the Human Environment, rather than a well thought-out course of action. It was seen as strengthening the EC, presumably at no great cost since hardly anybody expected environmental affairs to emerge as a major government priority.

The political mandate was picked up by a small group of EC bureaucrats. It became the germ cell of a substantial program of regulation, research, and policy development within the EC. Two motors appear to have sustained this effort despite continuing, sometimes vigorous opposition from within the ranks of the EC bureaucracy itself: unchanging public support and the growing recognition that the goals of economic integration were unattainable without attention to the environmental dimension of the economies.

"Europe" can mean quite different things to different people. The EC includes twelve quite heterogeneous countries whose interests can diverge significantly when it comes to the environment: the United Kingdom is a highly industrialized island state with a temperate climate; Germany, a continental country with shared natural resources linking it to all its neighbors, is part of the three major international river basins of Europe; Italy is an industrialized country with long ocean borders and a Mediterranean climate; Spain is a rapidly industrializing country that shares a peninsula with less developed Portugal; Denmark and the Netherlands are smaller countries with strong environmental constituencies, closely linked to their neighbors. The position of these countries differs on many significant environmental issues, exemplified by attitudes toward water management, air pollution control, toxic substances control, and global warming.

In the Northern countries, water quantity is not a pressing issue while water quality is; the Mediterranean countries tend to transfer water pollution to the ocean and worry primarily about water supply. The United Kingdom, with short swift rivers that regenerate rapidly, can maintain good ambient water quality with relatively modest effort and can discharge to the ocean from many locations. Germany, on the other hand, is faced with a situation where even heroic water treatment results in unsatisfactory surface water quality in some rivers. Thus, the United Kingdom tends to emphasize environmental quality objectives over strict emission standards while Germany takes the opposite approach. The challenge the EC faced when it launched its environmental program was to find a regime that ensured and could accommodate both approaches. The initial approach allowed countries to pick either method of control and imposed an obligation on the EC to establish "equivalent" standards for emissions and for quality objectives. This quickly proved to be an impossible undertaking and ultimately countries began moving toward the only environmentally sound approach, namely to use these two methods in tandem to achieve both adequate environmental quality and reasonable levels of economic equity. Despite these confusions, the EC has had noticeable impacts on water quality management in several countries. The 1976 compromise included provisions to make information on water quality publicly accessible. Similar provisions were being planned by the British government of the day. When the government changed and sought to draw back from the projected changes, it found that EC law forced it to go ahead. Several years later, in the process of privatizing the water supply companies, the British government again discovered that EC law represented a critical barrier to its plans since the EC would not permit the transfer of regulatory functions to private agents. Furthermore, measures needed to meet EC water quality standards represented a sizable charge against future earnings of the companies, effectively depressing their market value. At the same time, the EC groundwater directive— more specifically its provisions concerning the concentration of nitrates in groundwater—is presently causing several EC countries to rethink their agricultural policies as over-fertilization threatens aquifers throughout the region.

These examples illustrate how typically local and regional concerns such as water quality management can impact the economic parameters for the countries of the EC and ultimately contribute to more equal conditions of competition. At the same time, they illustrate the complexity of creating an appropriate body of international regulation to go along with the steady liberalization of the movement of goods and services within the EC.

The major parameters of air quality management are by now well-established. It requires the control of emissions from energy use and of toxic substances from point and nonpoint sources. The fact that the EC was based on coal and nuclear energy could lead to the conclusion that it would have an active energy policy. Until recently, that has not been the case. The interests of Member States have not converged.

Until the early 1980s, this divergence extended to the control of atmospheric pollution, with Germany and the United Kingdom combining to render impossible effective controls of acidifying emissions from power plants. All countries worked together to hinder rigorous controls on automobile emissions by leaving the task of European harmonization of automobile emission standards to the Economic Commission for Europe (ECE) where an obscure committee, including both Eastern and Western European nations, consistently agreed to standards that reflected engine design criteria rather than emission control objectives.

This deadlock was broken in 1982 when Germany, Austria, and Switzerland discovered extensive forest dieback, which was widely attributed to acid rain. Switzerland was the first country to reject the ECE standards by requiring catalytic converters in new cars. Germany changed from being an opponent of controls on acid rain to a vigorous proponent, in particular by introducing tight, state-of-the-art controls on sulfur dioxide and nitrogen oxide emissions from fossil fuel power plants. It immediately sought to impose these emission standards on all other Member States of the EC; but while its change of heart broke the deadlock in the EC, its approach found no favor.

The German controls effectively required a retrofit of desulfurization and denitrification equipment on all major oil- and coal-fired power plants with a significant remaining useful life. Such a retrofit reduced emissions but was hardly the most economically efficient approach to the problem. In a country like Germany, with dense population and high levels of industrialization as well as a "balanced" budget of long-range imports and exports of air pollutants, such measures could be justified.

These measures could not be justified in the United Kingdom (which exported a large proportion of its emissions, some of which were deposited in the ocean), in Portugal (with limited levels of industrialization), or in the Netherlands (which had adopted more control measures against acidification than other continental countries). After arduous negotiations, an extraordinary compromise emerged that specified essentially the German standards for new combustion plants but allowed countries wide latitude in pursuing agreed-upon levels of emission reductions from current levels. Indeed, Portugal was allowed to double its total emissions while the EC average was to drop by almost 58 percent by the year 2003.

The process of transforming a German initiative into a European measure illustrates in a remarkable fashion how environmental management techniques that may be appropriate within a national context produce undesirable distortions when applied internationally. In a similar fashion, the initial U.S. approach to controlling CFCs by banning "nonessential" uses in aerosols proved unacceptable at the international level; the Montreal Protocol was based on the EC approach of controlling production but strengthened by adding use controls and imposing surprisingly severe limits—at least by the standards of 1987.

Hazardous waste management represents a particularly thorny problem in relation to trade liberalization. It is remarkably difficult for proponents of free trade to recognize that to succeed in their overriding goal they must ensure that trade in hazardous waste is rigidly controlled; otherwise waste management scandals risk bringing the structure of trade liberalization into disrepute. The EC went through the entire cycle, including a false start involving liberalized movement of hazardous waste. This proved a mistake when forty-one drums of waste contaminated with dioxin, originating from the Italian town of Seveso, simply disappeared from the face of the earth despite EC rules governing export and documentation. As a result, a regime evolved that is based not only on prior informed consent—like the Basel Convention on the Control of Transboundary Movements of Hazardous Wastes and their Disposal—but includes the right of Member States to license the import, export, and transit of hazardous wastes. Despite these restrictions, illegal transport of waste continues to be discovered, most recently into the countries of Central and Eastern Europe.

The linkages between trade and environment have been particularly evident in the area of toxic substances control. The EC has established two major directives, one for the control of certain particularly hazardous substances, and one for the packaging, labeling, and notification of substances. The latter, also known as the Sixth Amendment, involves a remarkable approach to testing and notification. It provides a "minimum premarket set of data" that all producers and importers of new substances must provide, as well as a carefully constructed sequence of decision points, based on volume of product marketed, where public authorities must decide whether to require additional testing. In return, it allows a manufacturer or importer to notify the competent authority in one country and then to market the product in all EC countries without any further controls, obligations, or paperwork. In effect, the authority that receives the notification acts as an agent for the competent authorities in the other countries. One result of this structure has been vigorous interaction among competent authorities to ensure that controls remain tight in all countries. In sharp distinction to the U.S. Toxic Substances Control Act (TSCA), the Sixth Amendment focuses on premarket notification rather than premanufacture, again reflecting the requirements of an international regime that would be overburdened by a requirement to act in response to production; it does not extend to significant new uses as TSCA does. The Sixth Amendment has initiated an intensive process of interaction between authorities in EC Member States that tends to use the more flexible instrument of EC Commission directives (roughly comparable to regulations in the United States) rather than the unwieldy Council directives, which are used for new binding legislation. This effectively creates a management structure for risks from the marketing and use of toxic substances that accompanies the trade liberalization process and allows it to proceed without undermining essential environmental safeguards.

The issue of climate change is quintessentially international because action by individual countries, certainly by individual EC countries, is manifestly futile. The global character of climate change should not, however, mask the degree to which measures that may be adopted can impact every facet of a society, down to individual communities and households. Consequently, the need to ensure that equal conditions prevail among countries with open borders is particularly strong, yet the style and substance of each country's environmental and economic policy must be integrated into the emerging structure. Recognition of this basic need has driven the EC to take an active role in climate negotiations from the outset. While countries can act on energy efficiency measures largely independent of each other (although voluntary harmonization organizations can play an important role), the adoption of carbon taxes or other measures to ensure the internalization of environmental costs associated with the use of fossil fuels requires broad coordination between countries because its effects are widespread and persistent and must be reflected in consumer prices if the desired effect is to be achieved.

The EC has agreed to a position in favor of carbon and energy taxes but has made them conditional on the adoption of comparable measures in other Organization for Economic Cooperation and Development (OECD) countries. This argument is flawed from a trade perspective because it assumes a level of open market access within OECD that is not currently available. In practice, trade borders still exist between many of the OECD countries—and wherever a trade border exists, it is possible to border-adjust for special measures such as carbon taxes, to rebate the carbon tax on export and to impose it on import, as the United States does in relation to the superfund tax. This implies that the EC position does not properly reflect the level of market integration but rather represents a political position to avoid rapid implementation of measures that have been agreed to in principle.

OTHER EUROPEAN INSTITUTIONS

The unity of the Nordic Council is attenuated by the fact that Denmark is a member of the EC while the other four members are not. In practice this means that the Nordic Council countries cooperate on policy initiatives but not in relation to trade. The importance of trade relations can be illustrated by Sweden's attempt to ban cadmium from its market and Denmark's efforts to follow suit. In 1979 Sweden decided that efforts to reduce the release of cadmium to the environment had failed and that only a ban on the use of cadmium as surface coating, pigment, or stabilizer could lead to the desired reduction in environmental exposure. Over several years, Sweden attempted to implement this ban, only to find that cadmium was in widespread use in industrial products and that exceptions had to be allowed for a number of products (military hardware and certain plastics in particular). Sweden's attempt to implement the ban caused environmental levels of cadmium deposition to fall only marginally. At the same time, Denmark pursued parallel policies but found it even harder to implement a ban within the EC. The Danish position was rendered more difficult by the fact that as much as half of all cadmium deposited on soils in that country was transported by atmospheric deposition from outside the country. The experience of these two countries shows how congruent environmental policies are essential to control pollution from industrial activities.

EFTA never developed a level of economic cohesiveness to require integration of policies such as environmental protection. Initially EFTA included Austria, Denmark, Norway, Portugal, Sweden, Switzerland, and the United Kingdom, countries with almost no shared environmental resources. At the same time, these countries (with the exception of Portugal) represent a homogeneous group in terms of environmental policy. Cooperation among them was unlikely to produce major environmental benefits because none of the countries required external pressure to adopt appropriate policies internally. Subsequently, three of these countries broke away to join the EC, leaving essentially a rump EFTA.

The aims of EFTA were more closely tied to economic cooperation without the goal of broad integration. It sought to promote a sustained expansion of economic activity, full employment, increased productivity, the rational use of resources, financial stability, and continuous improvement in living standards. The reference to "rational use of natural resources" indicates an evolution with respect to GATT and the European Economic Community, but it reflects primarily the concerns of resource poor European countries about access to natural resources rather than any concern about environmental management. Over the thirty years of its existence, EFTA has not found it necessary to establish an environment committee. Despite its slightly different mandate, and despite high levels of environmental concern in its member countries, EFTA's approach to environmental issues is more akin to GATT. The EFTA Secretariat was located in Geneva in proximity to GATT. However, based on a full treaty, EFTA was able to develop a more differentiated institutional structure than GATT.

Similarly the countries of the former Soviet bloc undertook only limited levels of cooperation on environmental affairs. Environmental concern carried no weight in the Council for Mutual Economic Assistance (CMEA, formerly known as COMECON), and pollution involved no penalty so that measures to reduce pollution were viewed as pure externalities with costs but no benefits. Lacking the corrective of public pressure that drew democratic societies back from the brink of environmental destruction that was threatening in the late 1960s, the Soviet system demonstrated the results of industrialization without environmental controls. The absence of environmental protection in most countries of the CMEA meant that there was no need for active cooperation within the trading bloc, although by 1990 even CMEA was planning a report on the environment and efforts to protect it in its member countries—a little like closing the stable doors after the horse has bolted. In the changing landscape of Central and Eastern Europe, the EC looms very large. Most of the newly formed countries are torn between the express desire of their citizens to see quick environmental improvements and the traditional economic advice that views environmental investments as unproductive. It will be critical for all of these countries to embrace both goals internally and in their trade relationships; the EC lead will be important in this respect.

Thus the most important European policy initiatives linking environment and trade took place within the EC. By now, the EC environmental policy transcends its origins as an offspring of economic integration. For many years, environmental management has represented an important activity in its own right within the EC and an independent factor of integration within the system. This was recognized in 1986 by the Single European Act. The act introduced a new title addressing the environment and clarified that environmental management within the EC serves not only the defensive purpose of avoiding distortions to international trade but represents a positive goal of improving environmental protection and contributing to the overall aims of the EC, including political integration.

Given this background, one might expect the EC to be at the forefront of the environmental debate in relation to international trade liberalization. This is not the case. To a certain extent, this is the result of the curious structure of GATT, which is an unratified agreement binding the executive branches of government. As a consequence, the EC is represented in GATT by the Commission of the European Communities rather than by Member States through the EC Council. The Commission is less publicly accountable, representing a further layer of public administration on top of the national authorities and exhibiting many characteristics of a civil service cut loose from the citizens it serves. Consequently, EC trade negotiators have even less reason than national trade negotiators to experience directly the pressure of environmental needs or to seek modifications in the international trade regimes to accommodate the environmental imperative.

WHAT LESSONS CAN BE DRAWN
FROM THE EUROPEAN EXPERIENCE?

A number of lessons emerge from the European experience with trade and environment. The first lesson is clearly that as trade liberalization advances, increased levels of integration of environmental management become necessary. In some instances the need is defined by the nature of trade and the characteristics of products moving in trade; in other instances the need is created by the fact that environmental problems left unmanaged internationally can put the entire trade regime at risk in terms of public support. Examples are the mismanagement of hazardous waste or inadequate protection of certain species that have high public visibility.

When comparing the intensive level of environmental action in the EC with the much less strong involvement of the EFTA states in environmental coordination, it becomes apparent that the degree and form of environmental action in relation to trade liberalization depends on the form and extent of the opening of borders and to some degree on the proximity of the participating countries. Whereas the EC represents a largely contiguous area (albeit not in any sense of the word an ecological unity), the EFTA was a disjointed group of countries (with Switzerland and Austria sharing a mountain border and Britain and Ireland sharing an island). Contiguous countries have the additional need to manage shared resources such as surface water, air pollution, or wildlife and suffer the environmental consequences of inadequate environmental management in addition to any economic impact that may exist. Moreover, citizens will organize across shared political boundaries, creating new and effective pressure for stronger environmental management. Countries that are distant, or at least sufficiently distant to permit environmental impacts to be mitigated and to render citizen action across borders difficult or impossible, will find that the linkages between trade and environment are more clearly limited to those aspects that are defined by goods in trade. These aspects include the characteristics of products and the need to ensure that controls are equivalent so that products entering trade are equivalent in terms of environmental impact and economic burdens. For this reason, the issue of harmonization has long been the focus of particular attention within the OECD.

The EC experience in particular points to innovative approaches to managing the environmental aspects of products entering international trade; by ensuring that measures in trading countries are equivalent, it is possible to share the regulatory burden and to reduce costs for manufacturers and importers. However, this requires a high degree of confidence in the ability of authorities in all countries to act in an equivalent manner.

The EC experience further illustrates differences between international and national environmental management. Repeatedly, management strategies that are effective in a relatively integrated national political and administrative structure prove impossible, inequitable, or ineffective in an international context. This can be seen in relation to such diverse issues as water quality management, air pollution control, toxic substances control, or the reduction of the use of chlorofluorocarbons. Learning to develop appropriate international approaches that complement national measures and provide an adequate level of assurance in terms of outcomes represents one of the most important challenges facing environment and trade policy makers in the coming years.

Finally the EC experience shows that the requirements of environmental management in a trade context are dynamic in nature and, consequently, the response needs to be the creation of a correspondingly dynamic process. Attempts to find solutions that deal with issues "once and for all" are bound to fail.

WHAT ARE THE PROSPECTS FOR FUTURE DEVELOPMENTS IN EUROPE?

The process of European integration is currently undergoing important changes. Within the EC, uncertainties remain whether the decisions envisaged in Maastricht in December 1991 can be implemented. The EC is moving toward close integration with the countries of EFTA with the creation of the European Economic Zone embracing both the EC and EFTA. Some EFTA countries have applied to join the EC as full members or are considering such a step. At the same time, the situation in Central and Eastern Europe promises to be a major issue for the EC for many years to come.

This uncertainty extends in some degree to the related environmental agenda. In some instances, the steps that are envisaged are likely to strengthen environmental management within the EC. Most EFTA countries are traditionally advocates of strong environmental protection. They already create pressures for more vigorous action. To a certain extent, the heterogeneity of the EC renders environmental policy making within the community difficult—but promises real benefits when agreement is reached because several countries will be induced to move farther faster than they would if left to their own devices.

EC environmental policy is liable to become the benchmark against which the countries of Central and Eastern Europe measure their own performance. At the same time these countries are also likely to exert pressure to reduce the salience of environmental requirements, arguing—as Greece, Portugal, and Spain have before them without success—that they need to first develop their economies. A widespread fallacy among economic policy makers is that environmental protection only sets in when a certain level of development has been reached (essentially a mirroring of the mistakes of the market economies in allowing unacceptable levels of pollution to develop before vigorous action was taken instead of seeking to learn from them). The EC will play a critical role in determining whether the Central and Eastern European countries can integrate environment and economy from the outset.

As a result of the debate concerning the Maastricht agreement, there has been a growing discussion on "subsidiarity," the principle that decisions should be taken at the lowest possible level of government. Applied to the EC, subsidiarity means that, in the words of the Single European Act, "[t]he Community shall take action relating to the environment to the extent to which the objectives [of the proposed action] . . . can be attained better at Community level than at the level of the individual Member State." This principle was already enunciated in the First Action Program and theoretically underlies all environmental measures of the EC. In practice, it remains difficult to determine the appropriate level of action. Since environmental phenomena respect no political boundaries, virtually any environmental issue can produce international effects. The region around Basel, where Switzerland, Germany, and France meet, demonstrates how even archetypically local issues such as the siting of industrial facilities and of major public works can engender multilateral international problems. At one level, any environmental issue can have an international dimension, and thus trigger EC action (since the Single European Act does not limit the EC to issues involving all Member States, it can at least in theory enter any matter that involves more than one). This makes a mockery of the principle of subsidiarity; it also flies in the face of a long tradition of environmental management that emphasizes the local over the regional and the regional over the global, even while remaining sensitive to the larger dimension of many localized issues.

A number of issues acquire particular saliency under the principle of subsidiarity: those that link environmental management to international economic policy, including trade, development assistance, structural adjustment, international finance, and technology transfer, whether within the EC or between the EC and third parties; those where the EC acting together can make a greater impact than individual Member States, for example all broader international environmental concerns; those that involve ecosystems of European significance, for example major river basins, migratory wildlife, transboundary air pollution; and the unhappy issue of hazardous waste that fits nowhere and provides the refuge of last resort to those determined to pollute rather than act responsibly for the environment. In practice, all these issues still make a major agenda for EC action.

A major unresolved issue with the EC and in its relations with other countries concerns the Common Agricultural Policy (CAP) and its impacts on the environment. While the CAP has come under attack from other countries because of its trade distorting aspects, in reality these represent but one element of an elaborate policy of subsidies, many of which are acceptable under GATT because they do not distort trade, even though they represent economically and environmentally distorting policies within the EC. It is conceivably possible to make the CAP GATT-consistent, while keeping in place extremely distorting subsidies such as those that exist in the United States for water use in agriculture. The relationship between the CAP and the environment has been analyzed for some years, but the precise mechanisms linking the two policy areas remain unclear. The assumption must be that removing many of the CAP subsidies will lead to environmental improvements while removing all subsidies will lead to environmental degradation. Thus, the environmental priority is for selective adjustment to agricultural regimes to ensure freer markets based on more complete internalization of environmental costs. That goal overlaps with the goals of trade liberalization; it is not, however, identical and the related conflicts have not yet been worked out.

Finally, it must be recalled that the environmental agenda is by no means closed. New approaches to environmental management are emerging that create closer links between environmental and economic policy, or that give meaning to the principle of prevention, enunciated in most environmental programs but rarely followed to its logical conclusion in practice. An example of the kinds of challenges emerging in Europe is the recently adopted German regulation on packaging waste. This regulation shifts responsibility for the reuse or recycling of packaging waste from the user to the manufacturer; it imposes percentage reductions in the amount of packaging waste that may go to landfills and forbids incineration as a form of reuse. If applied properly, this regulation will transform the packaging industry in Germany; it will also create new and complex requirements for those wishing to sell on the German market, requirements that may appear to some as non-tariff barriers to trade. The EC and other European institutions will need to grapple with these issues as they emerge.

9

Free Trade and Environmental Enhancement: Are They Compatible in the Americas?

Ambler H. Moss, Jr.[1]

INTRODUCTION

T wo events in the summer of 1992 must be seen, in retrospect, as having set important parts of the Western Hemisphere agenda for the Clinton administration even before it was elected. Both were milestones along the path toward what world consensus has deemed primary post-Cold War objectives—environmental protection and accelerated development.

THE UNITED NATIONS CONFERENCE ON THE ENVIRONMENT AND DEVELOPMENT AND THE NORTH AMERICAN FREE TRADE AGREEMENT

The first event was the United Nations Conference on Environment and Development (UNCED), held in Rio de Janeiro in June 1992. With 118 heads of state and government present, 172 of the 178 member nations of the United Nations (UN) represented, and over 10,000 delegates of countries and nongovernmental organizations in attendance, it was the largest international conference in history. The second event was the completion of negotiations for the North American Free Trade Agreement (NAFTA), announced by the governments of Canada, the United States, and Mexico in August 1992 and signed in December 1992.

There was a time not long ago when most people assumed that environmental protection and development were at least somewhat incompatible, if not mutually exclusive. People interested in trade and development tended to look at environmental regulations as disguised protectionism or barriers to progress. Environmentalists looked more toward limiting growth and development as the only means of saving the Earth from destruction.

As UNCED demonstrated, a large number of the world's nations no longer regard development and environmental protection as mutually incompatible or antagonistic, but, on the contrary, as capable of being mutually reinforcing. Furthermore, a comprehensive treatment of environmental concerns was an important part of NAFTA negotiations. U.S. Trade Representative Carla A. Hills told the Senate Finance Committee in September 1992 that NAFTA would do more to improve the environment than any other trade agreement in history. Whether or not such language is an exaggeration, this certainly was not the case with NAFTA's predecessor, the U.S.-Canada Free Trade Agreement. In that agreement, environmental issues were deliberately left out, to be treated separately. Many environmentalists on both sides of the border were unhappy at how these issues had been shunted aside. Some members of the environmental community were pleased at how squarely NAFTA addressed environmental issues.

This is not to ignore continuing sharp controversies concerning specific policies and measures to be taken. Splits within the Bush administration prevented the United States from taking a leadership position at UNCED or even, in the case of the Convention on Biological Diversity (Biodiversity Convention), from signing an important document agreed to by the great majority of delegates. James Gustave Speth, currently the Administrator of the United Nations Development Program, said that the United States found itself continuously out of step and isolated at UNCED. The main problem seems to have been the inability of William Reilly, head of the U.S. delegation and then Administrator of the U.S. Environmental Protection Agency, to obtain any clear direction from the administration on several crucial issues. This was through no fault of his own; in fact, after the conference he publicly expressed his frustration over the inattention and low priority assigned to these issues by Washington. Those familiar with executive branch politics were impressed with his outspokenness; presidential appointees have been sacked for much lesser offenses.

It became clear at UNCED that an ongoing debate between North and South over the financing of environmental protection will be a continuing feature of the negotiating landscape. A complete impasse was avoided at UNCED by skillful eco-diplomacy which extracted certain promises of greater funding through national development assistance and through multilateral negotiations. It remains to be seen, however, whether the promised funds will be forthcoming.

Nevertheless, people and governments around the Americas, where there is now a proliferation of environmental groups, have become highly sensitive to the rapid destruction of the environment and to the fact that such a situation cannot be continued if human civilization is to survive. That understanding is encompassed in the notion of sustainable development. The World Commission on Environment and Development report, *Our Common Future,* defined sustainable development as "development that meets the needs of the present without compromising the ability of future generations to meet their own needs." UNCED, even if it did not usher in a millennium of sustainable development, was the major consciousness-raising event to date, giving a strong impulse to carry its substantial commitments forward.

EARLY INTERNATIONAL EFFORTS

It must be appreciated that the environmental consciousness of the world has come a long way since UNCED's predecessor conference held twenty years earlier, the United Nations Conference on the Human Environment in Stockholm (the 1972 Stockholm conference). Ecologists of the day were few and largely from the scientific community. Representatives of developing countries were often hostile to what they saw as plots by industrialized countries to keep them primitive. Industrialized countries were only beginning to understand the ultimate results of massive pollution in terms of quality of life. Out of the Stockholm conference came an important institution, however, the United Nations Environment Programme (UNEP), which would assert a leadership role in the development of international environmental accords.

Most of the environmental agreements negotiated during the 1970s and 1980s were the direct result of the "agenda-setting" function of

UNEP. Two of the overarching problems of world ecology—ozone depletion and global warming—are issues on the world agenda only because of UNEP's extraordinary role. Its greatest achievements have been the Vienna Convention for the Protection of the Ozone Layer and its successor, the Montreal Protocol on Substances that Deplete the Ozone Layer (Montreal Protocol).

Development as it is taking place today is clearly not sustainable—we need look only at our own Western Hemisphere as an example. Add to the equation present population trends, and the projection becomes even more alarming. The world population of approximately 1.5 billion in 1900 and 5.3 billion today may, according to UN projections, reach 8.5 billion by the year 2025. Its ultimate stabilization point is unknown. The UN projects the number of people living in "absolute poverty" by the year 2025 to be 1.5 billion. In our own hemisphere, Mexico's population is expected to grow during this period from 88 million to 150 million, and Brazil's from 150 million to 246 million.

Given such realities, no one can question the necessity of development. The semi-desertified landscape of Haiti is an example of the fact that abject poverty and underdevelopment is one of the environment's worst enemies. It is impossible to demand any environmental awareness from a population whose only daily objective is survival. On a different scale, survival is also the response of peoples who are rapidly destroying tropical rainforests all over Latin America. Clearly, development solutions have to be found through cooperation, and on a global scale.

In the United States, as in other countries, the need to reconcile the twin objectives of development and environmental protection is moving us away from the more simplistic theories of the 1980s, what President Ronald Reagan called "the magic of the marketplace." From the environmental side of that particular worldview, the marketplace could regulate a theoretically limitless supply of resources and continue to dispose its wastes into a theoretically limitless "sink." The demise of Reaganomics, largely formalized by both political parties in the 1992 presidential campaign, implies the insertion of a social component into an essentially free-market strategy. It may also imply the addition of an industrial policy. A pending question is how quickly the transition can proceed toward effective adoption of sustainable development as a national policy.[2]

In the world today, and particularly in the Western Hemisphere, trade is seen as an important component of development. In Latin America, a commonly shared view of economic development emphasizes growth through the private sector, the freeing of markets, shrinking of government, privatization of state-owned enterprises, attraction of foreign investment capital, and the liberalization of international trade. This restructuring is the antithesis of prevailing Latin American policies during the 1970s and 1980s. Those decades were generally characterized by policies of import substitution and high tariff barriers, the development of state-owned enterprises and, in some nations, the discouragement of and frequent hostility toward direct investment by foreigners. Debt financing, which banks and governments later came to regret, was the source of capital during those years, not private direct investment.

SUSTAINABLE DEVELOPMENT AND LATIN AMERICA

On June 27, 1990 President George Bush introduced the Enterprise for the Americas Initiative; its most innovative feature was the proposal for the creation of a free trade zone encompassing the entire Western Hemisphere. That concept was warmly received in Latin America. It represented recognition and acceptance of Latin initiatives that were already well under way. Free trade accords all over Latin America have been and are being negotiated—the Common Market of the Southern Cone (MERCOSUR), made up of Argentina, Brazil, Paraguay, and Uruguay; trade liberalization among the countries of the Andean Pact; a renewed Central American common market; the Caribbean Economic Community; a Mexican-Chilean free trade agreement; and, most recently, accelerated negotiations between Colombia and Venezuela toward a common market, to be joined by Ecuador.

Latin America has realized the need for transition to sustainable development in a number of ways. The General Assembly of the Organization of American States, pursuant to Resolution 1114 of June 8, 1991, called upon member states to review their environmental laws, needs, and capabilities. Following UNCED, the Latin American Economic System (SELA), an important nongovernmental organization based in Caracas, Venezuela, called for careful review of UNCED and its resolutions. SELA is evaluating the impact of Agenda 21, UNCED's most important action plan, as well as assessing the financial resources needed to achieve Agenda 21's recommendations. It has also recommended a "technical study" on the concept of sustainable development, in light of the many different ideas on the subject, including those contributed by Latin America.[3] The United Nations Commission on Latin America and the Caribbean, based in Santiago, Chile, is performing similar work.

Both Latin America and the United States are interested in global trade liberalization through the long-running Uruguay Round of negotiations under the General Agreement on Tariffs and Trade (GATT). Success in the round will clearly benefit both the United States and Latin America. Unfortunately, the talks have repeatedly been stalled or suspended by such controversies as that between the United States and the European Community (EC) over farm subsidies. An ultimate failure of the Uruguay Round could mean the division of the world into competitive trading blocs. This threat may well have been a conditioning factor that led to the Enterprise for the Americas Initiative—the United States may need a trading bloc to call its own.

Despite stubborn opposition from labor and some adversely affected industries, President Clinton entered office with the assurance that mainstream U.S. opinion recognized economic interdependence as a fact of life, and that free trade and the creation of jobs were linked. U.S. exports to Mexico are the best example. Due to the Mexican trade liberalization measures under Presidents Miguel de la Madrid and Carlos Salinas de Gortari, exports to Mexico from the United States increased from $12 billion in 1986 to over $40 billion in 1992. According to an accepted "rule of thumb," each increment of $1 billion creates 20,000 additional jobs in the United States.

Under the best of circumstances, expanded international trade can be used to help the environment. It can "harmonize standards upward" to those of the most environmentally sensitive partner; the automobile industry is a good example. Trade can help to terminate subsidies, especially in agriculture, which are especially environmentally destructive. It can also put more financial resources into the hands of environmental enforcement agencies that lack resources, especially in the less developed world. Mexico is a prime example. Only with the advent of NAFTA was Mexico's environmental protection authority given adequate funding, a requirement for U.S. environmentalists to support the agreement.

It does not follow necessarily and automatically, of course, that the environment is safe from degradation by NAFTA. Citizens in both the United States and Mexico have expressed concern that "dirty" industry would simply migrate to Mexico, creating pollution havens there and eliminating U.S. jobs at the same time. There are strong arguments to the contrary, however, supported by the World Bank, the Inter-American Development Bank, international business associations, and most economists. They say that if care is taken and if Mexico's 1988 environmental laws are enforced, then increased trade through NAFTA will actually benefit the environment. Not only will increasingly more resources be put into the hands of environmental enforcers, but businesses will also be able to afford clean technology in their processes. It is likewise argued that economies of a similar level can more easily harmonize production standards. From years past, in the absence of a NAFTA, the Mexican side of the U.S.-Mexico border has accumulated a number of well-documented environmental horror stories. NAFTA may help to get the mess cleaned up.

Of course, to secure the support of the environmental community, President Clinton recognized even before his election that a supplemental agreement would be required to enhance the environmental provisions of NAFTA. That agreement, along with the one on enforcement of labor standards, will now form the complete NAFTA package, which still faces considerable difficulty in obtaining Congressional approval.

According to the American Chamber of Commerce in Mexico, multinational firms moving into Mexico during its restructuring over the last few years tend to be good environmental citizens. They respect local environmental laws and work to raise compliance within the business community to prevent unfair competition, among other reasons. Developed countries are also in a good position to benefit from the rising environmental standards in the developing world. Only developed countries have the environmental technology available to supply these emerging markets. If NAFTA works in this way to pursue both objectives of development and environmental protection, why not move beyond NAFTA into the rest of the hemisphere?

Implementation of a Western Hemisphere free trade area was provided for by the incorporation of an "accession clause" in NAFTA. Although this makes it possible for other countries to incorporate into NAFTA, in fact any new entry would require the same Congressional approval process as NAFTA itself. The U.S. market is of course the big trade prize for Latin America. In this sense, NAFTA is important as the beginning of North-South trade negotiations in which the environment can become a major beneficiary. It must be seen as such an opportunity even though there is an absence of quantitative analysis showing definitively the effects of NAFTA on the environment.

ELEMENTS OF ENVIRONMENTALLY
SOUND TRADE AGREEMENTS

Certain environmental criteria should be embodied in trade negotiations, both now and for the future Western Hemisphere free trade area. First, the U.S. government should clearly, and with one voice, adopt the principle of sustainable development as the organizing principle not only of trade agreements but also of bilateral or multilateral investment agreements that may be signed in the future. Other Western Hemisphere governments should be invited to adopt the principle to guide their negotiations.

It necessarily follows that environmental concerns should be integrated into the actual text of future free trade agreements. The model to follow is NAFTA, not the U.S-Canada Free Trade Agreement. In looking toward an eventual Western Hemisphere system, it would be helpful if current regional or bilateral agreements among Latin American and Caribbean countries fully addressed environmental concerns, so that these issues are not confronted for the first time in negotiations with the United States.

Although sustainable development will continue for some time to be subject to varying technical interpretations, it should be accepted as the overall guiding principle for trade and development in the world. From this, it flows logically that certain basic principles should be the subject of the international trade policies of the United States. Some of these are:

• *The Polluter Pays Principle* — requiring whoever causes damage to the environment to pay for its restoration, as the most efficient way to internalize real costs.

• *The Precautionary Principle* — calling for immediate cost-effective measures to prevent environmental damage when there is evidence of a significant or substantial environmental threat.

• *Priority of prevention* — favoring those measures needed to prevent possible environmental harm rather than providing for after-the-fact rectification of the damage.

• *Transparency and public participation in environmental and trade processes* —offering the general public access to information upon which a decision is based and giving it the right to participate in the process itself.

• *Dispute resolution* — subjecting environmental disputes that arise out of trade agreements to a separate and comprehensive dispute resolution process. Participation in these processes should involve scientists and environmental experts, not only lawyers and economists, as is the case in dispute resolution under GATT.

Much of the increased trade and investment contemplated to take place between the United States and Mexico is already a reality, even though the formal agreement has not yet been approved by Congress. Nevertheless, it is not too soon for the Clinton administration to undertake a study of desirable criteria to be included in free trade agreements with other Western Hemisphere countries. Discussions of these criteria could take place with potential free trade partners, encompassing an evaluation of environmental implications in future agreements. This process would be similar to what is going on with the economic restructuring of Latin American and Caribbean countries. In effect, economic reforms constitute building blocks toward a free trade agreement even before formal negotiations commence. Environmental reforms can play the same role.

In contemplating future agreements, it should be recognized that cooperative efforts to advance environmentally sound actions are vastly preferable to sanctions and penalties. As trade sanctions are likely to be applied, it is important to avoid protectionism creeping in under the guise of environmental protection; examples of such problems exist in the EC, even where countries deal with each other on a roughly equal economic footing. In the Danish Bottles case, the Court of Justice of the EC upheld Denmark's ban on non-returnable containers. Exporters to Denmark had complained that the ban was a simple restraint on trade, not a primarily environmental regulation.

In this respect, it would also be helpful to study an amendment of GATT, updating it to take into account environmental concerns. A number of environmental agreements provide for some form of trade sanction to enforce compliance. If challenged, these agreements could be nullified by GATT rulings. GATT was negotiated in the late 1940s when environmental awareness was largely limited to health and safety concerns.

It is thus important that GATT be amended to recognize the enforcement of environmental agreements and national laws. One constructive proposal is for GATT to sponsor negotiations for a new environmental code that would "set out minimum levels of pollution control and environmental quality." Violations of the code could be defined as countervailable subsidies under GATT.

Special environmental problems will arise in a world of greatly increased trade and environmental consciousness for which, at present, no effective control or sanctions are provided. The transport and disposal of toxic wastes and hazardous materials is one such problem. It is especially acute as a North-South issue because considerable amounts of these substances have been sent from developed countries to be dumped in developing countries in recent years. The Basel Convention on the Control of Transboundary Movements of Hazardous Wastes and Their Disposal, opened for signature in March 1989 (signed, but not yet ratified, by the United States), may prove to be an insufficient instrument by itself. Rather than prohibit any actions, that agreement simply requires "prior informed consent" and will be difficult to enforce. As a stopgap measure, many developing countries have obtained specific agreements from developed countries concerning national prohibitions of such exports to their countries.

THE FUTURE OF TRADE AGREEMENTS AND ENVIRONMENTAL PROTECTION

Looking to the future, what hope can we derive from the relationships among trade, development, and the environment that emerged at UNCED in Rio? The fact that the conference was held in Brazil was indicative of Latin America's new environmental consciousness and a contrast with the 1972 Stockholm conference. Latin America, once considered by the United States largely within the Cold War context, is now seen as an environmentally sensitive area.

The nonbinding Rio Declaration on Environment and Development, signed at UNCED, places human beings at the center of sustainable development concerns and emphasizes that environmental protection is an indispensable part of the development process. It stresses that the eradication of poverty must be a concern of the entire world and that the least developed countries deserve special consideration. Its principles argue for global consensus as opposed to unilateral action by individual nations.

The two legally binding conventions signed at UNCED—the Biodiversity Convention and the Framework Convention on Climate Change—provide for the transfer of technology and for scientific and technical cooperation between developed and developing countries. While recognizing the sovereignty of each state over its own natural resources, these agreements nevertheless move environmental concerns further toward a system of global governance in which individual states must behave responsibly.

Perhaps the greatest contribution of UNCED was Agenda 21, which was drafted during the preparatory period before the meeting. It is a vast strategic plan to reverse environmental deterioration, advance the world toward sustainable development, and clean up the global environment. Although a nonbinding document, Agenda 21 is a long-term agenda-setting action plan. It recognizes the elimination of poverty as essential to the implementation of sustainable development policies and encourages the efficient use of resources in doing so. It considers trade liberalization to be a catalyst for sustainable development. The rationale is practical—an open international trading system would improve the access of developing countries to international markets and eliminate certain current distortions in trade. Removing subsidies and tariffs, and including environmental costs of production in prices, are essential components of sustainability; they can also help the developing world.

UNCED clearly illustrated that there are environmental problems that confront the world as a whole, such as global warming and ozone depletion, while there are others that are more particular to individual countries or regions. One of these particular problem areas is deforestation, a practice of which developed countries have long been guilty. In response to deforestation, UNCED adopted a Statement of Principles on Forests, which applies to temperate-zone as well as tropical forests. South America today encompasses about 48 percent of the Earth's remaining forests; Brazil's Amazon alone contains one third of the world's forested area. The carbon dioxide absorptive capacity of forests make them critical components in the control of global warming caused by the emission of greenhouse gases. Yet the forests of Latin America are disappearing at an alarming rate of 8.4 million hectares per year, or an annual disappearance of 0.9 percent annually of the tropical forest in South America.

Deforestation in Latin America constitutes not only the destruction of a valuable natural resource, but also the burning of rainforest is responsible for 7 percent of the total global emissions of carbon dioxide along with resulting soil loss and degradation. Additionally, the biodiversity of the region, unsurpassed by any other part of the world, is also at risk. The current rate of ecological destruction could lead to the extinction of between 100,000 and 300,000 species within the next forty years. Latin American deforestation is clearly a problem common to both North and South.

Additional funding will be required to address all of the issues raised at UNCED. A part of the solution would be to increase the use of debt-for-nature swaps, using Latin America's enormous external debt of over $400 billion. In many countries, external debt can still be purchased on the secondary market at very favorable prices. Official debt waivers dedicated for environmental protection, such as that begun on limited terms in the Enterprise for the Americas Initiative, can also be increased.

At this writing, it is impossible to predict in which decade of which century the world might expect to attain the state of sustainable development. We do not yet even have a clearly defined and quantifiable definition of the term itself. But the process of recognizing sustainable development as a necessary and urgent objective has begun. An improvement of the world's international trade practices—the elimination of tariffs, quotas, subsidies, taxes, and other charges which work against that goal—are on the negotiating table today. A great deal of progress is being made, and it deserves to be supported.

NOTES

1. The author wishes to acknowledge the assistance of Rosa Lopez-Gaston, a North-South graduate assistant, in the preparation of this article.

2. Gareth Porter and Janet Welsh Brown, *Global Environmental Politics* (Boulder, Colo.: Westview Press, 1991), discuss the "paradigm shift" now under way (pp. 26-30). This book is recommended as a useful "primer" on the interplay of environmental issues in contemporary international global environmental action, from the "incremental change approach" (largely the present one), to the "global partnership approach," to the "global governance approach." The last is not altogether imaginary. Effective U.N. authority was seriously proposed at a conference in The Hague in March 1989 by the prime ministers of France, the Netherlands, and Norway and signed by 24 heads of state, although it was opposed by the United States, the Soviet Union, Britain, China, and Japan (p. 153).

3. Latin American Economic System (SELA), *The Environment and Development,* Document SP/CC/XVIII.O/DT No. 8 (September 1992). The study emphasizes that "the starting point for a policy of sustainable development is people; sustainable development cannot exist in an environment of grinding poverty; and human development must be its cornerstone, along with the rational use of resources."

10

A Business Perspective on Trade and the Environment

Robert J. Morris

I n discussing the approach of business to the trade and environment issue, it is important to acknowledge that "business"—taken as a whole—encompasses enterprises whose understanding of, and commitment to, sound environmental management practices varies from the exceptionally high to the virtually nonexistent. However, that comprehension and commitment has been increasing dramatically in recent years, especially among the more internationally competitive companies. It is primarily with the views and activities of that group that this chapter will deal.

For these enterprises, the conclusions put forth in the 1992 World Bank *Report on Development and the Environment* are the bedrock on which their approach to resolving the problem raised by the interaction of trade and environmental policies and objectives rests. The report convincingly demonstrated that "economic development and sound environmental management are complementary aspects of the same agenda. Without adequate environmental protection, development will be undermined; without development, environmental protection will fail."

These observations may strike most people as self-evident, but the fact is that many in the environmental movement do not accept them at all. Thus, when business points out that an open, rule-based trade system is an indispensable condition for promoting the economic growth that will best assure environmental protection, there is as yet no workable consensus that would permit business and most in the environmental community to agree on what those rules should be. That is not to say that dialogue is

121

impossible; it is simply to acknowledge that what may seem obvious to some as a point of departure is often not seen that way at all by others.

BUSINESS EFFORTS TO
IDENTIFY PRINCIPLES AND RULES

The only practical way to develop a coherent and effective set of principles and rules is for those on each side who do believe a consensus is necessary to lay out the problem as they see it and the solutions that would permit it to be managed. Business has begun this process over the last few years, using a variety of instruments to articulate its concerns, views, and the commitments many companies are prepared to accept on a voluntary basis.

For example, the International Chamber of Commerce (ICC), with representation in over 100 countries, has been actively promoting environmental awareness among its membership for more than twenty years. In 1984 it took the initiative, jointly with the United Nations Environment Programme (UNEP), of organizing the first World Industry Conference on Environmental Management (WICEM). In preparation for the second of these conferences, held in Rotterdam in April of 1991, the ICC took the lead in developing for the first time a set of principles that world business would propose to governments as public policy guidelines to deal with the trade and environment relationship. After discussion at Rotterdam, the ICC issued a formal set of recommendations on these issues in October of that year. What follows draws extensively on that statement as well as further refinements that American and other business organizations have brought to it over the last year. In this business effort, individual American companies and associations, especially the U.S. Council for International Business (the U.S. affiliate of the ICC and the Business and Industry Advisory Committee (BIAC) of the Organization for Economic Cooperation and Development (OECD)), have played an active and often leading role.

The ICC statement of October 1991 begins with the following declaration of principle:

> Growth is necessary to improve welfare and to provide the conditions and resources to enhance environmental protection. Trade ensures the most efficient use of resources, is indispensable to

economic growth, and [sic] therefore a necessary element in enhanced environmental protection. Economic growth, opening of markets, and environmental protection are complementary and compatible objectives.

Internationally competitive business believes that open markets are the most—and perhaps only—effective stimulus to the development of new products and technologies needed both to lower costs and to promote wider use of products and processes that will reduce environmentally destructive and wasteful practices. Open trade, buttressed by multilaterally agreed-upon rules that constrain arbitrary government actions, is the best way to assure that markets are in fact open to competition.

Those who argue that trade fosters environmentally unsound production or environmentally unsustainable exploitation of the world's resources often find themselves aligned with, and their arguments co-opted by, those whose main objective is to restrict competition in order to maintain a dominant market position. Environmentalists need to be wary of alliance (even inadvertent) with protectionists, not because it may not be politically advantageous in advancing their views (it often is), but because protectionism and uncompetitive markets will ultimately deprive society of the resources needed to achieve their environmental protection goals.

A recent example will serve to illustrate this point. On November 20, 1992 OECD organized a consultative meeting that brought together representatives of business and industry from several OECD member countries and government officials participating in OECD's joint working group on trade and the environment. Before that meeting, the BIAC (the organization that formally represents business and industry interests to the OECD) had agreed on a policy statement that reaffirmed business's opposition to the use of countervailing duties to offset the alleged competitive advantage of imports from countries whose producers have not had to operate under as strict an environmental regulatory regime as that of the importing country. This principle, incidently, was also set forth in the 1972 OECD *Declaration on Guiding Principles on Trade and Environment* (1972 OECD *Guiding Principles*).

During the consultative meeting, a representative of a European steel company complained that his enterprise was facing unfair competition from producers in Eastern Europe that did not have to meet the strict environmental standards required of his firm. While his call for countervailing tariffs was rejected by most of the other business representatives at the meeting as both unnecessary and unworkable, the incident underlined the fact that some in business are prepared to harness the cause of environmental protection to the more dubious cause of commercial protection. As the GATT Secretariat report of February 1992 on trade and the environment noted, "biases that protectionist interests introduce into the environmental policy package increase the cost of environmental improvement and slow its implementation."

If the protectionist solution is not the answer, what is? Business believes that it has to be found in measures that can best provide for clarity of policy and certainty of implementation in accordance with rules that minimize distortions in open markets. Broadly, these measures are the rules on which GATT is built:

- Nondiscrimination among outside suppliers;
- Treatment no less favorable than that accorded national products or producers;
- Transparency in rule making and implementation;
- Orderly processes for resolving disputes among what must in any case remain sovereign nations; and
- Disciplines that deter violation of agreed-upon rules, or that impose clearly defined penalties, should a sovereign country conclude that its interests require it to act contrary to a previously accepted rule.

Clearly, business would prefer that countries abide by the rules they have negotiated. Consistent failure to do so simply creates greater uncertainties in markets. It undermines the confidence that business needs to undertake new investment and develop the new technologies that are needed to promote sustainable development and the economic prosperity that alone will guarantee it. Perpetually hungry and impoverished people will simply not put a very high value on protecting their own or anyone else's environment.

If a rule-based system is a vital component to the success of the mission to promote growth and environmental protection, can we be satisfied with the rules we have, or are new rules needed? The answer business gives is that we need to preserve what we have as an essential foundation, but that new circumstances, the challenges of increasingly globalized markets, and the growing demands for new and often widely disparate regulations to protect environmental resources demand new rules and responses from governments as well as business.

Responsible business will do its part; for example, over a thousand large corporations and business associations have endorsed the Business Charter for Sustainable Development put forward by the ICC at the Rotterdam WICEM meeting in 1991, and more are signing on as it becomes widely known. The charter is a set of sixteen principles concerning responsible environmental management and practices that companies agree to employ in their own operations. Many companies have gone further in developing their own codes of conduct. Certainly, more need to get involved in these and comparable programs, but no one would argue that voluntary efforts by business are enough to deal with the complex environmental challenges that the modern industrial society creates. Governments clearly have obligations to legislate or regulate when specific environmental problems and society's interest demand a common response that voluntary efforts alone cannot assure, or when a common set of rules needs to apply to all market participants.

That said, business also understands that objective environmental conditions and society's preferences for managing the risks that are posed to the environment can vary considerably among different countries, and that the regulations and standards that each country adopts to meet its own conditions or preferences will inevitably create problems for international trade. While internationally active business would prefer that such regulations and standards be harmonized internationally to the maximum extent possible, it also realizes this will not always be possible (perhaps in some cases not even desirable). Governments must, in consequence, develop clear rules and procedures for dealing with the effects of different policies and standards on trade and investment if we are to maintain an open system governed by effective rules.

Broadly, there are three main areas where business—at least as represented by the ICC and the U.S. Council for Business Investment—believes new or clearer rules are required.

First, it is necessary to create rules regarding the setting of nationally or internationally harmonized standards for products or the production processes designed to render certain products "fit for use." In particular, a consensus about the use of scientific principles and practices in developing new standards and the elaboration of criteria that will apply in resolving disputes about the unnecessarily trade-restrictive effects of national standards are needed to adapt the GATT dispute settlement system to contemporary reality.

Second, the international commitment to the Polluter Pays Principle, first elaborated by the OECD in 1972, must be strengthened and extended. The principle needs to be clarified to assure that its focus remains on the avoidance of targeted government subsidies that help finance the costs to specific enterprises in meeting new environmental regulations and thereby creating a market-distorting advantage over nonsubsidized competitors.

Third, it is necessary to promote adoption of multilateral agreements to deal with efforts to protect resources that are part of the global commons, or for regional agreements to deal with problems that are transboundary in scope. The provisions of such agreements may involve departure from GATT rules and, if they do, business needs to know the rules governments will apply to deal with such inconsistencies. Finally, business believes that such extraterritorial problems can only be effectively dealt with through international agreements, not through the unilateral imposition of extraterritorial jurisdiction that ignores the fact of sovereignty and often puts business in an impossible position of conflicting legal requirements.

There are many other issues that will need to be addressed by governments, in GATT or elsewhere, as they move to elaborate new international rules to deal with trade and the environment. Business will, of course, want to be consulted about these efforts and contribute to them. But for now the three areas outlined above are those around which business believes the highest priority work needs to be done.

In approaching that task, several American businesses have taken an increasingly active interest and have laid out various proposals that they believe merit careful consideration, both by their counterparts in the environmental community and by the governments who will have to negotiate the specifics. The following sections spell out in greater detail many of the proposals that have been endorsed by the members of the U.S. Council for International Business, and that have been broadly supported by the ICC and BIAC organizations at an international business level. While they are by no means the last business word on these issues, they constitute the first detailed elaboration of a business "agenda" on trade and environment issues, and as such are a step toward development of the kind of consensus that many of us believe will be a major economic and social responsibility for all countries in the decade ahead.

In laying out its agenda on particular issues, business has also developed certain general principles or guidelines that it suggests should constitute the framework within which its specific recommendations for dealing with problems of standards, dispute settlement, subsidies, and competition should be accommodated. They address both the questions of the design and implementation of trade policies that reflect environmental concerns, and the design and implementation of environmental policies that minimize trade distortions. Both are essential to a balanced approach to trade and environmental problems. The components of this general framework recapitulate several of the points made earlier in this chapter but are worth recalling again to set the context.

The development of trade policies that reflect environmental concerns has been hotly debated lately. Business believes that such measures should not constitute a means of arbitrary or unjustifiable discrimination or a disguised restriction on international trade. This chapter has previously warned against the danger of an environmentalist alliance with protectionists. While business would prefer that trade measures not be used to enforce environmental policies, it recognizes that such measures may often be an inevitable consequence of differences in national approaches or in implementing the obligations of an international agreement on a specific environmental problem. Therefore, when such measures are deemed necessary, their use should be consequent upon internationally agreed-upon procedures and should be subject to the rules embodied in GATT regarding transparency, national treatment, and nondiscrimination.

Business does favor the use of multilateral agreements to deal with environmental management issues involving transboundary or global ecological problems. In particular, business endorses the commitment undertaken at the meeting in February 1992 of the United Nations Conference on Trade and Development, and later reaffirmed at UNCED, that "unilateral actions to deal with environmental challenges outside the jurisdiction of the importing country should be avoided." In negotiating such international agreements, governments should include provisions, where relevant, implementing such principles as the Polluter Pays Principle, the use of sound science, and proportionality between objectives sought and the trade measures employed. Finally, trade measures contained in such agreements should be the least trade-restrictive necessary to achieve their objective.

Turning to the development of environmental policies that minimize trade distortions, business believes that environmental policies should rely to the maximum extent possible on market-oriented measures that encourage innovation by industry to find the most cost-effective ways to achieve environmental goals. The greater the reliance on market policies and instruments, the less the scope for distortion in international trade and investment flows. Harmonization of policies using economic instruments that harness market forces to achieve the goals of regulatory efforts should be encouraged. Among economic instruments, there should be a preference for those involving the least market distortion. Thus, for example, the choice embodied in the U.S. Clean Air Act for the use of tradeable permits is preferable to the proposals under discussion for a carbon or broad-based energy tax, which is burdened with market-distorting effects on competitiveness.

Business has also endorsed the use of life-cycle analysis in the development of environmental policies. It believes that this kind of comprehensive overview is necessary to identify those points of intervention that are most cost-effective and least disruptive of trade.

In addition to these general propositions as the outline of a workable framework within which governments can develop mutually compatible trade and environmental protection policies, business has also set out a series of more specific recommendations to deal with those issues it believes merit the priority attention of governments. The main reason for this priority is that the rules and policies (or lack of them) that governments apply in setting product or process standards, in resolving disputes that arise over the trade effects of national differences, and assisting or not assisting enterprises in meeting new regulations and standards, directly impact how businesses organize their investment, production, and marketing strategies and can become significant factors influencing international trade and investment. Some rules already exist on these issues but greater clarity is needed in all three areas.

HARMONIZING (AND RATIONALIZING) ENVIRONMENTAL STANDARDS

Harmonization of standards, or mutual recognition of essential requirements, is a desirable goal and a useful way to minimize distortions in international trade and investment. Business believes that standards, whether national or internationally harmonized, should be based on sound scientific knowledge and data. However, it does not believe that differing national standards need to be harmonized down to the lowest common denominator. Various factors may well justify national standards that seek to achieve higher levels of protection than those accorded by internationally agreed-upon standards. Some of these factors were listed in the 1972 OECD *Guiding Principles* and remain valid today. They include, as examples, different pollution assimilative capacities, different social objectives and priorities, and different degrees of industrialization and population density.

In keeping with the reality that standards may well differ internationally, business believes that GATT rules should also not require adoption of lower standards in cases where a sub-national authority has set a standard that requires a higher level of performance or protection than that required by the country's national standard. California's air quality and auto emission standards are a case in point. However, while such local standards may be entirely appropriate, they should not create unnecessary trade barriers, should have a solid scientific basis, and should be applied in accordance with other GATT rules (for example, national treatment and nondiscrimination).

Standards should be based whenever possible on objective criteria and required performance rather than on particular design or technology specifications (which could be used by a country to favor a national supplier over the foreign competition). They should balance the protection sought with the costs involved and should be reassessed periodically to incorporate advances in scientific knowledge and to monitor their effectiveness. Obsolete standards too often risk deteriorating into trade barriers on which domestic industries become dependent.

SETTLEMENT OF DISPUTES

The process by which disputes over conflicts between trade and environmental policies and goals are resolved should be made more transparent. Business, unlike some environmentalists, does not insist that intergovernmental disputes over the effects of these policies be conducted as if in an open court. However, dispute settlement bodies (including GATT panels) should be permitted to invite comments by interested nongovernmental experts at the start of the process and to provide an opportunity for comment before any final report is submitted for adoption.

Business has also recommended that the various dispute settlement processes should distinguish between the functions of risk assessment and risk management. The former should require that the standard be based on sound science, while the latter recognizes that the degrees of risk acceptable to particular countries may legitimately vary among them. Thus, dispute settlement bodies should be required to reach separate judgments about the scientific basis of the standard in dispute and about whether it is unnecessarily trade restrictive in implementing a particular country's risk management preference.

Reflecting this distinction, business has proposed criteria that would assist the dispute resolution body in making the judgments suggested. As regards judging the scientific basis for the standard in dispute, the body should consider the latest scientific data and knowledge in the field (for which expert evidence is likely to be critical), the feasibility of the standard, and the experience gained in the application of the standard in question, and standards in effect in other countries used for similar purposes. As regards judging whether a standard is unnecessarily trade restrictive, the body should determine whether the effects on trade are only incidental, whether the burden on imports is excessive in relation to the environmental benefit, and whether the legitimate environmental objective could not be promoted by a measure with a lesser impact on trade. It is encouraging to note that the Uruguay Round draft agreement released in December 1991 by the GATT Secretary General includes several of these concepts in the text relating to standards; the recommendations above would make the concepts more operational by giving clearer guidance to participants in the dispute settlement process.

THE 1972 OECD GUIDING PRINCIPLES

Business believes that the 1972 OECD *Guiding Principles,* which first codified the Polluter Pays Principle as an internationally approved concept, remain valid and that they should be re-endorsed by OECD governments. In doing so, some further clarifications on the following issues are desirable.

Subsidies designed to assist particular sectors or enterprises to meet new environmental protection standards or regulations undercut the Polluter Pays Principle by preventing the market mechanism from incorporating environmental protection costs in product prices. Such subsidies should continue to be actionable under GATT if they cause injury to other parties.

The Polluter Pays Principle should be applied in ways that do not create additional distortions in international trade and investment. In particular, the principle should be interpreted to mean that environmental measures or regulations, especially liability measures, should be forward-looking to the greatest extent possible—designed to deter future environmental damage. Application of such measures to remedy existing damage shifts resources away from resolution of the environmental problem and allocates them to transaction costs, chiefly litigation.

The recommendation in the 1972 OECD Guiding Principles against import levies or export rebates to compensate for differences in environmental policies among countries should be re-enforced. Governments should recognize that differences in policies or standards may often be justified for a variety of reasons, including differences among countries in political decisions about managing environmental risks. However, the competitive advantages that occur for these reasons should be no more countervailable than any other legitimate source of competitive advantage among nations or differences arising from different domestic political preferences. Thus, where a country considers stricter standards for production plants and processes to be necessary for environmental reasons, the imposition of such standards should not be made contingent upon, or give rise to, the introduction of compensating, discriminatory levies on the import of goods produced using less stringent standards. To the extent that such differences are judged to be problems requiring temporary trade restrictive action (for example, to facilitate structural adjustment), other instruments, such as the safeguard processes set forth in both GATT Article XIX and U.S. trade law (Section 201), should be used.

COUNTERVAILING DUTIES

There is growing sentiment in the environmental community for the use of countervailing duties on imports to force countries with different (lower) standards or regulations to raise them to the highest levels. Though not advocated for protectionist reasons, the effect is protectionist. However, the argument against use of this technique does not depend on an anti-protectionist sentiment alone. The problem is that it would be virtually impossible to quantify the alleged advantage conferred on the products from lower standard countries. Further, even if an objective system could be devised, there would have to be different levels of duty charged both by product and country of origin. And if you allow an equalization tax for lower environmental standards, then why not for differences in wage rates, or tax systems, or social safety net programs, or . . . (fill in your favorite cause).

Whether limited to the environment or expanded to include almost anything else, the result would be an almost infinitely complicated matrix of charges levied on virtually all traded goods by most countries from almost all sources; clearly, the end of any kind of open world trade system and the collapse of much transnational commerce. All this because of alleged competitive advantages (which most objective studies show to be marginal for most products) or in the interest of achieving a global uniformity, which is neither necessary to meet most environmental protection needs nor possible in a world of diverse and sovereign nations. I hope that even our European steel colleagues will eventually admit that such a "solution" is really global commercial anarchy.

CONCLUSION

These are the main recommendations that American business has put to the U.S. government. A similar set of proposals has been endorsed by the BIAC as the basis for updating and expanding upon the 1972 OECD *Guiding Principles*. Finally, international business has made it clear to governments of all countries that it is more than willing to work with them in the development of creative and effective solutions to these problems. It would welcome a dialogue for this purpose with those environmental organizations that are prepared to work with business on the basis of agreement to the principle that economic development, open trade, and environmental protection can and indeed must be complementary and mutually compatible objectives for economic activity and public policy. Nothing less will meet the needs of either business or environmentalists.

11

Foreign Direct Investment and Environmental Protection in the Third World

Norman A. Bailey

INTRODUCTION

D uring the early 1970s when environmental concerns were first injected into the international economic agenda, it was considered a reasonable assumption that the volume and composition of international investment flows would change in response to international differences in environmental cost controls. One of the earliest studies, Charles Pearson's *Implications for the Trade and Investment of Developing Countries of United States Environmental Controls*, expressed skepticism about this assumption.[1] That skepticism was empirically vindicated in later years.

At the present time, after almost two decades of extensive environmental protection legislation in the Organization for Economic Cooperation and Development (OECD) countries, environmental concerns have returned to the world economic agenda, seriously affecting the General Agreement on Tariffs and Trade (GATT) and the North American Free Trade Agreement (NAFTA) negotiations. Environmentalists want GATT's trade rules to be turned into instruments of environmental enforcement, primarily against non-OECD nations still far behind in environmental protection legislation. The environmentalists' voice has been amplified by an opportunistic alliance with protectionist interests in the developed sector. They claim that environmentally indifferent free trade will destroy local habitats, the global living environment, and ultimately possibly the whole biosphere.

Opposing the environmentalists are the trade interests represented by GATT (to which environmentally unconcerned Third World governments are attempting to attach themselves). At the behest of the international business community, GATT warns that turning GATT rules into tools of environmental enforcement would have an effect similar to the Smoot-Hawley Tariff Act of 1930, destroying the world economy.

Technically, the battle is in part being fought at the GATT negotiations over the issue of "harmonization of standards." Three possibilities present themselves to world trading partners. The trading partners will harmonize their environmental standards covering products and production processes, either according to the lowest common denominator of environment-insensitive partners, according to the highest environmental standards of the OECD nations, or by effecting a compromise between low and high standards.

Thus, the question first posed in the 1970s arises again: How will the flow and volume of international investment, especially to Third World countries, be affected by these developments? Examination of the available (and inadequate) literature leaves no doubt that the development-versus-environment debate has produced one dramatic shift of opinion among experts and is, at the present time, undergoing a second, more spectacular shift that promises to have far-reaching consequences in our understanding of the impact of direct foreign investment on Third World environments.

First, contrary to the widespread assumptions of the 1970s, detailed empirical studies conducted during the 1980s have demonstrated that the environmental deterioration in the Third World is caused primarily by local, low-technology economic activities and by low per capita incomes, but not by advanced-sector/transnational investments in those regions.

Second, further empirical studies have shown that transnational corporations and advanced-sector direct investments in the Third World have, on the whole, maintained higher environmental protection standards than host governments and are not responsive to environmental cost differentials in their decisions of where to locate their activities. Contrary to popular assumptions, transnational corporations have generally not sought "pollution havens" in less developed countries.

As a result, the eminently reasonable argument is now advanced that higher levels of economic activity will result in improvement, not deterioration, of environmental conditions. This argument is presented as a formal thesis by GATT and as a favored hypothesis by numerous studies sponsored by the World Bank and some United Nations organizations. The first empirical studies in support of this argument have been presented, and more comprehensive ones have been urged and are being carried out at present. A tentative, yet impressive, theoretical framework has been proposed that is sufficient to stimulate and inform further empirical studies.

TRANSNATIONAL INVESTMENT AND POLLUTION

Despite recent and current arguments by converging protectionist and environmentalist lobbies surrounding the NAFTA negotiations, numerous empirical studies have established that transnational corporations do not tend to relocate their operations simply in order to take advantage of more lax environmental regulations elsewhere. A useful survey of the earlier of these studies is presented in Charles Pearson's *Environmental Standards, Industrial Relocation and Pollution Havens,* which summarizes the state of research as of the date of publication (1987) as follows:

> Despite difficulties with the data and analytical techniques, some reasonably strong findings emerge. First, environmental control costs are a small fraction of production costs in virtually every industry, and the effect on trade is correspondingly small . . . Second, there is no evidence of widespread reallocation of production by [multinational corporations (MNCs)] on the basis of environmental cost considerations . . . Third, efficiency in granting of permits and stable, predictable environmental regulations are important . . . Fourth, there is weak evidence . . . that MNCs may have an inherent advantage over local firms in meeting environmental control regulations.[2]

A more recent, and rather thorough and comprehensive survey of the literature conducted in 1991 by the World Bank's Judith M. Dean, concurs that "there is no *a priori* reason to believe that increased output [in less developed countries due to laxity of environmental controls] in the environmentally abundant country will be captured by multinationals as opposed to domestic firms. There is also no *a priori* reason to believe that less developed countries are relatively environmentally abundant compared to developed countries."[3] Dean's survey also places considerable emphasis on a 1988 study by Jeffrey Leonard of the efforts of four countries, Ireland, Spain, Mexico and Romania, which at an earlier point in time attempted to offer themselves to foreign investors as "pollution havens" but discovered that "the absence of pollution controls were not substantial enough to alter the locational preference of multinational firms."[4] Numerous other studies support the conclusion that transnational corporations, which account for 75 percent of world trade, are not engaged in evading environmental controls by relocating to environmentally lax Third World countries, as empirical investigations since the 1970s have found that no relocations of this type take place.

This, however, is not to argue that transnational corporations are environmentally benign by merely "not being there." The available evidence suggests that they tend to be relatively more beneficial environmentally to their host Third World or developing country than domestic companies in comparative fields. Notable among the studies that indicate this are the United Nations Center on Transnational Corporations' 1991 *Benchmark Corporate Environmental Survey,* which found that "three-quarters of the respondents are using company-wide environmental policies going beyond those required by national legislation."[5]

FOREIGN DIRECT INVESTMENT MAY REDUCE THIRD WORLD POLLUTION LEVELS

Under the reasonable hypothesis that increased Foreign Direct Investment (FDI) raises, over time, the per capita gross national product of the recipient country, it may now be argued that there is a high likelihood that FDI will improve, rather than worsen, the quality of environment in the Third World. Indeed, Marian Radetzki's paper contributed to the November 1991 World Bank symposium on International Trade and Environment, put forward a concept, labelled by its author the "intensity of use hypothesis," according to which higher per capita incomes correlating with technological progress will have a tendency to reduce the wear on the environment per unit of finished output over time.[6] Although at the time of its writing in 1991, this hypothesis still lacked empirical verification, the author followed the generally accepted practice of considering the "environment," under any of its numerous definitions, as a further "factor of production," in addition to the classical factors of physical labor, physical capital, and land. Then, by viewing the environment as "material," Radetzki drew an analogy between the behavior of this "material's" intensity of use and that of materials in industrial processes about which there existed adequate quantified empirical studies. In the case of these industrial processes, the intensity of use of base materials tends to grow in the early stages of the given industry's technology, but then, past a certain point of technology maturation, this intensity begins to diminish. Similarly, Radetzki argued, the "environment," however defined, undergoes intense wear in lower technology economies, and, when the technological base of the given economy advances past a certain point, the intensity of environmental wear, measured in environmental wear per constant dollar of Gross Domestic Product (GDP) produced, begins to decline.

Radetzki thus constructs a curve in which intensity of environmental wear is plotted against per capita GDP (on the reasonable assumption that different per capita GDP levels correlate with different levels of technological sophistication). This curve has an inverted U-shape with the upward slope corresponding to low GDP per capita and the downward slope to high GDP per capita (see figure). The turning point between high intensity environmental wear and abated environmental wear is hypothesized at an income level of about $5,000 to $6,000 per capita. Economies below this level of income are subjecting the environment to great strains, and economies above this level of per capita tend to improve their environment.

This hypothesis, of course, though based on a solidly rational methodology, runs contrary to what had come to pass as conventional environmental wisdom of the 1970s, which had argued that more technology is bad for the environment; it even runs against the compromise reached in the 1980s that had argued that technological advances need not be detrimental to the environment. Here the argument is that the more technology advances beyond a certain level, the better it is for the environment.

An interesting piece of empirical support for this hypothesis, regarding urban air quality worldwide, was supplied a few months later, in the February 3, 1992 advance release of the "Trade and the Environment" chapter of GATT's annual International Trade 1990-1991 report. In it are the results of the data collected by the Global Environmental Monitoring System of the World Health Organization and the United Nations Environment Programme in the course of monitoring sulfur dioxide and suspended particles in the air over cities around the world. The GEMS data

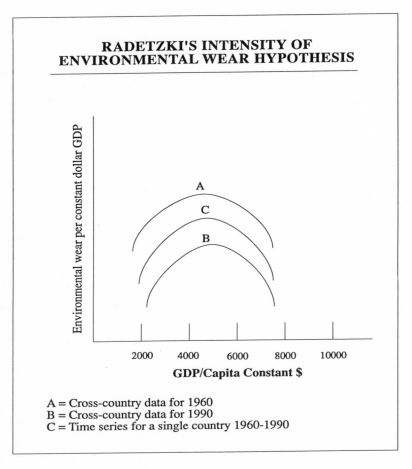

**RADETZKI'S INTENSITY OF
ENVIRONMENTAL WEAR HYPOTHESIS**

A = Cross-country data for 1960
B = Cross-country data for 1990
C = Time series for a single country 1960-1990

correlated exactly as the "intensity of environmental wear" of Radetzki had predicted: an inverted U-shaped curve with the turning point at $5,000 GDP per capita.

This finding alone is ample justification for encouraging more comprehensive empirical investigations aimed at proving (or disproving) the Radetzki hypothesis. Its implications are quite far-reaching, not only with respect to policies of environmental protection, trade, and investment, but also with respect to broader issues in both the physical sciences and in philosophy of science—issues that have only been alluded to or lightly touched upon by the environmental debate. The hypothesis implies, perhaps without its author's suspecting it, an underlying ontological compatibility between "nature" in the larger sense and "human nature," or cognitive human activity exercised upon non-rational nature, which had been merely surmised in philosophical speculations of earlier ages, and is at present being considered anew in contemporary discussions of the philosophy of science (as in the recent discussions of the "anthropic principle" in modern physics). A quantified, empirical investigation into the Radetzki hypothesis would have payoffs not only in the consideration of environmental policy, but also in broader fields of inquiry.

Half of this hypothesis, the half pertaining to the low GDP per capita region of the curve, hardly requires any further empirical verification. The ecological problems in the underdeveloped world are to a large extent explained by low income levels. The recent literature in the field universally embraces the assertion that there is no a priori reason to assume, as had been the case in the early days of the environmental debate, that underdeveloped countries are more environmentally rich than developed countries—and it often is the case that they are environmentally worse off.

In addition, low GDP per capita countries lack:

- A sense of urgency regarding environmental protection;
- Technical and educational means for implementing environmental control legislation; and
- Populations with the cultural standards required for handling modern technologies.

Moreover, they have empirically been shown to concentrate their economic effort in pollution-intensive industries.

The Bhopal case dramatized the adverse relations between environmental soundness and a low-income, low-technology-affinity culture. An authority on the case, Thomas N. Gladwin, who places the legal culpability squarely on Union Carbide, identified ten causal factors that led to the catastrophic accident in 1984:

1) Encroachment of densely populated shantytowns composed of poor illiterate people right near the boundary of the plant;
2) Absence of a highly educated pool of workers and high turnover among employees;
3) Weak enforcement of relatively lax health, safety, and environmental laws;
4) Nepotism and cozy ties between plant management and local politicians;

5) Import controls that could block or delay the procurement of key parts of equipment;
6) Absence of a deep commitment among workers to the importance of preventive maintenance;
7) Regulations mandating labor-intensive rather than capital-intensive operations, making safety dependent on proactive manual, rather than passive mechanical, operations;
8) Regulations requiring significant participation of local owners and partners whose regard for safety and environmental protection could be different from that of the foreign enterprise;
9) Regulations constraining the firm's ability to lay off workers and close the plant if it became uneconomical; and
10) Public transportation, communication, health, and safety systems that could inhibit proper emergency evacuation and relief efforts.[7]

All the causal factors that contributed to producing that environmental catastrophe are, without exception, poverty-induced, demonstrating that poverty not only causes environmentally unsound resource allocation, but also has the capacity to turn a piecemeal, one-time attempt at technological modernization, such as the Union Carbide investment in India, into an ecological disaster of first rank.

Thus, the low GDP per capita region of the inverted-U curve depicting the Radetzki hypothesis is amply verified by empirical data. What the hypothesis needs is verification of the high GDP per capita region of the curve and a study of the conditions that produce the turning point. In this respect, it should be noted that a variety of inverted-U curves have been hypothesized, which have failed to be verified by empirical research, but none of these bears upon the methodological characteristics of Radetzki's own inverted-U curve. Whereas others simply correlate income levels with environmental degradation, Radetzki proposes to correlate technology-level-determined incomes with intensity of environmental wear.

Characteristically, a study of toxic emissions from manufacturing correlated merely with GDP, while confirming the inverted-U curve in data comparing different countries at any one time, failed to confirm it for data of a single country over a prolonged period of time, suggesting that the mere increase of GDP, due, for example, to the expansion of non-polluting industries such as services, does not necessarily correlate with lower pollution. If evidence is eventually collected that verifies correlation of higher income levels generated by higher technological cultures with lower environmental wear, the current debate over the relationship between development and environment may be substantially reformulated.

Mankind's historical experience with industrialization, one of a mere 200-plus years, may not warrant the generalization that any technological advance causes environmental damage, though this has been the experience of the now advanced nations. If past a certain point there occurs a qualitative shift away from pollution-intensive processes, then our prevailing notions of technology dissemination, international investment, and world economic relations will be correspondingly revised. It may also be the case that the mechanisms of the free market may already be at work revising them. In all the literature available, there has been no attention paid to the experiences gained by the miracle economies of the 1980s, the East Asian "tigers" that attained prodigious advances in GDP per capita without undue dependence on pollution-intensive industries.

ENVIRONMENT AND FOREIGN INVESTMENT: CHICKEN OR EGG?

There are two logical questions to ask concerning the relation between foreign investment and environmental quality: Does less environmental protection promote foreign investment in Third World countries? Does more foreign investment inhibit environmental protection in the Third World?

Regarding the first question, all empirical studies to date answer in the negative—environmental laxity has not resulted in attracting more foreign investment. These findings have vindicated the original hypothesis, formulated by Pearson in the 1970s, that "the low ratio of direct environmental control costs to value of output for the more highly processed goods (fabricated metals, machinery, and transports) indicates a relatively low incentive to establish production abroad."[8]

Thus, the second question becomes the one of interest, as the Radetzki inverted-U curve suggests that increased foreign investment into the Third World may well become the vehicle for improving environmental conditions. Although a thorough empirical verification of this hypothesis is required, there are other factors that suggest that this may indeed be the case.

One such factor is the increasingly changing practices of the financial communities of the United States, Europe, and Japan, which are basing their global investment decisions in accordance with environmental regulatory considerations. As a result, if Third World countries were to receive foreign investments, the likelihood is great that those investments will accord with the higher environmental standards of OECD countries, and foreign investment will become a vehicle for exporting environmental soundness.

Another such factor is the greater economic efficiency, and hence profitability, of environmentally sound advanced production technologies. These economic advantages make environmentally sound production technologies more attractive to international investors than older, less economically efficient technologies. This environmental/economic advantage effect has been hypothesized in the case of paper and pulp, one of the world's most pollution-intensive industries.

Thus, if in the context of the current debate over harmonization of standards, the environmentalists' demand for adoption of the higher standards is ceded. Third World nations that would suffer from the measure might demand reciprocity of a greater advanced-sector commitment to direct investments in their economies. Or they might simply offer more attractive conditions for foreign investments. It has been suggested that in countries where national policies promote internationally competitive industrial growth, "firms tend to adopt low-polluting production technologies."[9] This suggests that policies promoting free movement of capital into the Third World would also promote environmental improvement.

Under the emerging pressure of these considerations, the United Nations Conference on Trade and Development (UNCTAD) is once again raising its advocacy for technology transfers to the Third World on grounds that such transfers will be environmentally sound:

> The need to improve the access of developing countries to these technologies must be underlined. In many sectors, environmentally sound technologies are simultaneously capital-, science-, and management-intensive . . . The transfer of obsolete technologies to developing countries should be avoided . . . The international dialogue on the transfer of technology, which has been pursued for many years in UNCTAD, could be revived around environmental concerns. [10]

Thus, it appears that a high probability exists that there is a genuine (objective though not perceived) convergence of interest among promoters of free trade, advocates of environmental protection, supporters of free international flow of capital, and advocates of Third World development. This probability will become a certainty when we can empirically ascertain that past a certain level of technological maturation, human economic activity becomes more environmentally sound.

NOTES

1. Charles S. Pearson, *Implications for the Trade and Investment of Developing Countries of United States Environmental Controls,* UNCTAD/TD/B/ C.2/150Add.1/Rev.1, Chapter III, esp. pp. 24-27 (New York: United Nations, 1976).
2. Charles S. Pearson, ed., *Multinational Corporations, Environment, and the Third World,* pp. 24-27 (Durham, North Carolina: Duke University Press, 1987).
3. Judith M. Dean, "Trade and the Environment: A Survey of the Literature," *World Bank Symposium on International Trade and Environment,* pp. 25-27 (1992).
4. Ibid, p. 33.
5. U.N. Center on Transnational Corporations, *Consolidated Executive Summary of the Benchmark Corporate Environmental Survey,* ST/CTC/SER.C/ 5, p. 3 (New York: United Nations, 1991).
6. Marian Radetzki, "Economic Growth and Environment," *World Bank Symposium on International Trade and Environment Papers,* p. 189 (November 21-22, 1991).
7. Charles S. Pearson, ed., *Multinational Corporations, Environment, and the Third World,* pp. 227-28.
8. Charles S. Pearson, *Implications for the Trade and Investment of Developing Countries of United States Environmental Controls.*
9. *Ibid,* p.275.
10. *Report to the Secretary General of UNCTAD to the Preparatory Committee for the United Nations Conference on Environment and Development,* par. 35-38 (New York: United Nations, July 10, 1991). It could be argued that the dissemination of technologies envisaged by UNCTAD could be better implemented by the free decisions of market forces rather than by the formalities of "technology transfers" implied by the agency's report.

PART III

Trade and Environment Conflicts

12

Problems with Free Trade: Neoclassical and Steady-State Perspectives

Herman E. Daly

INTRODUCTION

No policy prescription commands greater consensus among economists than that of "free trade based on international specialization according to comparative advantage." Free trade has long been the "default position," presumed good unless proven otherwise in specific cases. This presumption should be reversed. The default position should be in favor of domestic production for domestic markets, with balanced (not deregulated) international trade, as a fall back alternative when domestic production is too inconvenient.

Three classes of argument are offered in support of this view. They correspond to the three basic goals of all economic policy: efficient allocation, just distribution, and sustainable scale. The first two are traditional goals of neoclassical economics; the third is newly recognized and is associated with the viewpoint of steady-state economics. Sustainable scale means that the scale (population times resource use per capita, or total resource throughput) of the economy relative to the containing ecosystem must be biophysically sustainable. In other words, the input of raw materials and energy must be within the regenerative capacity, and the output of waste materials and energy must be within the absorptive capacity, of the ecosystem. In the first section, the three types of argument will be discussed to the extent possible within the neoclassical frame of reference. In the second section, the idea of scale will be expanded into a discussion of the steady-state economy. The concluding section explains further implications for the free trade debate.

ARGUMENTS IN FAVOR
OF DOMESTIC PROTECTION

EFFICIENT ALLOCATION

A clear conflict exists if a nation follows a domestic policy of internalization of external costs into prices, and, simultaneously, an international policy of free trade with countries that do not internalize their external costs into their prices. The cost-internalizing country should be allowed to employ a tariff to compensate for the higher cost—not to protect an inefficient industry, but to protect an efficient national policy against standards-lowering competition. This does not imply the imposition of one country's environmental preferences or moral judgments on another country. Each country sets the rules of cost internalization in its own market. Whoever sells in another nation's market must play by that nation's rules of cost internalization, or pay a tariff sufficient to remove the competitive advantage of lower standards as a price of admission to that market. For example, tuna sold in the United States, whether by U.S. or Mexican fishermen, must count the cost of limiting the kill of dolphins associated with catching tuna, as required by the Marine Mammal Protection Act (MMPA). Tuna sold in the Mexican market, whether by U.S. or Mexican fishermen, need not include that cost. Each country sets its own rules. There would be no imposition of standards or "environmental imperialism."

Competition can reduce prices in two ways: by increasing efficiency, or by lowering standards. The lower standards refer to the failure to internalize social and environmental costs. Costs to the firm are reduced by low pollution control standards, low worker safety standards, low wages and standard of living for workers, and, among others, low health care standards. Free trade is not enough to avoid standards-lowering competition. Attaining cheapness by ignoring or externalizing real costs is a sin against efficiency. Even the General Agreement on Tariffs and Trade (GATT) makes an exception for prison labor, recognizing that requiring citizens of one country to compete against foreign prison labor is carrying standards-lowering competition too far. However, no similar exception is made for child labor, uninsured risky labor, or subsistence wage labor. Protection of a truly inefficient industry against competition from a truly more efficient foreign competitor—what is usually meant by "protection"—is very different from protecting an efficient national policy of full cost pricing against standards-lowering competition from nations that, for whatever reason, have lower standards of living for workers, and lower environmental, safety, and health care standards.

Standards-lowering competition exists within, as well as between, nations. Profit-maximizing firms in competition always have an incentive to externalize costs to the degree they can get away with it. Within nations there is a large legal, administrative, and auditing structure designed precisely to keep costs from being externalized, that is, social and environmental standards from being lowered. But there is no analogous body of law and administration internationally. There are only national laws, and they differ widely. If firms are allowed to produce under the most permissive standards and sell their product without penalty in countries with higher standards, they succeed in externalizing costs and bringing pressure to bear on the high-standards country to lower its standards—in effect "imposing" their lower standards.

JUST DISTRIBUTION

According to the doctrine of comparative advantage, free trade between rich and poor countries will benefit both. The factor-price equalization theorem recognizes that the laboring class in the high wage country will see their wages fall, but the total gains from trade are supposed to be enough to compensate them, if it were decided to do so. An explicit assumption of the comparative advantage argument is factor immobility between nations, in particular international immobility of capital. When capital is mobile internationally, it follows absolute advantage, just as it does within a nation. Only if capital cannot cross national boundaries in pursuit of absolute advantage is there any reason for it to follow the logic of comparative advantage in its allocation within the nation. Once capital is mobile internationally, as it certainly is today, then all the comforting assurances of comparative advantage are irrelevant. Furthermore, the tendency to wage equalization becomes much stronger when freely mobile capital is added to the free flow of goods. When capital flows abroad, there is no longer the same opportunity for new employment domestically as there was when capital remained at home and specialized according to international comparative advantage. Capital now leaves the country, and national labor has fewer employment opportunities. It is worth remembering that the vast majority of citizens are wage earners. Even if free trade and capital mobility raise wages in low-wage countries, and that tendency could be thwarted by overpopulation and rapid population growth in low-wage countries, they do so at the expense of labor and to the benefit of capital in the high-wage countries, thus increasing income inequality in the high-wage countries.

Neoclassical economists admit that externalities resulting from overpopulation can spill over to other nations, and thus provide a legitimate reason against free immigration, however uncongenial to liberal sentiments. But externalities of overpopulation, in the form of cheap labor, can spill over into other countries through free migration of capital just as much as through free migration of labor. The legitimate case for restrictions on labor migration are therefore easily extended to restrictions on capital migration.

SUSTAINABLE SCALE

The answer often given to the allocation and distribution problems raised above is that growth will take care of them. The allocation problem of standards-lowering competition will be dealt with by harmonizing all standards upward. The distribution problem of falling wages in high-wage countries will be only temporary. The neoclassical faith is that growth will eventually raise world wages to the former high-wage level and beyond. The third goal, sustainable scale of total resource use, forces us to ask what will happen if the entire population of the earth consumes resources at the rate associated with current real wages in high-wage countries. This question is central to the steady-state paradigm, but remains unasked in the neoclassical view, or is given the facile answer that there are no environmental limits.

Steady-state economics suggests the following answer: the regenerative and assimilative capacities of the biosphere cannot sustainably support even present levels of resource use, much less the many-fold increase required by "upward harmonization" of consumption standards. Still less can the ecosystem afford the upward harmonization of standards for an ever-growing population striving to consume ever more per capita.

This heretofore unrecognized limit to development puts a brake on the ability of growth to wash away the problems of allocation and distribution raised by free trade with free capital mobility. In fact, free trade becomes a recipe for standards-lowering competition leading to the downward harmonization of efficient allocation, equal distribution, and ecological sustainability.

In the face of these enormous problems, what is the appeal of ever larger free trade blocs to corporations and governments influenced by corporations? There are, of course, gains in efficiency from greater specialization under free trade, but these are small compared to the losses just discussed. The big attraction is that the larger the free trade area and the larger and more footloose the corporation, the less it will be responsible to any local or even national community. Increasingly, the corporation will be able to buy labor in the low-wage markets and sell its products in the remaining high-wage, high-income markets. The larger the market, the longer corporations will be able to avoid the logic of Henry Ford—that he had to pay his workers enough for them to buy his cars. In a big trading area, you can go on for a long time making cars with cheap labor in one place and selling them to the remaining high-wage earners somewhere else. The larger the free trade bloc, the longer you can get away with depleting resources and absorptive capacities in one area in order to enjoy the benefits produced from these costs in a well-preserved environment somewhere else. The larger the trading area, the more feasible it is to separate costs and benefits spatially, thus avoiding the discipline of cost internalization geographically. That is why transnational corporations like free trade, and why workers and environmentalists do not.

The correct name for "free trade" (who can oppose freedom?) is "deregulated international commerce," which should serve to remind us that deregulation is not always a good policy. Recall recent experience with the deregulation of the savings and loan institutions, the junk bond financed leveraged buyouts, and the current instability in our banking and airline industries. Any profit-making entity has an interest in externalizing costs. Regulation is needed to keep costs internal, so that cost reductions come from true improvements in efficiency, rather than from simply throwing the costs on to others in the form of lowered standards. Again, the point is not to deny that there are gains from international trade. Rather it is to agree with Keynes that there are also gains from national self-sufficiency accompanied by balanced trade in items that are inconvenient to produce nationally:

I sympathize, therefore, with those who would minimize, rather than those who would maximize, economic entanglement between nations. Ideas, knowledge, art, hospitality, travel—these are the things which should of their nature be international. But let goods be homespun whenever it is reasonably and conveniently possible; and, above all, let finance be primarily national.[1]

THE STEADY-STATE PARADIGM AND FREE TRADE

Although the allocation and distribution arguments can be made within the standard neoclassical paradigm, the scale argument, as we have seen, requires some degree of acceptance of the steady-state paradigm. Since the latter view is not as familiar as the former, it will be developed in this section.

The pre-analytic vision from which steady-state economics emerges is that the economy, in its physical dimensions, is an open subsystem of a finite, nongrowing, and materially closed total system—the Earth's ecosystem or biosphere. An "open" system is one with a "digestive tract," that is, one that takes matter and energy from the environment in low-entropy form (raw materials), and returns it to the environment in high-entropy form (waste). A "closed" system is one in which only energy flows through, while matter circulates within the system. Whatever flows through a system, entering as input and exiting as output, is called "throughput." Just as an organism maintains its physical structure by a metabolic flow and is connected to the environment at both ends of its digestive tract, so too an economy requires a throughput, which must to some degree both deplete and pollute the environment. A steady-state economy is one whose throughput remains constant at a level that neither depletes the environment beyond its regenerative capacity, nor pollutes it beyond its absorptive capacity.

The following diagrams depict the vision of the economy as an open subsystem, in two versions: the "empty" world and the "full" world. Of course, the world was never really empty or full in any absolute sense—only relatively empty of human beings and their furniture (manmade capital) when it was relatively full of other species and their habitats (natural capital). Years of economic growth (the conversion of natural into manmade capital) has changed the basic pattern of scarcity. The role of the limiting factor to further economic expansion has shifted from existing manmade capital to remaining natural capital.

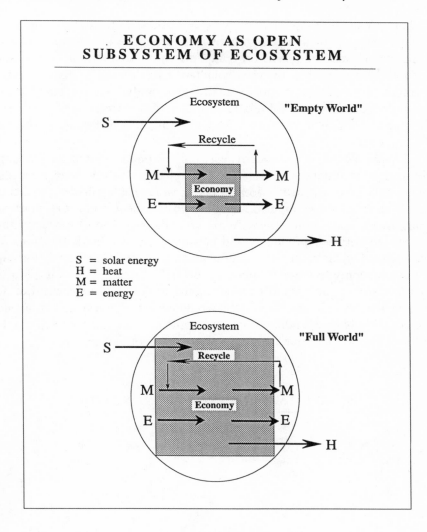

Growth of the subsystem is effectively limited by the complementary relation between manmade and natural capital. If the two forms of capital were good substitutes, then natural capital could be totally replaced by manmade, and the only limit to expansion of manmade capital would be finiteness of the containing system. But in fact, the two forms of capital are complementary. Manmade capital loses its value without a complement of natural capital. What good are fishing boats without populations of fish? Saw mills without forests? And even if we could convert the whole ocean into a catfish pond we would still need the natural capital of solar energy, photosynthetic organisms, nutrient recyclers, and so forth. The economists' emphasis on competition, or substitution, to the near eclipse of cooperation, or complementarity, in technical relations among factors of production is analogous to their preference for competition over cooperation in social relations. It also results from "analytical convenience," which seems to have become a higher value than congruence with the facts.

The pre-analytic vision underlying standard economics is that the economy is an isolated system: a circular flow of exchange value between firms and households. An "isolated" system is one in which neither matter nor energy enters or exits; it has no relation with its environment, and for all practical purposes has no environment. While this vision is useful for analyzing exchange between producers and consumers, and related questions of allocation and distribution, it is quite useless for studying the relationship of the economy to the environment (scale). The analogy is as if a biologist's vision of an animal contained only a circulatory system, but no digestive tract or lungs. The animal would be an isolated system. It would be completely independent of its environment. If it could move, it would be a perpetual motion machine. Its size would not matter.

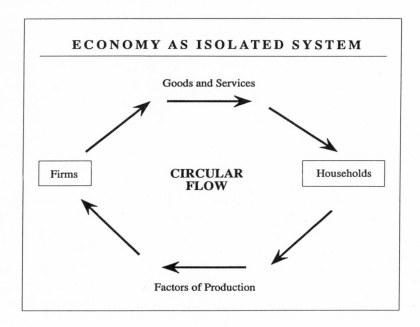

Economists are interested in scarcity, and as long as the scale of the human economy was very small relative to the ecosystem, one could abstract it from the throughput, because no apparent sacrifice was involved in increasing it. The economy has now grown to a scale such that this is no longer reasonable. We have also failed to make the elementary distinction between *growth* (that is, physical increase in size resulting from accretion or assimilation of materials), and *development* (the realization of potentialities or evolution to a fuller, better, or different state). Quantitative and qualitative changes follow different laws. Conflating the two, as we currently do in our measure of economic activity, gross national product, has led to much confusion.

The usual pre-analytic vision, the one that supports most neoclassical economic analysis today, is that the economy is the total system and nature is the subsystem. The economy's growth is unconstrained by any enveloping natural system. Nature may be finite, but it is just a sector— the extractive sector—of the economy, for which other sectors can substitute, without limiting overall growth in any important way. If the economy is seen as an isolated system, then there is no environment to constrain its continual growth. But if we see it as a subsystem of a larger, but finite and nongrowing ecosystem, then obviously its growth is limited. The economy may continue to develop qualitatively without growing quantitatively, just as the planet Earth does, but it cannot continue to grow. Beyond some point it must approximate a steady state in its physical dimensions. Sustainable development is development without growth, in other words, a physically steady-state economy that may continue to develop greater capacity to satisfy human wants by increasing the efficiency of resource use, by improving social institutions, by clarifying ethical priorities, but not by increasing the resource throughput.

IMPLICATIONS FOR TRADE POLICY

In the light of the growth versus development distinction, let us return to the issue of trade and consider two questions: What is the likely effect of free trade on growth? What is the likely effect of free trade on development?

Free trade is likely to stimulate throughput growth. Trade offers the possibility of importing environmental carrying capacity in the form of raw materials and waste absorption capacities in exchange for production. It allows a country to exceed its domestic regenerative and absorptive limits by importing these functions from other countries. That tends to increase throughput, other things being equal. But it could be argued that the country exporting carrying capacity might have had to increase throughput even more had it produced the products domestically rather than importing them. Nevertheless, trade does postpone the day when countries must face up to the discipline of living within natural regenerative and absorptive capacities, and by doing that probably serves on balance to increase throughput growth and environmental degradation. Free trade also introduces greater spatial separation between the production benefits and the environmental costs of throughput growth, making it more difficult for the latter to temper the growth of the former. Furthermore, as a result of the increased integration caused by trade, countries will face tightening environmental constraints more simultaneously and less sequentially than they would with less trade and integration. Therefore, there will be less opportunity to learn from other countries' prior experience with controlling throughput. In sum, by making supplies of resources and absorption capacities everywhere available to demands anywhere, free trade will tend to increase throughput growth and with it the rate of environmental degradation.

Will free trade tend to increase resource efficiency and reduce environmental damage for any given level of welfare? In the preceding paragraph it was noted that trade could increase resource efficiency through specialization. But there are other likely consequences as well. Trade increases competition to lower costs. Costs can be reduced by true improvements in technical efficiency, or by externalization from the ledger of the firm to the public at large by lowering social, environmental, and safety standards. In other words, as already discussed, competition can be either "efficiency-increasing" or "standards-lowering." Standards-lowering competition to keep or attract footloose capital by reducing wages, medical insurance, environmental standards, and so forth, is not unknown. Cost externalization is socially inefficient. A country trying to internalize external costs cannot accomplish that efficient policy if it enters into free trade with countries that do not internalize their external costs. Reduced efficiency results in a higher throughput for any given level of welfare, other things being equal.

In addition, a conflict arises between static and dynamic efficiency promotion. For example, trade in toxic wastes promotes static efficiency by allowing the waste to be disposed of wherever it costs less, according to today's prices and technologies. But a more dynamic efficiency would be served by outlawing the export of toxins, in effect internalizing their cost to their country of origin, that is, not only to the firm but also to the country under whose laws the firms operates. This creates an incentive for the firm and nation of origin to find technically superior ways of dealing with the toxins they produce, or of redesigning processes to avoid their production in the first place.

In conclusion, the allocative, distributional, and scale problems stemming from free trade in today's world are sufficient to reverse the traditional default position in its favor. Measures to further globalize and integrate the world economy should now be treated as a bad idea unless proven otherwise in specific cases.

NOTES

1. J.M. Keynes, "National Self-Sufficiency," *The Collected Writings of John Maynard Keynes*, vol. 21, ed. Donald Moggeridge (London: Macmillan and Cambridge University Press, 1933).

13

Trade and the Environment: The False Conflict?

Jagdish Bhagwati

INTRODUCTION

I nternational trade and the environment are arguably the most important issues on the global economic agenda for the last decade of this
millennium.

The United Nations Conference on Environment and Development
(UNCED), which met in Rio de Janeiro for nearly two weeks of June
1992, was a dramatic demonstration of the urgency and seriousness with
which we consider environmental issues today. The "mother of all conferences," UNCED was a blockbuster event that even a reluctant President Bush eventually was constrained to attend. It is truly hard to imagine
that a conference could attract over three thousand accredited nongovernmental organization (NGO) representatives, eight thousand official delegates, and, quite astonishingly, over one hundred heads of state. And then
again, even serious business was transacted, chiefly the signing of two
major global treaties, one on climate change and the other on biodiversity.

Besides, Agenda 21 was adopted, plotting a plan of action to garner the
energies and define the programs of the community of nations on ecological issues for years to come. We are now in the aftermath, with performance and its monitoring being negotiated at the United Nations. We can
indeed be confident of global action with the elevation of Senator Al
Gore, a committed environmentalist, to the vice-presidency in the new
U.S. administration, with Japan's active leadership on the issue as well,

and with the growing voice of the environmental NGOs in defining the policies of nations around the world.

The swift rise of environmental concerns on the global agenda coincides with the enhanced importance that questions of international trade have now acquired, which is reflected in the Uruguay Round of multilateral trade negotiations. The Uruguay Round is now entering its seventh year of negotiations. The eighth round of negotiations since the General Agreement on Tariffs and Trade (GATT) was signed in 1947, the Uruguay Round does not quite parallel UNCED, because the latter was laying the foundation for a major new agenda while the former is augmenting the architecture of an institution and a regime that has long been in place.

But the Uruguay Round is still ambitious in scope. It brings new sectors (services, for example) under the discipline of GATT and strengthens disciplines on old sectors (like textiles and agriculture). Of all the rounds to date, it is also the one where the greatest number of the world's nations, 108 in all, are engaged in negotiations. This is not just for the trivial reason that there are now more nations than before, but also because nearly every country today sees advantages accruing from international trade and wants to play where the action is. While there is a school of thought in the United States, located at MIT, which has delivered itself of sentiments that GATT is dead or should be killed, and that regionalism and aggressive unilateralism by the United States are the wave of the future, the fact is that this remains a foolish position. It has also been until now a fringe position. But the populist themes that were struck in the recent U.S. election that suggested U.S. departures from a policy of adherence to an open, multilateral trading system, and the early selections of managed trade proponents as key professional economists in the new administration, have raised questions about whether the Clinton administration will continue full support for the GATT system. It is hard, however, to imagine that President Clinton would so readily squander the legacy of U.S. leadership in crafting and sustaining the multilateral trading regime.

Both trade and environment thus occupy frontally the global agenda in the 1990s. Yet, lest you think that this makes for harmony among the supporters of free trade and better environment, you are sadly mistaken.

Trade is essentially aimed at exploiting markets, whereas the environment is traditionally outside their purview. The cause of trade is pursued principally by corporate and multinational interests, while the environment is espoused mainly by NGOs that are generally suspicious of these interests. For these reasons, and because trade is an old concern where debate and resolution were defined in ways that made little adjustment for the environment, which is a new concern, the intersection of the two issues has inevitably been marked by friction. Indeed, although light may soon be replacing heat on the question, extreme fears have arisen among several environmental groups that trade and GATT are environment-unfriendly. In turn, pro-trade groups and interests have often reciprocated with similar fears: that the environmentalists' demands cannot help but undermine the possibility of gainful trade.

I might recall the time in 1991 when the GATT Dispute Resolution Panel on the U.S.-Mexico tuna-dolphin case found in favor of Mexico on the issue of the U.S. Marine Mammal Protection Act (MMPA), under which the United States was embargoing imports of Mexican tuna because they were caught in purse seine nets that cruelly killed dolphins in greater number than the U.S. law permitted. The panel ruled in favor of Mexico chiefly on the grounds that the United States could not suspend Mexico's trading rights by unilateral legislation proscribing production methods outside of its jurisdiction. The environmentalists' frustration with GATT then turned swiftly to anger. It was denounced as GATTzilla, evocative of the Japanese monster Godzilla, a double threat in its gargantuan size and in its subliminal allusion to the yellow peril. A blitzkrieg of condemnatory advertisements and communications in the western media followed, threatening retribution and talking of GATTastrophe.

But must the partisans of the two great issues of the 1990s be at loggerheads? Like a good liberal intellectual, I would like to believe that all good things go together. I do believe indeed that the conflicts between the two groups are greatly exaggerated. But, when the misunderstandings have been cleared up, there do remain areas of conflict—between the issues, and among different countries—the resolution of which will require imagination, craftsmanship, and goodwill. In this chapter, I propose to address just these questions, of compatibility and of conflict, between the interests of the trading system and of environmental protection.

COMMON FALLACIES

While the debate on trade and the environment is now fairly sophisticated in informed circles, and I shall presently consider the principal issues, we are not entirely free from the baleful influence of fallacious arguments that assert that there are several necessary conflicts between the pursuit of free trade and of the cause of environment. Permit me therefore to recount and refute the most insidious of these fallacies, especially as they appear to be so plausible and consonant with common sense.

FALLACY 1: FREE TRADE WILL HARM THE ENVIRONMENT BECAUSE IT IS AIMED AT EFFICIENCY AND ECONOMIC GROWTH WHEREAS GROWTH LEADS TO ENVIRONMENTAL DEGRADATION.

The evidence on whether freer trade leads to more growth is still debated by economists, like much else in economics. But I would say that the postwar experience certainly makes that link appear pretty plausible. And certainly countries around the world today are acting on that policy judgment as they give up inward-looking policies of the postwar years and seek integration into the world economy.

But it is incorrect to assume that the growth of per capita income necessarily, or even overwhelmingly, damages the environment, for several reasons.

- Increased income per capita, aside from *directly* reducing poverty by creating jobs, will reduce poverty *indirectly* as well by enabling the state to raise revenues to pay for "basic needs" programs. Similarly, it would help pay for pollution control and remedial clean-up.
- Again, if the demand for better environment is income-elastic, the growth of per capita income would translate the added resources for potential pollution control and environmental use (that growth makes available) into actual expenditures toward that purpose. While the evidence is only casual rather than systematic, it appears that the amount of organized activity for environmental causes is greater in the richer than in the poorer countries. I should stress however that this will not always be so. Ideas spread quickly and this diffusion has no relationship to per capita incomes. Indeed, we now know from the work of the political scientist Myron Weiner, that in regard to policies promoting compulsory primary education and banning the use of child labor, the international diffusion of ideas crisscrossed the pecking order of per capita incomes.
- At the same time, even if the rich countries had both greater resources to tackle problems such as environmental pollution and more

articulate and effective organizations demanding that these issues be addressed, the reduced levels of pollution may still be higher, in absolute terms and also as a proportion of GNP, than in poor countries simply because the rich countries also produce more pollution in the first place. In other words, the increase in the supply of pollution more than offsets the increase in (effective) demand to reduce it.

Thus, one may well find that *specific* types of pollution fall as per capita incomes rise, as indeed is the case with sulfur dioxide pollution, except for per capita incomes below $5000 in urban areas across the world, according to a much-cited study by my former student Professor Gene Grossman (co-authored with Professor Alan Krueger). But nothing *general* could be asserted for pollution of all kinds, obviously. Growth can then be asserted to be *tightly linked* neither to the improvement of the environment nor with its degradation.

FALLACY 2: FREE TRADE DIRECTLY CAUSES MORE ENVIRONMENTAL DAMAGE THAN SELF-SUFFICIENCY OR PROTECTION.

But if trade, via growth, may improve (rather than harm) the environment, it may also do so directly, when compared to protection. The often-expressed fears that free trade or trade liberalization will harm the environment are not based either on logic or on facts; the reality again is complex.

It is of course obvious that trade will enable the import of pollution-control technologies and pollution-free processes using products and goods causing less pollution. Thus, for instance, trade in low-sulfur coal can help the users of domestic high-sulfur coal shift from the latter to the former.

If these benefits of trade are obvious, it is less obvious, but no less true, that protectionism can harm the environmental objectives and freer trade can help them. Two examples illustrate:

- The 1991 GATT report on *Trade and the Environment* (the first such single-theme analysis of a topic of critical importance to the world trading system to be regularly included as a part of GATT's Annual Report, and also issued as a report by itself) shows how agricultural protection shifts agricultural production from efficient producers in low-income countries to inefficient producers in high-income countries. In turn, this is likely to cause more environmental damage because of the greater use of chemical fertilizers and pesticides in the richer countries. Again, the evidence suggests that variations in agricultural output in the poor nations, in response to price changes (induced by trade liberalization or otherwise), are primarily via changes in capital and labor use and not through change in quantity of land used, so that the loss of forests due to trade liberalization is not a problem either.

• Another example comes from automobile protection in the rich countries. It is well known that the exports of automobiles from Japan have been restrained during the 1980s by the imposition of voluntary export restraints by the United States and the European Community (EC). Research by yet another former student of mine, Professor Robert Feenstra, has shown that these restraints shifted the composition of Japanese exports to the United States from small to large cars. The larger cars, in turn, were fuel-inefficient compared to the smaller cars. Thus the net result may well have been that while protection reduced the overall purchases of cars, the shift to larger cars resulted in more carbon dioxide in the air rather than less. Free trade in cars may well have been the better environmental policy.

THE GENUINE PROBLEMS

But if the stereotypical fears of free trade are to be rejected, there *are* genuine problems that we must confront. To understand them, however, it is necessary to remember a fundamental distinction of analytical importance between (a) environmental problems that are intrinsically *domestic* in nature (though they may be "internationalized" for reasons I will discuss); and (b) those that are intrinsically *international* in nature because they inherently involve spillovers across national borders.

Thus, if India pollutes a lake that is wholly within its borders, that is an intrinsically domestic question. If, however, she pollutes a river that flows into Bangladesh, that is an intrinsically international question. So are the well-known problems of acid rain, ozone layer depletion, and global warming. These latter, intrinsically international problems of the environment raise questions that interface with the trade questions in a more complex way than the former, intrinsically domestic problems, and I shall address them at the end of this chapter.

"INTRINSICALLY DOMESTIC" ENVIRONMENTAL PROBLEMS

A country's solution to intrinsically domestic environmental problems should reflect her own resources, her technical know-how, and her tradeoffs between income and pollution of several varieties. Her solutions should thus be within her own traditional jurisdiction. As long as the environmental question is intrinsically domestic, one may wonder why anyone should object to the conduct of free trade with a country on the grounds that her preferred environmental solution makes free trade with her unacceptable. Yet the fact is that they do. And the objections are directed not merely at free trade, but also at the institutional safeguards and practices, as at GATT, which are designed to ensure the proper functioning of an open, multilateral trading system that embodies the principles of free trade.

In essence, these objections take the following four forms:

- *Unfair Trade*—If you do something different, and especially if you do what appears to be less concerning the environment than I do in the same industry or sector, this is considered to be tantamount to the lack of "level playing fields" and therefore amounts to "unfair trade" by you. Free trade, according to this doctrine, is then unacceptable as it requires, as a precondition, "fair trade."
- *Losing One's Higher Standards*—Then again, environmentalists fear that if free trade occurs with countries having "lower" environmental standards, no matter what the justification for this situation, then the effect will be to lower their own standards. This will follow from the political pressure brought to bear on governments to lower standards to ensure the survival of their industry.
- *Imposing One's Ethical Preferences on Others*—Environmentalists also often want to impose their ethical preferences on other nations. Free trade with nations that do not comply with one's preferences (as in the non-use of dolphin-entangling purse seine nets in catching tuna or leghold traps in hunting for fur) is then objectionable because either trade should be withheld as a sanction to induce or coerce acceptance of such preferences or trade should be abandoned, even if it has no effective consequence and might even hurt only oneself, simply because "one should have no truck with the devil."
- *Constraining One's Freedom to Pursue Domestic (Intra-Jurisdictional) Environmental Objectives*—Finally, many environmentalists consider the trade-regulating institutions such as GATT to be pro-

trade and anti-environment because these institutions are regarded as constraining the freedom to pursue even purely domestic environmental objectives. The interests of the environment are seen as being sacrificed when they conflict with those of trade, as they occasionally do.

I will now consider each of these contentions, in turn. I might add that I will conclude by arguing that some of these positions have cogency whereas others do not; and that some institutional changes are in order to bring harmony between environmentalists and free traders.

Unfair Trade

The objection to free trade when differences in environment regulations make for alleged differences in international competitiveness is probably the most potent objection today. There are efforts under way in the U.S. Congress, for instance, to impose "countervailable duties" on imports of products made abroad by industries that have lower environmental standards than in the United States, by calling it "social dumping" or "environmental dumping" and treating the matter as one where the country with lower standards is effectively unfairly subsidizing her production by not meeting the environmental standards of the United States. For instance, Senator Boren of the Senate Finance Committee made a statement on October 25, 1991 proposing precisely such a countervailable duty on the grounds that:

> We can no longer stand idly by while some U.S. manufacturers, such as the U.S. carbon and steel alloy industry, spend as much as 250 percent more on environmental controls as a percentage of gross domestic product than do other countries . . . I see the *unfair advantage enjoyed by other nations exploiting the environment* and public health for economic gain when I look at many industries important to my own state of Oklahoma. . . [1]

These demands, which are now also finding their way into demands at the GATT for amendments that would establish "international standards" on environmental regulation and GATT-legal countervailable duties against nations that do not meet them, altogether ignore the fact that the precise choices that a nation makes in intrinsically domestic environmental regulation must reflect her own economic conditions and social preferences. For instance, polluting now, growing faster, and cleaning up later may be more economical for a country. Or for specific environmental choices, a country may prefer to spend on clean-up or prevention in one industry rather than in another, reflecting her own evaluation of environmental impacts in these different industries.

In short, the notion that "international standards" should be set for all, or that the United States should have the power to countervail any "social dumping" it deems to be occurring abroad, ignores the fact that there are legitimate reasons for diversity in environmental regulation across countries. In the economists' jargon, diversity of environmental regulations internationally reflects underlying diversity of endowments, technological know-how, and preferences over time and currently between income and pollution of several different varieties. Differences in competitiveness that arise from such environmental regulatory differences are thus part of the case for gainful trade among countries; the more different the environmental regulations are, the greater the gains from trade are likely to be.

But the complaints and political pressures brought by specific industries regarding "unfair trade" by countries with differential and "lower" environmental standards compared to one's own remain a potent force on the political scene. They have now become part of the more general case for what the Americans call "level playing fields"—that is, competition subject to common rules and handicaps.

Demands for harmonization of all kinds of domestic policies are growing apace: in environment, in labor standards, in competition (antitrust) policy, in technology policy. Without such harmonization, it is increasingly asserted that free trade cannot be "fair," and countervailable protection becomes necessary. There are many reasons for this trend which pose a real threat to free trade because, in the end, countries are not likely to become clones of each other in domestic objectives and policies. But the chief reason lies, in my view, in the intensification of competition that the globalization of the world economy has brought about.

With industries everywhere increasingly open to competition, thanks precisely to our postwar success in dismantling trade barriers, with multinationals spreading technology freely across countries through direct investments, and with capital more free than ever to move across countries, producers now face the prospect that their competitive advantage is fragile and that more industries than ever before are "footloose." There is therefore much more sensitivity to any advantage that one's rivals abroad may enjoy in world competition, and a propensity therefore to look over their shoulders to find reasons why their advantage is "unfair."

The notion of unfairness is also attractive to those who seek relief from international competition. If you go to your Congresswoman and ask for protection because the competition is tough, it is going to be difficult to get it. After all, many of them have been sufficiently educated, or perhaps brainwashed (depending on your point of view) into thinking that protection, while not a four-letter word, is not something you want to embrace if you aspire to anything like statesmanship. But if you go to her and say that your successful rival is playing by "unfair" rules, that is just music to protectionist's ears. In the United States, in particular, the "unfairness" notion can take you very far since the economic and social ethos reflects notions of fairness and equality of access (rather than success) more than anywhere else.

The fact that the United States has also been undergoing the "diminished giant" syndrome, vis-à-vis the Pacific nations and her fear of consequent deindustrialization, has also made the American politicians more susceptible to these "unfair trade" arguments from interested lobbies. The continuing dominance of the United States in setting the world's trading agenda powerfully reinforces, in turn, the trend toward "fair trade" and "level playing fields."

While the "unfair trade" argument for rejecting free trade with countries with different environment standards is therefore part of the generic and more general demands for harmonization and level playing fields in world trade, environment (whose protection is legitimately a virtue in itself) brings to this trend additional arguments with perhaps even more powerful appeal.

Fear of Losing One's Own Standards

Chief among these arguments is the fear that competition with the imports and exports in third markets from countries with lower standards will put pressure on domestic industries, triggering political action by them to lower standards down to the levels abroad. Having seen former U.S. Vice President Quayle's Competitiveness Council do precisely this, the environmental NGOs in the United States, and their friends in the EC and elsewhere, have come to see this as a real threat to their goals if free trade is embraced and harmonization *up* is not imposed simultaneously by coercion on foreign countries, especially the poor ones. As Walter Russell Mead put it in a much-cited article in *Harper's* magazine:

> Either the progressive systems of the advanced industrial countries will spread into the developing world or the Third World will move north. Either Mexican wages will move up or American wages will move down. Environmentalists, labor unions, consumer groups, and human-rights groups must go global—just as corporations have done.
>
> This concern reflects at the global level the debate within the EC: the fear that the Common Market's free trade and free capital flows will lead to harmonization *down* of standards "from below" and the efforts of many in consequence to impose harmonization at a *higher* level of standards "from the top."[2]

In fact, these concerns now also cut across to the effects of free trade and capital flows on the real wages of workers—an issue that became important in the recent presidential election in the United States. The Clinton campaign focused not just on the failure of the Bush administration to revive the economy; it also made much of the so-called structural problem that is defined by the stagnation of real wages of unskilled workers during the 1980s.

At least one of the candidates for explaining this phenomenon has been the integration of the world economy and the competition in regard to poor countries with abundant unskilled labor. I doubt the importance of this explanation myself, but it has powerful appeal. In fact, some of the attempts at globalizing the higher environmental and labor standards, with the latter coming uncomfortably close to also raising wages in the industrial sectors of the poor countries on human-rights and labor-rights grounds, can be seen as indirect ways of trying to reduce the perceived threat to real wages of the unskilled in rich countries from free trade with (and capital outflows to) the poor countries.

But if this explanation is really bought, then we are back to the old concerns that free trade with the poor countries will truly act like free immigration from them; the immigration would directly depress workers' wages, free trade would indirectly do so. Interestingly, in the animated British debate prior to the passage of the 1905 Immigration Act, the free traders were also free immigrationists, and the protectionists were also for restrictions on immigration. Immigration was even described as "free trade in paupers."

If I may complete this thought, the growing sentiment that free trade with the poor countries will increasingly depress rich countries' real wages should eventually lead not to protection that few would want, but to palliatives like the imposition of harmonized-up environmental and labor standards, and attempts at restricting capital outflows to them (synonymous in politics with "losing jobs") by way of direct foreign investment. I predict that we will also increasingly witness attempts at encouraging and even forcing population control in these countries.

Many liberal economists have traditionally contemplated the possibility that free immigration will depress wages and then gone on to argue that therefore free immigration requires that the poor countries restrict their population. But if free trade will do the same, or similar, harm to workers' wages, the same thought will strike the policymakers fairly soon. I believe population control is good for the poor countries anyway. But I would not be surprised if, despite the opposition of the religious right in the United States that the Bush administration caved in to, the Clinton administration now actively pushes for population control abroad. Let me return however to the environmental question.

Imposing Ethical Preferences on Others

Behind the environmental argument against free trade is also the zeal to impose one's ethical preferences on other communities and nations. But the use of *state power* in the shape of trade sanctions to force others into accepting one's own idiosyncratic choice of ethical concerns seems wholly inappropriate. Let me explain.

For instance, one can appreciate that Americans are particularly touched by dolphins being caught cruelly in purse seine nets set for tuna. But I wonder when I see on television an interview with the man who brought this to national attention by filming the dolphins in distress; he is, I think, eating fish in the wilds. If Americans have their dolphins, the Indians have their sacred cows. Animal rights activists object to American slaughterhouses. Others may see in Robert Redford's film, *A River Runs Through It,* not rapport with nature, but violation of it with cruelty to the fish that twists and turns, writhing in agony on the fisherman's line.

The moral militancy that motivates some of the environmental NGOs seeking unilaterally imposed trade sanctions on others who do not share their particular preferences or "values" has begun to turn off even other NGOs, especially in n the poor countries that see "eco-imperialism" when the strong nations use trade power to force their preferred values on the weaker nations. The equally autonomous values of the weaker nations, however, cannot be forced upon the stronger nations in the same way. NGOs of the poor countries deny that the NGOs of the strong nations have a monopoly on virtue. And some charge hypocrisy when they see asymmetrical efforts by these latter NGOs at home and abroad even on broadly shared values. Why, they ask, is the U.S.-based global warming-conscious Greenpeace agitating about rainforests in the poor countries instead of concentrating on raising U.S. gas prices to international levels?

Thus, permit me to quote the most radical of today's pro-environment NGOs in India on this issue, in an editorial entitled "Trade Control is not a Fair Instrument" in the country's leading environmental magazine, *Down to Earth*:

> . . . in the current world reality trade is used as an instrument entirely by northern countries to discipline environmentally errant nations. Surely, if India or Kenya were to threaten to stop trade with U.S.A, it would hardly affect the latter. But the fact of the matter is that it is the northern countries that have the greatest impact on the world's environment and yet, their past record in their own countries . . . is nothing to be proud of . . . [T]he instruments that need to be devised for . . . a system of global discipline must be fair and equally accessible to all. Reinforcing [through unilateral muscle-flexing by rich-country NGOs and their governments via trade sanctions] the power that already flows in a northern direction cannot improve the world.[3]

The 1991 GATT report on *Trade and the Environment* drew attention not to the disturbing asymmetry of power to enforce effectively the "values" of the North versus the equally autonomous "values" of the South. Rather, it advanced the "slippery slope" scenario that if any country could suspend another's trading rights in products produced in an "unacceptable" fashion (when no international physical spillovers could be cited as a possible justification and only "values" were at stake), the result was likely to be a proliferation of trade restrictions without any discipline or restraint:

> . . . it is difficult to think of a way to effectively contain the cross-border assertion of priorities. If governments suspend the trading

rights of other nations because they unilaterally assert that their environmental priorities [in other words, "values"] are superior to those of others, then the same approach can be employed on any number of grounds. Protectionists would welcome such unilateralism. They could exploit it to create embargoes, special import duties and quotas against rivals by enacting national legislation that unilaterally defines environmental agendas that other countries [with different "values"] are likely to find unacceptable.

Changing the world trading rules so as to permit the suspension of trading rights of others by individual contracting parties, based simply on the unilateral and extraterritorial assertion of their environmental priorities, undoubtedly would be difficult because many countries would consider such a change to be a big step down a slippery slope.[4]

These views concerning unilateralism to impose one's values on others acquire yet greater cogency when we recognize that there are alternative ways in which one's values can be indulged and propagated.

Most important, if your values are good, as with human rights, they will spread because of their intrinsic appeal. Mahatma Gandhi's idea of nonviolence spread far and wide, not because India had economic power to force it on others or because Western NGOs urged trade sanctions against their own nations to canvass its adoption. It spread simply because of its inherent and powerful moral attractiveness.

Contrast this with the following argument advanced by the able and insightful policy analyst Steve Charnovitz in defense of biodiversity: "There are important medical reasons to preserve biodiversity. But there are also important moral reasons. Geopolitical boundaries should not override the word of God who directed Noah to take two of every living creature into the Ark 'to keep them alive with you.'"

I must confess that, as a Hindu, among nearly 800 million on this planet, I find this moral argument less than persuasive. It leaves me cold just as the display of Christian zeal at the Republican convention in the recent U.S. election left me hot under the collar.

Moreover, there are alternative private options available to propagate your particular ethical preferences if greater activism is desired. Nothing today proscribes NGOs in the U.S., for example, from financing NGOs in Mexico to bring pressure on their government to change its attitude on purse seine nets, thus changing the balance of forces in Mexico away from more productive tuna fishing that benefits Mexico economically and toward "dolphin-safe" fishing that benefits the dolphins instead.

Then again, voluntary private boycotts can be a potent instrument as well. A longstanding tradition permits such boycotts. Provided labeling requirements that permit consumers to make the choices in the marketplace between, say, "dolphin-safe" and "dolphin-unsafe" tuna are allowed, these boycotts will provide an important option.

This option is not the same as proscription, of course. Environmentalists will thus note that labeling may be ineffective because "consumers may act *rationally* in calculating that their individual purchase of environmentally unfriendly products . . . would have only a negligible effect" and that "consumers may act *irrationally*" by not appreciating the ecological importance of avoiding the consumption of the offending product.

Then again, there are bound to be substantive disagreements about the nature and extent of labeling: "dolphin-unsafe" labeling may be objected to as too pejorative and "Tuna from Mexico" labeling may be considered too weak. The problems that have plagued the labeling issue for a variety of questions within United States itself, both in terms of its design and its uniformity versus diversity among the different States of the Union, will not go away at the international level; if anything, they will be more fiercely debated.[5]

While there are factors that weaken the efficacy of the voluntary-boycott prescription, we must also consider two offsetting factors that strengthen it instead. Boycotts in rich countries with big markets, even when leaky, can carry disproportionate clout. Moreover, the funds at the disposal of some of the environmental NGOs and certainly in their aggregate (as demonstrated when they carry enormously expensive full-page ads simultaneously in newspapers such as the *New York Times*, the *Washington Post* and the *Financial Times*) are evidently large relative to what the poor countries they occasionally target can muster in defense of their own practices and preferences.[6] One might also add that the passionate zeal with which these boycotts are advocated, and the occasional willingness to portray those that disagree as morally defective, add to their potency as weapons.

The unilateral, governmental imposition of trade sanctions against other nations simply with a view to coercing them into accepting one's idiosyncratic "value" preferences seems therefore to be unwise on three principal grounds:

- It is essentially intransitive, with each nation able to say its specific values are better than another's; it thus creates the potential for chaotic spread of trade restrictions based on self-righteousness, compounded by a likely encouragement of the process by protectionists;
- It is inherently asymmetric toward poor nations with less economic clout, implying that the economically strong nations are also morally superior and their governments must not be constrained by multilateral rules from coercing others into conversion; and
- There are alternative, private options that can be used to create a multilateral consensus of shared values, based not on the sword but on precept, example, and even private retribution via boycotts.

Even though some of the environmental NGOs in the United States in particular, and perhaps elsewhere too, are skeptical or scornful of them, it is noteworthy that these arguments are spreading within the international community. Thus, Steve Charnovitz has recently complained, "the GATT's campaign against unilateralism is having some impact. Earlier this year, the United Nations Conference on Trade and Development adopted a resolution stating that 'unilateral actions to deal with environmental challenges outside the jurisdiction of the importing country should be avoided.' The Rio Declaration repeats this statement."

I will argue later that some ways will have to be found to accommodate less-than-universal environmental agreements that use well-defined trade restrictions and sanctions, when the problems at hand involve *physical spillovers* across countries (as with global warming). But I have little doubt that unilateral actions designed simply to impose "values" on others through the use of trade sanctions are unwise. I am therefore only delighted that this view is gaining ground.

Something more needs to be said, however. Suppose that your intention in denying Mexico access to the U.S. market is not to change Mexican fishing of tuna in a "dolphin-safe" direction, but simply to avoid eating a "defiled" product that offends your moral values.[7] Should you then be forced into consuming Mexican tuna? That would seem a tall order to many.

But there is an answer to this objection. Nothing in current or prospective GATT rules forces you into this offensive option. For, you could certainly compensate the country whose trading rights (i.e., access to your market) are being denied or suspended by *either* offering other concessions or (in the odd manner of GATT procedures) having the other country withdraw some "equivalent" concessions of her own to you or, better still (in a manner advocated by some), through cash compensation for the gains from trade lost by the other country.

Confronted by this argument, some environmentalists are offended. "Why should we have to pay for our principles?" The answer is, "that is a small price to pay if the alternative (of unilateralism) has the many drawbacks that were noted earlier." If it is right in the Christian tradition to buy indulgences to pay for one's vice, perhaps one should not object to a proposal to pay for one's virtue. At least, the former is for personal gain, the latter (if you accept my arguments) for social gain.

Charnovitz also appeals to "original intent" to argue that the original signatories to the GATT, and earlier practice in some cases, permitted exceptions to market access based on extrajurisdictional exercise of "values" in cases such as the prohibited U.S. landing and sale of U.S. sponges from the Gulf of Mexico gathered by "certain harmful methods [such as] diving or using a diving apparatus." I am assured by academic legal experts on the GATT, however, that the GATT's "original intent" is not unambiguously inferred in this as in many other instances.

John Jackson, one of the leading authorities on GATT law, has thus noted that:

> It has been argued [by Charnovitz] that the drafting history of the GATT would lead to an interpretation of Article XX that would permit governments to take a variety of environmental measures and justify them under the general exceptions of GATT. While this view is interesting, and the research is apparently thorough, it is not entirely persuasive and overlooks important issues of treaty interpretation. Under typical international law, elaborated by the Vienna Convention on the Law of Treaties, preparatory work history is an ancillary means of interpreting treaties. In the context of interpreting the GATT, we have more than forty years of practice since the origin of GATT, and we also have some very important policy questions. . . Thus, unlike certain schools of thought concerning U.S. Supreme Court interpretation of the U.S. Constitution, it is this author's view that one cannot rely too heavily on the original drafting history.[8]

In any event, I find it ironic that the liberal environmentalists who would ordinarily oppose the appointments of "original intent" judges on the Supreme Court should endorse this juridical approach in seeking to prevent the GATT from pursuing (what I have argued are) sensible interpretations of its laws on environmental issues.

Constraining One's Freedom to Pursue Domestic (Intrajurisdictional) Environmental Objectives

But environmentalists are also worried, with a little more cogency, about the roadblocks that current and prospective GATT rules can pose for environmental regulations and standards aimed entirely at domestic production and consumption, matters that are conventionally and properly within domestic jurisdiction.

Now, as long as these rules are applied without discrimination between domestic and foreign suppliers and among different foreign suppliers, there is really little that GATT rules can do to prevent a country from doing anything that it wants to do. For domestic conservation, safety, and health reasons, under Articles XX(b) and XX(g), a contracting party of GATT can even undertake discriminatory, selectively targeted, trade-restraining action, subject to safeguards.

Thus, if you insist on safety belts or airbags in cars, you can impose them on cars as long as both imports from all sources and domestic production are symmetrically treated. The same is true for requiring catalytic converters to reduce environmentally harmful emissions.

The most significant and contentious conceptual question arises when you have a rule that says that consumption (from both domestic and foreign sources) of a product will be restricted if the product is produced using a *process* you disapprove of. Objecting to a process used in a foreign (or, strictly, non-domestic) jurisdiction is, under GATT rulings, not acceptable. There are two types of such process-related problems that we might distinguish:

(1) where the process used is objected to because of "values": for example, purse seine nets or leghold traps; and

(2) where the process used is objected to because it creates cross-border physical spillovers such as acid rain or global warming.[9]

I have already indicated that official trade restrictions under category (1) are properly dismissed as inappropriate unilateralism and the refusal by GATT panels to endorse such actions is good law. But, as I will argue presently, the presence of cross-border physical spillovers raises more legitimate worries about altogether ruling out process-related trade restraints, and appropriate changes in GATT law will be necessary in this class of cases where it seems evidently inappropriate to prevent nations from any use of trade restraints to limit the physical harm being imposed on them by other nations whose trade accentuates this harm.[10]

Leaving this thorny question aside for the present, it would appear that GATT rules should cause no problems for environmentalists. Thus, the GATT report on *Trade and the Environment* argues that:

> Under GATT's rules, governments can employ many different measures to protect and improve the local environment. Thus, sales taxes on products that can create pollution (those containing chlorofluorocarbons, for example), deposit refund schemes for recyclable waste (bottles, scrap cars), or favorable tax treatment of environmentally friendly products (lead-free gasoline, solar panels for home heating) and other nondiscriminatory measures ensuring a pattern of domestic consumption that minimizes pollution would not normally be open to challenge.

There is also nothing in GATT that prevents contracting parties from taxing or regulating domestic producers who engage in polluting activities—even to the extent of prohibiting the production and sale of particular goods. For instance, ceilings on air pollution levels and levies on companies that discharge pollutants into lakes and rivers are fully consistent with GATT rules.

In certain cases, even a measure taken for environmental protection purposes that would otherwise violate GATT obligations not to discriminate may be permitted under Article XX of GATT. The narrowly defined exceptions in Article XX permit a contracting party to place health, safety, or domestic resource conservation goals ahead of nondiscrimination, but only when certain conditions are fulfilled. In general, these conditions ensure that a trade measure is necessary for the achievement of such goals—and that these goals are not used as a pretext for reducing competition from imports.

GATT rules, therefore, place essentially no constraints on a country's right to protect its own environment against damage from either domestic production or the consumption of domestically produced or imported products. Generally speaking, a country can do anything to imports or exports that it does to its own products, and it can do anything it considers necessary to its own production processes.

Alas, that is not the end of the matter for the environmentalists. For, as the GATT *Trade and the Environment* report suggests, even if a regulation or a standard were set in an apparently nondiscriminatory fashion, other issues may arise:

- In reality, is its intention to discriminate against imports rather than to reach the stated (environmental or other) objective?
- In practice, even if the intention is truly to reach the stated goal, is the choice from different ways to reach that goal in favor of a regulation or standard that effectively discriminates most, rather than least, against imports?
- Then again, especially when safety and health standards are set (as with phytosanitary standards), there have been increasing demands for "scientific tests" as a precondition for the imposition of such standards, so as to make these palatable to other trading nations who might see their resulting loss of markets as otherwise unreasonable.

These are perhaps the three most contentious issues today, where the trading interests see the reasonableness of current and prospective GATT procedures designed to ensure as much freedom of access to markets as possible, and where the environmental interests see in the same procedures an unreasonable bias against themselves. In all three areas, GATT permits challenges to be mounted by contracting parties to be mediated by dispute settlement panels and for codes and rules that define how the panels might adjudicate these disputes. Let me say a little about each of these three issues.

(a) The Intention Issue Economists have long recognized the intention issue. Thus, the classic instance we regale our students with relates to Gottfried Haberler's example of the provision in the German tariff, dating from 1902 and valid decades later. The tariff was clearly meant to apply to Switzerland and Austria, relating to "brown or dappled cows reared at a level of at least 300 meters above the sea and passing at least one month in every summer at a height of at least 800 metres."[11]

Within the environmental field, a fine example where the United States is the aggrieved party is provided by the Canadian province Ontario's 10 percent tax on beer cans but not bottles, on environmental grounds. Even if the U.S. authorities did not challenge the objective of restricting the use of cans,[12] they could legitimately note that the law was likely to have been motivated by the desire to discriminate against foreign beer supplies who (unlike local rivals) predominantly used cans rather than bottles, combined tellingly with the fact that the use of cans for other products such as soups and juices (where Ontario producers would have been affected) was not proscribed.

It is hard to see how a good, open trading system cannot permit member countries to examine the bona fides of environmental (and other) regulations in this way. Surely, given the ease with which regulations and standards can be misused for protectionist purposes, *some* mechanism must exist for grievances to be aired and adjudicated. The GATT dispute settlement mechanism, albeit improved as contemplated in the Uruguay Round and further in the direction of greater transparency, is sufficiently objective and neutral between contracting parties to provide a better method for dealing with the problem than national procedures that would always be suspect as influenced by national political considerations.

(b) The Alternative-Measures Issue   There are more difficult issues however, when the question of the use of alternative ways of reaching an environmental objective is raised.

It seems totally sensible that, if alternative ways of meeting an environmental objective exist, a contracting party should be asked to choose one that infringes least on another's trading rights. In fact, this view seems embodied in GATT's Article XX(b) that allows even discriminatory trade restrictions against another contracting party if the measures are deemed "necessary" to protect human, animal or plant life or health.

Two different views of the matter, however, can be taken in interpreting what is "necessary." Thus, in the case of Thailand's restrictions on importation and internal taxes on cigarettes, a GATT Panel decided that Thailand should use the "least GATT-inconsistent" measure to achieve its domestic objective. Then again, one could consider a "least-trade-restrictive" test that, of course, will not necessarily coincide with the "least-GATT-inconsistent" test.[13]

Aside from the greater difficulty of determining what greater and lesser GATT-consistency means, the economic superiority of the test that requires least damage to trade is manifest. In fact, the December 1991 draft of the proposed Uruguay Round treaty adopts the latter test; it is built into the GATT Standards Code and also into the Sanitary and Phytosanitary Decision. It is also the test used in the GATT panel decision in 1992 on alcoholic beverages where the United States lost. The laws in five states that required a common carrier to enforce their tax and alcohol policy were held to be unacceptable because "the U.S. has not demonstrated that the common carrier requirement is the least trade restrictive enforcement measure available to the various states and that less restrictive measures, e.g., record-keeping requirements of retailers and importers, are not sufficient for tax administration purposes."

This test seems reasonable, of course. The objections to it amount mainly to objections to the methods by which the beverage panel arrived at the judgment that less-trade-restrictive measures to achieve the same objectives were available in that instance. But there are indeed inherent difficulties in defining the set of alternative policies that, with differential trade impact, would achieve identical environmental (or other domestic) objectives. It is hard to imagine *identical* results on these objectives from alternative policies, though *similar* results can sometimes be deemed possible (though, here too, judgments will differ sharply in many cases).

In the end, any practical enforcement of the "least-trade-restrictive" test for evaluating the acceptability of an environmental regulation or standard will likely force the adjudicating panel into evaluating, implicitly or explicitly, *tradeoffs* between the cost in trade disruption and the cost in reaching the environmental objective. This is a phenomenon and a problem that economists, who accept free lunches but do not believe in them, have no difficulty recognizing.

The jurisprudence, by necessity, if not by choice, will have to move in the direction of evaluating and deciding upon the solution to such tradeoffs. Thus, under EC law, in the case involving Denmark's laws concerning disposable beer cans, the European Court of Justice seems to have explicitly considered such a tradeoff between the interests of "free movement of goods" (and consequent trade benefits) and "environmental protection."

It is natural therefore that environmentalists and trade experts who seem to occasionally attach opposing weights to the environmental and the trade benefits of any regulation or standard will worry about what weights the adjudicating panels will choose in reaching their decisions. If disputes are to arise between nations, and tests of "necessity" that imply weighing alternative policies leading to different tradeoffs are to be utilized, it is not illegitimate for the environmentalists to seek improvements in the dispute settlement process that would give them greater access in terms of standing and make the procedures more transparent than hitherto at the GATT.

A complementary policy of prevention rather than cure would also be useful as we move increasingly into this difficult and contentious area. The input of "principally affected" trading countries into the setting of domestic environmental and other regulatory standards, such that the policy alternatives are discussed and adopted in light of such input, would help to reduce to an irreducible minimum conflicts that the judicial process must address and resolve. Instances of such international input into domestic setting of standards are not lacking; the United States, worried by the trade-restrictive implications of EC standards-setting procedures, has indeed gained some access to the EC processes. But clearly more institutionalized and satisfactory procedures for doing so, available to weak and not just to strong nations, would appear to be a most useful innovation.

(c) The Scientific Test Issue   The use of scientific tests to determine whether a product can be proscribed, even on a nondiscriminatory basis between imports and domestic production, creates yet another important source of disagreement. Suppose that the United States uses Alar to spray apples and that the EC does not. Suppose then that, faced with agitation from consumers who consider Alar-sprayed apples to be a hazard to their health, the EC bans their sales. The U.S. industry and government can then be expected to demand that the EC justify, through the use of a scientific test, its fear that Alar-sprayed apples are a hazard.

Although this case is hypothetical, the EC-U.S. conflict on EC's proscription of hormone-fed beef is not. In this instance, the U.S. beef producers that used hormones and the biotech industry that had invented and now produced the hormones were pitted against what they considered to be a wholly unscientific fear of hormone-fed beef among Europeans. The United States went to the length of trade retaliation under Section 301; the EC in the end did not counter-retaliate; and the matter was not taken to the GATT dispute settlement process for adjudication, with both the EC ban and the U.S. retaliation continuing in place. Given the high probability that a scientific test criterion would have been required by a GATT dispute settlement panel, it is likely that the EC would have lost the case.

But the case was an early warning sign of the tension between commercial and environmental interests on this issue. Admittedly, even hard science is not hard enough most of the time. The many who are convinced of a hazard to their health, no matter what the *current* preponderance of scientific opinion, might well turn out to be right after all. Then again, even if scientists were agreed on measuring the risk from any event or act of consumption or production, the subjective reaction of different people to the objective risk may vary greatly and, in fact, does.

It is tempting then to say, "let any regulation pass, regardless of the scientific test, no matter that it reduces another's access to one's market." But we are back then to the "slippery slope" scenario. Without the restraining hand of current science, the itch to indulge one's fears could be overwhelming.

The solution may then well be to institutionalize, which is what in effect happened with the hormone-fed beef case. Have the scientific test; if you lose, "pay up" (as the EC did) if you do not wish to change your regulation or standard; or settle by shifting your regulation or standard so as to move broadly in the direction of achieving your objective by alternative policies (for example, labeling hormone-fed beef as such rather than proscribing it altogether and then undertaking education, propaganda, and boycotts against its use).

(d) The Circumventing Democracy Issue I would be remiss if I did not also note the increasing appeal to some environmentalists of the notion that "the process of negotiating international agreements [as the GATT's Uruguay Round] is less subject to public scrutiny, and therefore a threat to democratic accountability" and, more specifically, that "trade liberalization [is] in part a strategy for circumventing health and welfare regulations."[14]

Robert Hudec's riposte to these arguments readily agrees that the democratic procedure of one's representative government negotiating international agreements may produce results that are different from those that result from a purely domestic legislative process. But he denies that the resulting rules, laws, and regulations are "inferior"—contrast what the domestically legislated Smoot-Hawley Tariff of 1930 did with what the internationally negotiated GATT has accomplished in the last four decades. Nor is it correct to assert that the international negotiations are less "democratic." For instance, Hudec argues:

International negotiations also affect the make-up of the electorate that expresses itself on these issues. When an issue of protection is taken up in isolation, be it a tariff or a needlessly protective health regulation, the economic interests harmed by that action—say, exporters who will be injured when foreign governments take similar action—often find themselves under great pressure not to intervene. It is often very bad public relations to butt in—to oppose a fellow citizen's petition for help from his/her government when you have no visible direct interest at stake. A trade agreement provides a setting which legitimizes such participation; it allows the exporter to be seen expressing support for some tangible national gain, in the form of foreign market access guarantees. In short, the trade agreement setting allows all the affected elements to speak.[15]

In my view, the enhanced attention to international effects and international interests makes the trade agreement setting a more legitimate forum for electoral expression of preferences than was the more intimate but patently misinformed process of direct democratic participation leading to Smoot-Hawley.

ENVIRONMENTAL PROBLEMS WITH INTERNATIONAL PHYSICAL SPILLOVERS

When, however, the environmental actions of one country spill over (physically) into another, the economic issues, and hence the questions regarding appropriate policy responses, get more complex.

The Issues

Take the simplest example where I create acid rain for you across our common border. Ideally, the appropriate (first-best) response would be for me to have a policy that taxes the producers for use of processes that produce the acid rain, thus "internalizing" the externality at issue. But suppose that I do not do that.

Free trade with me then will benefit you in the usual way, but with an important difference. If it leads to an expansion in use of acid rain-producing processes because the products using them are produced in greater volume now, then your gains from trade are offset by the damage from increased acid rain. You may even be immiserized by such free trade.

Given that I will not tax the acid rain-producing process, you would then want to consider alternative second-best responses within your own jurisdiction. Thus, an appropriate import tax would reduce your gains from trade but also reduce the damage from the acid rain. The suspension of my unrestricted access to your markets in products using acid rain-producing processes would seem logical and indeed sensible in this instance.

This simple example shows that the GATT rule prohibiting the use of trade restrictions to object to processes used abroad, invoked in the recent tuna-dolphin panel decision, is unlikely to appear sensible when cross-border physical spillovers are at issue.

Now that science is increasingly establishing plausible evidence of more such physical spillovers, the question will certainly have to be addressed anew. Safeguards such as scientific tests, as in the case of domestic regulations and standards that I discussed earlier, would have to be put in place, in case trade restraints are to be allowed. I should imagine that the possibility of (second-best) remedial action at the GATT in this fashion may even encourage the offending party to adopt appropriate (first-best) remedial action within its own jurisdiction to restrict the emission of cross-border pollution.[16]

But this example was an easy one. Suppose that, as in global warming, several countries are emitting carbon dioxide and methane that are creating a planetary problem affecting almost all (though the impact is most adverse on those who expect to be submerged by rising oceans, partially or even wholly, whereas a few cold-afflicted countries might even profit from rising temperatures).

A cooperative solution to such problems is itself hard to devise for several reasons. The economists will be tempted to allocate any targeted reduction of global warming among the different countries according to a cost-minimization principle: the marginal opportunity cost of everyone's contribution should be equalized. Such a solution however is only an efficient solution; it says nothing about equity. It may imply that Brazil should forgo cutting down many forests and the United States should do little about reducing carbon emissions from driving cars, since the initial cost per unit of global warming-prevention is less in Brazil than in the United States. But this would imply that Brazil makes the most effort, and the United States the least, resulting in an efficient but inequitable solution in terms of who bears the burden of reducing global warming.

Thus, consider Figure 1(a). The horizontal axis measures the quantity of global warming prevented and the vertical axis represents its marginal cost. The marginal cost curves for Brazil and the United States are depicted. If the targeted volume of prevention is OQ1, then clearly the entire prevention will be concentrated in Brazil, the total cost incurred in (and by) Brazil being the striped area under Brazil's marginal cost curve, if an efficient, global cost-minimizing solution is to be adopted.

In Figure 1(b), where the targeted volume of prevention is OQ2, OQ will be assigned to Brazil and QQ2 to the United States, and again the Brazilian cost, OQRB, will exceed the cost for the United States as represented by the hatched area QQ2SR. Evidently, in each illustrated instance, the poorer country winds up with the greater cost burden than the richer country in an efficient solution. The efficiency-equity conflict, in the absence of transfers from the rich to the poor nations, becomes salient. The poor countries can be legitimately expected (as at UNCED) to demand transfers of funds if efficient environmental solutions seek to impose inequitable burdens on them.

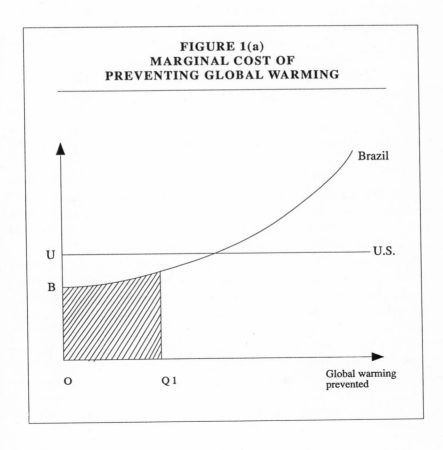

FIGURE 1(a)
MARGINAL COST OF
PREVENTING GLOBAL WARMING

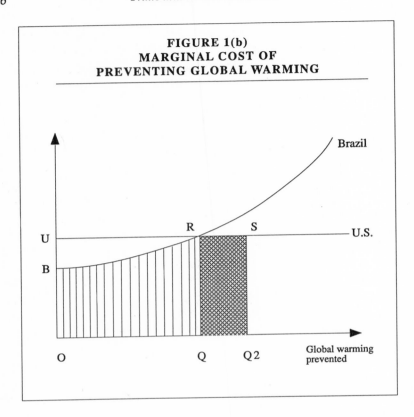

**FIGURE 1(b)
MARGINAL COST OF
PREVENTING GLOBAL WARMING**

In addition to this efficiency-based "flow" argument, the poor countries also make an equity-based "stock" argument: that the rich countries' past policies have "used up" the global commons and accentuated the global warming crisis, and hence they should contribute disproportionately to the current costs of prevention (at the margin).

These considerations explain why cooperative solutions to problems such as global warming and ozone depletion have proven hard to negotiate. In addition, there are the usual difficulties created by diverse scientific views[17] and by differing assessments of the risks posed even when the science is agreed upon.

Thus, in the case of these problems, nations can have legitimate objections to the solutions being urged upon them by other nations. The solutions may not merely be to problems whose scientific validity and implications are disputed but they may also be inefficient or, if efficient, may be inequitable.

The use of trade restrictions to chastise those who do not go along, condemning them as "rejectionists" or "free riders," would then be unjust. This constitutes a legitimate argument against the unilateral use by countries—for example, the Netherlands in seeking to suspend the imports of logs from countries without policies to "sustain" their tropical forests—of trade restrictions for solutions to global problems that are not demonstrated to be efficient and equitable. If such trade restrictions are to be accepted, then it is necessary that they be justified before an impartial adjudicating body such as perhaps a GATT dispute settlement panel, as required in order to secure an efficient and equitable solution to a global environmental problem rather than as an instrument to impose an inefficient and inequitable solution on another trading nation.

In principle, the same observations apply when a subset of the world's trading nations, or GATT contracting parties, reaches a multilateral agreement (such as the Montreal Protocol on Substances that Deplete the Ozone Layer) and then seeks to restrict the trading rights of nonmembers. The motivation behind the trade-restricting provisions in these treaties is evidently to prevent their efficacy from being undermined by trade between members and nonmembers of the compact.

Because these treaties generally have several participants and have therefore undergone a process of negotiation and persuasion, and because they are generally open to universal membership, one may be inclined to accept their denial of trading access to nonsignatories when this denial can be argued to be necessary for making the (global) objective of the treaty viable.

Where the membership is large enough to make a GATT waiver under Article XXV possible, the issue is moot in any event. But few treaties can be expected to reach the two-thirds majority of the votes cast, with the added requirement that the majority must constitute more than half of the contracting parties, for the GATT waiver to be invoked.

Suggestions for GATT Rules

I would then conclude, for these cross-border physical-spillover problems, that:

- The GATT rules need to be amended to allow countries to object to imports of goods using production processes that create cross-border spillovers;

- Safeguards will however have to be built in for countries whose trading rights are thus to be qualified;
- These safeguards should include the intention, alternative measures, and science tests that currently and prospectively are used in the GATT (as discussed earlier);[18] and
- The safeguards should also include an obligation to demonstrate that the trade restriction is designed to promote or sustain an environmental solution that is both efficient and equitable among the contracting parties.

These rules should encourage the signatories to the multilateral environmental treaties to ensure that these principles are already reflected in their own negotiations and treaty making. I would also suspect that purely unilateral measures would generally fail to meet these standards, leaving the arena to more broad-based, multilateral endeavors. Both would be desirable developments.

NOTES

1. Statement of Senator David L. Boren, Senate Finance Committee, *International Pollution Deterrence Act of 1991* (Oct. 25, 1991).

2. "Bushism, Found: A Second-Term Agenda Hidden in Trade Agreements," *Harper's*, p. 44 (Sep. 1992).

3. "Trade Control is not a Fair Instrument", *Down to Earth*, p. 4 (Aug. 15, 1992). The magazine is published in New Delhi and enjoys a large circulation.

4. General Agreement on Tariffs and Trade (GATT), *Trade and Environment Report*, pp. 33-34 (1992).

5. The recently activated GATT Group on Environment Measures and International Trade has among its tasks the examination of the trade effects of packaging and labeling requirements intended to protect the environment. It has been examining the packaging and labeling questions in depth.

6. It is not just that poor countries are financially strapped. It is also that few Parliaments would sanction expenditure of the huge amounts of money that are needed to take out ads in the Western papers and to hire lobbyists in Washington. The only democratic exception seems to be Mexico which had,

at the end of 1991, as many as seventy-one lobbying firms in the United States registered as "foreign agents" acting on behalf of NAFTA.

7. So, you are not a "consequentialist" but one who has an "absolute" moral value. You may not expect to change Mexican behavior; you may even be hurting only yourself. But you may be doing what you think duty or virtue compels.

8. John Jackson, "World Trade Rules and Environmental Policies: Convergence or Conflict?" *Washington and Lee Law Review*, vol. 49, pp. 1241-42 (1992).

9. Nearly all cases fit into one or both of these categories. Thus, if chickens are raised in undersized cages, this may be objected to as cruel, fitting it into category (1). If you overfish in the commons to which I have access, that fits into category (2). If you use your forests in an "unsustainable" way, I may object to it because I think that is bad *per se*, i.e., category (1), or because it affects global warming and hence me, i.e., category (2), or because of both reasons.

10. Such use must, however, be regulated in a way that ensures symmetry of rights, equity, and efficiency. Devising appropriate procedures and rules to regulate the use of such trade restraints is a challenge for the architects of the new GATT system.

11. Gottfried Haberler, *Theory of International Trade*, p. 339 (London: William Hodge & Co. Ltd., 1936). Haberler cited this amusing case as an instance of the manner in which countries evaded the obligation of the Most Favored Nation clause.

12. As argued below, a challenge to recycling and packaging requirements cannot be ruled out on the grounds that alternative, less trade-restricting measures are possible and should be undertaken.

13. Steve Charnovitz, "GATT and the Environment: Examining the Issues," *International Environmental Affairs*, vol. 4, no. 3, pp. 213-14 (1992). For the Thailand case, see GATT, *Basic Instruments and Selected Documents*, 375/200 (Geneva: 1990).

14. This was the issue addressed to a panel of trade and legal scholars at the Conference on "The Morality of Protectionism" at the New York University Law School in November 1992. It is quoted in Robert Hudec's excellent contribution, "'Circumventing' Democracy: The Political Morality of Trade Negotiations." *New York University Journal of International Law and Politics*, in press.

15. Hudec, *ibid.*

16. Whether it will, of course, depends on the relative distribution of the costs and benefits between the countries from the two alternative courses of action. It would also depend on imponderables such as the relative economic strengths of the two countries; a powerful offending nation may exercise retribution or offer incentives in unrelated areas.

17. Jessica Tuchman Matthews has argued that the scientific dissent on global warming is only about its size and speed. But surely that makes all the difference, because if the process is very slow and small in magnitude, the contention that technical revolutions that may reverse it quickly and effectively will have time to emerge may be more readily agreed to, obviating the need for emergency action now.

18. I agree with Charnovitz, that "where environmental threats are particularly serious or irreversible, GATT should adopt the precautionary principle, erring on the side of prudence."

14

Why Environmentalists Are Angry about the North American Free Trade Agreement

John Audley

In the words of a former "environmental president," most environmentalists can be classified as "the spotted owl crowd." But as this now former president learned, to simplify so complicated an issue as environmental concern is dangerous indeed. Environmentalists' interests are more far-reaching and comprehensive than this rhetoric would indicate. Not tied to a specific sector within the economy or society overall, environmentalists' interests lie within concerns we all have in common: protecting our air, water and soil quality, or protecting biological diversity. The "constituents" of the environmental movement understand neither the political divisions that define participatory democracies, nor the conflicts between the need for economic development and environmental protection. Because they have no voice of their own, they are subject to the decisions of humans, who do not often take the interests of the silent environment into consideration.

In defending this silent interest group, most environmentalists seek a balance between human activity and concern for the environment. Few advocate the extremes of the deep ecology movement, where civilization would return to some "state of nature," coexisting with one's ecosystem. In all probability this condition never existed; or if it did, returning to an earlier period fails to recognize that humans and the environment interact in a continuously changing relationship.

What environmentalists seek are policy decisions that recognize the importance of balance between narrowly defined human concerns, and

191

concerns for the long-term sustainability of the Earth. President Bush ignored these concerns when he developed his agenda for trade policy. He first resisted the link between trade and the environment, then relegated the environment to parallel tracks not tied to trade negotiations, and finally cloaked the North American Free Trade Agreement (NAFTA) in "green language" in the final days of negotiations. Ultimately, President Bush failed to meet the minimal environmental requirements of "no more harm to the environment through trade agreements" demanded by environmentalists. His failure to meet these minimal standards now jeopardizes the success of NAFTA negotiations, and puts President Clinton in a difficult position relative to promoting both economic development and environmental protection. The task for President Clinton is to determine whether resolving the environmental problems in NAFTA are possible through side agreements only, or whether more substantial renegotiations of portions of the agreement are required. So far, President Clinton has steadfastly maintained, rightfully or wrongfully, that side agreements are sufficient for the task.

THE UNION OF TRADE AND ENVIRONMENTAL POLICY

NAFTA marks the first time in the history of trade negotiations that environmental concerns were part of the negotiation process. Among the first initiatives to give formal attention to the relationship between trade policy and environmental protection was the 1987 Brundlandt Commission *Report on Environment and Development*. In the report, the Commissioners urged that the Uruguay Round of the General Agreement on Tariffs and Trade (GATT) should "reflect concern for the impacts of trading patterns on the environment and the need for more effective instruments to integrate environment and development concerns into international trading arrangements." In its 1992 report on trade and the environment, the U.S. Office of Technology Assessment acknowledged that conflicts between environmental principles and trade objectives are increasing. However, addressing these conflicts requires more than just a reliance upon market mechanisms. The World Bank's 1992 *Report on Development and the Environment* asserts that it is the government's role to ensure that industries around the world conform to environmental policies because "private markets provide little or no incentive for curbing pollution."

Despite assertions by international organizations such as the World Bank and reports by the U.S. government, the Bush administration began NAFTA discussions by refusing to acknowledge the link between trade and the environment. U.S. Trade Representative Carla Hills argued that environmental issues have no place in trade agreements. Rather than address environmental concerns directly in NAFTA, the Bush administration relegated them to a "parallel track," one that would run concurrently, but not conflict with, slow, or halt progress on the trade agreement. To gain enough environmental support for extending fast track authority with respect to GATT and NAFTA, President Bush promised to include five environmental advisors in the public sector advisory system for trade policy. Unfortunately, this eleventh hour conversion only marginally changed the negotiating agenda for the United States, and the Bush administration continued on its path toward free trade with little change in its original direction.

Despite the Bush administration's initial unwillingness to link trade and the environment, environmentalists continued to participate in the discussions surrounding trade. The reason for this interest is that environmentalists recognize that trade agreements have the potential to address one of the major enemies of the environment—poverty. Written correctly, trade agreements can help to alleviate poverty by promoting broader distributions of the benefits of a technological society.

Trade is one component of the principle of sustainable development, a principle which argues that natural resources should be used by societies. Sustainable development places one condition on the scale of use; consumption should "meet the needs of the present without compromising the ability of future generations to meet their own needs." This was articulated in the World Commission on Environment and Development's report, *Our Common Future* in 1987. Promoting the principle of sustainable development is where environmentalists began in their discussion of NAFTA. Developing the best strategy to transform so broad a principle into practical policy recommendations was the next step.

THE "MINIMALIST" APPROACH TO NAFTA: NO MORE HARM TO THE ENVIRONMENT

With the help of hindsight, environmentalists had three options by which to pursue their collective objective of sustainable development. Given the position of the administration, environmentalists could have selected a "kill" strategy, standing in opposition to any trade agreement offered by President Bush. This strategy obviously was not selected by even the most ardently concerned environmental organizations, specifically because it conflicts with the principle of sustainable development.

The second option available to environmentalists was to promote NAFTA as a positive instrument for implementing environmental principles. Using this strategy, environmentalists would have used NAFTA as a vehicle to promote many of the global changes necessary for long-term protection of the environment. Environmentalists would have urged that NAFTA include provisions to adopt "environmentally consistent accounting methods," where industry would internalize the cost for reducing natural capital stocks or damaging others. This strategy was also not selected by environmentalists. Policies supporting fundamental global change are not yet fully developed, and currently lack the interest of either federal or industry officials. Adopting a strategy like this would have resulted in the same consequence for environmentalists as the "kill" strategy; environmentalists would not have been included in negotiations.

Instead, environmentalists adopted a third strategy, best described as a "minimalist" strategy. Its objectives are the least trade prohibitive of the three. Environmentalists asked the president to minimize any more harm to the environment through bi-national trade. Working together, environmentalists drafted a series of documents that made the strategy functional.

THE ENVIRONMENTAL STANDARD FOR NAFTA

Behind the efforts of organizations like the National Wildlife Federation (NWF), which was one of the first national environmental organizations to commit itself to trade policy analysis and was one of the key environmental advisors to President Bush, environmentalists commented on the directions of negotiations, and provided substantive policy recommendations. Despite the secretive nature of trade negotiations, some information was shared with environmentalists during routine meetings with trade officials. In addition, officials in Canada leaked an early version of the agreement, and a number of environmental organizations had an opportunity to comment on it.

By the beginning of spring 1992, negotiations had proceeded far enough for environmentalists to develop a specific set of conditions for their support of NAFTA. Working in coalition, environmentalists produced three documents outlining their concerns. The first document, NWF/Pollution Probe-Canada's, *Bi-National Statement of Environmental Safeguards that Should be Included in NAFTA*, was completed in May 1992. Nine other groups in the United States and Canada signed this document. Other groups wished to elaborate further the principles in the paper and continued to work on a second document, the Natural Resources Defense Council's *Environmental Safeguards for the North American Free Trade Agreement*, completed in June 1992. This paper was endorsed by twelve U.S. environmental organizations. Finally, just prior to the release of NAFTA in August, eleven groups endorsed the Center for International Environmental Law's *Preliminary Overview of Environmental Concerns Arising from the NAFTA*. Although each of these three documents differ to some degree in scope and emphasis, they are all linked by a number of basic principles. These principles make up the heart of the environmental concerns in NAFTA.

First, environmentalists expressed concerns over the enforcement of domestic environmental laws. Historically, trade agreements suffer from the inability to enforce their own rules; more recently, concern has developed over their influence on the enforcement of domestic regulations. Recognizing the concerns over sovereignty, environmentalists recommended that NAFTA establish a North American Commission on the Environment (NACE). It was envisioned that the commission would have the power to monitor and report on the enforcement of environmental regulations throughout the free trade area, and would have the power to investigate environmental violations. Some described the commission as operating like a general accounting office, with the power to publish the performance records of industries and governments regarding domestic environmental law. Others sought a commission with "real teeth" or the power to sanction in some way.

The second concern involved maintaining each nation's right to set environmental regulations that are higher than those currently accepted by other trading partners. Much of the environmental discussions surrounding the Uruguay Round of GATT negotiations focused on apparent conflicts with domestic standards set to protect the environment, food quality, or exposure to potentially harmful substances. One of the goals of the Uruguay Round is to "harmonize" these standards between countries to avoid unnecessary barriers to trade. Environmentalists feared that the direction of this harmonization may be downward, and that there is a tendency for trade experts to dismiss health and safety standards as mere non-tariff barriers to trade, which should be minimized or eliminated to facilitate trading. Environmentalists argued that NAFTA should specifically state that governments have the right to set their own health and safety standards, regardless of existing international standards or those accepted by trading partners.

Finally, environmentalists argued that NAFTA's procedures and administration, as well as its dispute resolution process, should be open to the widest degree of public access and participation possible. Traditionally, trade agreements have established administrative and dispute resolution processes that are far removed from the eyes and ears of the citizens whose lives are directly affected by their decisions. This kind of secrecy resulted in a GATT panel decision that declared portions of the U.S. Marine Mammal Protection Act of 1973 (MMPA) to be "GATT inconsistent" because it "unjustly" required nations whose industries provide tuna to U.S. markets to avoid the unnecessary slaughter of dolphins. The uproar over this decision resulted in Congressmen Henry Waxman's and Richard Gephardt's sponsorship in the 102nd Congress of a resolution urging President Bush not to send any trade agreement to Congress that threatens existing environmental policies. The resolution overwhelmingly passed the House.

Environmentalists believe that the democratic process helps protect the environment because it holds the actions of elected and appointed officials accountable to citizens. Procedural democracy in the dispute process and procedures of NAFTA were therefore part of the message from the environmental community.

As an aside to the principles in NAFTA, environmentalists also insisted that NAFTA include adequate funding mechanisms to ensure proper installation of environmental infrastructure, to assist in enforcement, and to pay for the clean-up of the U.S.-Mexican border. There is a long-overdue "debt" to border communities because of a long-standing lack of environmental protection. According to the American Medical Association, environmental degradation related to industry location on the U.S.-Mexico border has turned the region into "a virtual cesspool and breeding ground for infectious diseases." Current estimates to clean up this crisis and create adequate infrastructures, such as indoor plumbing and sewage systems, range from $6 billion to $9 billion. Environmental groups insisted that, before trade is expanded, adequate revenues to correct the border crisis need to be guaranteed.

These benchmarks—enforcement, participation, safeguarding the authority of state and federal governments to set environmental, health, and safety standards, and adequate funding for environmental infrastructure—were used by environmentalists to judge NAFTA when it was released in September 1992. They reflect the broad consensus of the environmental community that trade is important, but that it also has a significant impact on people and their environment. It is by these benchmarks that the environmental community has overwhelmingly determined that NAFTA is an unsatisfactory trade agreement.

"ENVIRONMENTAL WINDOW DRESSING" OR THE "GREENING" OF TRADE AGREEMENTS?

With the exception of NWF, no U.S. environmental organization was ready to endorse NAFTA as presented by President Bush to Congress. Attitudes ranged from calling for renegotiation to regarding NAFTA as unfinished business. There are a number of reasons for the environmentalists' dissatisfaction.

NAFTA negotiators directed a great deal of their efforts to satisfy environmental concerns in the chapters on food safety and technical standards. Despite these efforts, serious questions remain in the mind of most environmentalists about the ability of existing environmental laws to withstand NAFTA's "necessary" and "appropriate" tests for environmental protection. While enabling legislation may be able to clarify these issues, whether NAFTA itself will impede future environmental protection remains uncertain.

Negotiators did agree to establish a NACE. The idea behind the commission is a promising one, supported by environmental organizations in all three countries. However, the agenda for discussion outlined by the State Department in late October 1992 indicates that the commission will lack any effective and substantive enforcement power. In December 1992, then U.S. Environmental Protection Agency Administrator William Reilly announced that negotiations to create the commission would cease until President Clinton took office.

In terms of the funding of border clean-up, participation in the administration and dispute settlement procedures, and enforcement, NAFTA fails to meet anyone's expectations. The burden of evidence proving an environmental regulation to be an illegal barrier to trade has apparently been shifted to the challenging party. But the dispute procedure remains secretive, and the Free Trade Commission (created by NAFTA) has the right to withhold information from publication if its members determine that publication is inappropriate. NAFTA does not address any issues of enforcement, making it virtually impossible to determine whether products entering the United States will meet the same production standards required of domestic manufacturers. Finally, U.S. Trade Representative Hills was quite specific in her refusal to consider funding issues as a part of NAFTA. In a letter to NWF's President Jay Hair, Hills claimed that any discussion of funding was a "nonstarter" between negotiating parties. The office of the United States Trade Representative (USTR) under the new leadership of Mickey Kantor has not yet addressed the funding issue.

By refusing to address issues of public participation and the funding of environmental projects, and by leaving so many environmental questions unresolved, the claim in the Preamble that NAFTA will "promote sustainable development" is difficult to take seriously. The unwillingness of the USTR to take seriously these concerns as they were expressed during congressional hearings in October 1992 demonstrates that President Bush has jeopardized the potential for trade agreements to promote more equitable distributions of wealth for citizens in all countries and to protect the environment. President Bush's signature on the agreement on December 17, 1992 has made it even more difficult for President Clinton to address properly these outstanding concerns and to help make NAFTA, at the very least, an environmentally neutral trade agreement.

The anger expressed by many environmentalists regarding the current situation over NAFTA stems from President Bush's actions. By utilizing a strategy of "trade versus the environment," he polarized concerned groups that should have been natural allies in the pursuit of economic development. Recognizing the importance of trade and the lack of solid evidence linking the two, environmentalists framed the least trade invasive test possible for evaluating the agreement. The "no harm" test did not ask NAFTA to become a positive vehicle for environmental goals; it was simply a request that NAFTA not further the environmental degradation resulting from multinational industrial behavior and the inability of national governments to monitor effectively these activities. Even this mild version of trade and environmental integration was not achieved by President Bush.

THE AGENDA FOR PRESIDENT CLINTON

As President Clinton now works to complete President Bush's trade agenda, he faces a difficult task. NAFTA will be a part of his overall economic package, one he hopes will revitalize the American economy by putting U.S. citizens back to work in high quality jobs. But as he picks up the pieces of President Bush's flawed NAFTA agenda, he runs the risk of dividing his supporters if he drops a seriously flawed trade agreement on Congress without some extensive repair.

President Clinton recognizes two important aspects of the task of completing NAFTA. First, he appears to recognize the extremely complicated nature of global economic integration. While expanded trade with other countries can create jobs, he has shown a sensitivity to the impact of capital mobility on the *quality* of jobs created in the United States. More service jobs, like those created during the Reagan/Bush years, do not serve the best interests of American people. He also appreciates the complicated relationship between the environment and trade. Lax environmental standards here and abroad not only harm our common environment, but they also create disincentives for responsible industrial behavior. Currently, these weak standards encourage behavior that irresponsibly uses natural resources and continues to degrade the environment.

President Clinton also appears to recognize that it is wrong to view a comprehensive national industrial agenda through the snapshot of a trade agreement with Mexico and Canada. NAFTA cannot be the focus of all our hopes and fears for the future, as President Bush envisioned. As then candidate Clinton said in a campaign speech on October 4, 1992 at North Carolina State University, "the shortcomings in the agreement are really a reflection, however, of the shortcomings in the Bush economic policy as a whole, not just in his approach to trade with Mexico or to world trade, but in the whole approach to the economy and the environment."

NAFTA should be a tool in President Clinton's agenda to rebuild the American economy and protect the environment, not the entire agenda. And as a tool, he should be willing to cancel the agreement if it cannot be made to protect the vital interests of America.

President Clinton outlined those vital interests in his October 1992 campaign speech. Of five interests important to the American people, three involved the environment: a guarantee to clean up the environment and provide adequate environmental infrastructure; a guarantee of protection for the democratic process (which environmentalists feel is key to protecting the environment); and an assurance that all imported agricultural products meet the same pesticide safety requirements as those grown by domestic producers.

To ensure that these environmental interests are protected in NAFTA, President Clinton suggested that, prior to the completion of NAFTA, the governments of Mexico, Canada, and the United States resolve two things. First, to protect against the negative side effects of expanded trade, there must be a NACE. It would be similar to the one currently proposed in name only, as President Clinton envisions a commission with the power to "provide remedies, including money damages and the legal power to stop pollution." He suggested that assuring the commission provide this kind of protection will be one of the jobs for Vice President Al Gore. Second, President Clinton advocates that the countries enter into supplemental agreements that will require each government to enforce its own environmental and worker standards. These agreements would provide the safeguards and remedies to ensure that laws are enacted: access to federal courts, public hearings, citizens' right to know, and the right to bring suit in domestic courts of law for failure to implement and enforce domestic environmental and worker safety protection.

President Clinton's plan for NAFTA is a bold attempt to link trade policy with environmental and worker protection. His call for the NACE, his demand that governments implement their own environmental laws, and his insistence that democratic principles underlie any agreement are all consistent with the "minimal test" advocated by environmentalists. Unfortunately, it appears that negotiations will fall short of President Clinton's vision for trade. To achieve his goals, President Clinton must take two steps. First, he must directly link the supplemental agreements to the language in the original agreement. Yet it remains unclear how he can achieve this goal without re-opening some aspects of the agreement. While a separate agreement guaranteeing the right of access to federal courts is important, it will not provide democratic access to the dispute resolution proceedings envisioned in NAFTA. President Clinton's environmental commission would be a revolutionary step toward establishing ecologically sustainable trade, but without some direct link to NAFTA it is difficult to see where the assurances of environmental protection will lie. Unfortunately, President Clinton has remained stubborn in his insistence to avoid even language clarifications to the text negotiated by President Bush.

Second, President Clinton must maintain his commitment to the principles he espoused during the campaign. He must ensure that the horrible conditions facing residents living along the U.S.-Mexico border are addressed as part of the negotiations, and he must ensure that industries cannot take advantage of lax enforcement of environmental regulations. Again, it appears that negotiations will fall short of his commitment. Due in part to the trade sanctions, and the strong resistance of the business community to endorse any kind of trade measure to promote environmental protection, it is unlikely that the supplemental agreements will contain any substantive means of promoting compliance with environmental laws. And second, the sheer magnitude of the environmental problems within the border region suggests a price tag in the range of $20 billion, an amount beyond the reach of the general revenues of any NAFTA country without infusions of resources directly tied to trade. Again, President Clinton seems to be willing to bow to the pressures of business, who refuse to consider any kind of revenue-generating mechanism associated with NAFTA.

Market access is often the most effective motivator for changes in behavior. Market access has induced Mexico to change its laws on investment, banking, insurance, and even to reconsider its laws on ownership and use of its vast petroleum reserves. Trade agreements can (and should) be used to change environmental behavior. Without some direct linkages to NAFTA, which would require renegotiating portions of the agreement, real assurances seem unlikely. Despite the rhetoric from both President Bush and President Carlos de Salinas of Mexico regarding renegotiation, the environment is the one area where Salinas indicated additional discussions might be necessary.

The paths facing President Clinton for achieving a successful NAFTA are difficult ones indeed. If he pursues President Bush's flawed trade agenda, he risks damaging vital U.S. interests, and perhaps a political battle in Congress that could put an end to *any* momentum he has built with the legislative branch. He can also pursue the parallel approach created by President Bush, and work hard at creating the assurances necessary to protect the environment through side agreements. This path has its dangers, for it may not provide the necessary links to NAFTA that promote environmental protection, worker safety, and economic growth. To achieve these ends, the president may be forced to renegotiate certain portions of the agreement, but this runs the risk of destroying a delicate agreement built on endless compromises between negotiators.

Whichever approach the president takes, his final product will be tested against the same "no more harm to the environment" standard used to evaluate earlier versions of NAFTA. But unlike President Bush, President Clinton has a better chance of balancing the need to promote economic development with environmental protection because he acknowledges the importance of effectively addressing the environmental concerns of trade. With the president's support, environmentalists will look toward creating a NAFTA that promotes economic development and environmental protection.

15

The United States Government, Public Participation, and Trade and Environment

Jan C. McAlpine and Pat LeDonne[1]

As trade and environment concerns began to overlap increasingly in the 1990s, one of the more intriguing areas of change in the development of U.S. government policy was the heightened public interest and participation in shaping U.S. international trade policy.

Beginning in 1991, the trade and environment debate in the U.S. played out through blaring international headlines and dramatic public advertisements. In the spring of 1992, posters mysteriously appeared in Washington, D.C. depicting GATTzilla, a monster chewing the globe, trampling the Capitol, and spewing DDT, while clutching a squealing dolphin. The headline blared "GATT is Coming, What You Don't Know Will Hurt You." Despite much speculation regarding its origin, no one stepped forward to claim responsibility for either the poster or for plastering it on the construction walls surrounding the building that houses the United States Trade Representative's (USTR) office.

The trade and environment issue created an intellectual firestorm among international policy wonks over which policy objective—trade or environment—is paramount. The debate, initially igniting over the negotiations of the Uruguay Round, the North American Free Trade Agreement (NAFTA) and the General Agreement on Tariffs and Trade's (GATT) tuna-dolphin panel report, went on to heat up discussions between government representatives in the Organization for Economic Cooperation and Development (OECD) and GATT.

Environmental and consumer organizations were originally concerned over the Uruguay Round and the possibility that existing U.S. environmental, health, and safety standards would be harmonized down to meet the requirements of the Codex Alimentarius Commission, the Geneva-based standard-setting organization. They grew even more wary of NAFTA.

As soon as it was apparent that President Bush would submit a request to Congress for extension of fast track authority, a coalition of public interest groups representing environment, labor, and consumer organizations rallied to urge Congress to reject the extension. They argued that NAFTA would encourage unsustainable growth and investment in Mexico, as well as provide companies operating in Mexico an unfair competitive advantage because of lower labor, environmental, and safety standards.

Congress sought assurances from President Bush that the agreement, if authorized, would address the environmental and labor concerns raised by the coalition. The White House responded with its "May 1 Plan" establishing the parallel track approach and placing the environmental and labor concerns separate and apart from the NAFTA negotiations. The assurances split the environmental coalition on whether or not the extension should be approved. Ultimately, Congress approved it. A number of environmental organizations, most notably the National Wildlife Federation, supported the extension.

In September 1991 a GATT dispute panel ruled that the United States had violated GATT law by slapping an embargo on Mexican tuna caught using purse seine nets, which result in the needless killing of dolphins. According to the panel, the United States violated GATT Articles III and XI by imposing a unilateral trade measure that discriminated against Mexico's "method of production" for catching tuna, to protect a species outside of its jurisdiction.

Although it may not have played out as an important issue in Peoria, this decision was a wake-up call for U.S. environmentalists who had never heard of GATT. Advertisements appeared in the *New York Times* and the *Washington Post* criticizing GATT for what was perceived as an attempt to undermine U.S. environmental law. It is interesting to note that the United States waited more than ten years before imposing the trade sanctions against Mexico as required under the Marine Mammal Protection Act—only after an environmental nongovernmental organization (NGO) won a lawsuit and the court ordered compliance did the United States act. Concurrently, environmentalists escalated their arguments opposing NAFTA and the "secret" manner in which the negotiations were being carried out. As public concern grew, Congress expressed reservations about supporting NAFTA for political reasons. The trade community reluctantly found itself addressing environmental issues and grappling with an extremely complex community of concerns.

INSTITUTIONAL DISSONANCE

Fundamental to the problems facing both the trade and environment communities are a number of structural problems that prevent the two groups from communicating clearly and negotiating fairly. Trade is often cited as the engine that drives the global economy, playing an important role in determining the economic relationships among nations. The trade community enjoys a long history of diplomacy, a tradition of in-ternational agreements, the institutional mechanism of GATT, a "gentlemen's agreement" for discussion and negotiation of international trade issues, and a relatively clear-cut idea of its clientele—business and industry.

Trade negotiations are conducted in a far more secretive manner than environmental policy making. This lack of transparency most concerns the environmental community. Trade negotiators are concerned that a more open process would result in undue influence by business lobbyists, as well as permit foreign competitors' access to sensitive information, placing their constituency at an unfair competitive advantage.

Trade policy negotiators and trade consultants initially tried to dismiss environmental concerns as an incidental, parallel track policy topic, or as a cover for protectionism. Trade is only about the trading of goods and services, or so the argument went, and it is not concerned with the environment. Environmental protection is a domestic issue and should be dealt with in that manner, said the trade community. International environmental concerns should be addressed through the appropriate environmental channels, or negotiated through multilateral environmental agreements, separate and apart from trade negotiations.

Environmental policy making, in a historical context, is relatively immature. Until recently, environmental policy has been dealt with uniquely at the national level. While environmental problems are increasingly global in nature, there is currently no effective institutional mechanism for achieving agreement on international environmental policies. Because the environmental community is somewhat fractured with regard to its philosophies and approaches, it is difficult to identify an environmental clientele.

Although environmental protection is innately for the well-being of humans, animal and plant life, as well as such intangibles as protection of the ozone layer, the environmental NGOs come closest to constituting an environmental clientele. A small exception to this is the environmental technologies, products, and services industry currently estimated at having a global market of $200 billion annually. However, this industry has competitive sectors and interests. These competing interests sometimes clash with longer-term environmental NGO objectives. They also preclude the industry from singlemindedly lobbying for environmental protection concerns in the trade and environment arena.

In the United States, environmental policy making is further complicated by the balkanization of environmental responsibility within the federal government. Agencies with responsibility for environmental policy include the Department of Interior, Department of Commerce and the National Oceanic and Atmospheric Administration, Department of Agriculture, Food and Drug Administration, Department of Energy, and the Environmental Protection Agency (EPA). In addition, the State Department has been given the responsibility of overseeing foreign policy decisions with regard to the environment.

Within the government, Congress has mandated the USTR to be the lead negotiating authority on trade. USTR ensures that U.S. interests are represented in the trade policy arena, both nationally and internationally. Although the Department of Commerce shares responsibility for trade matters with USTR, there is a much clearer delineation of roles and responsibility between the two agencies as compared to those agencies that share responsibility for environment. These two agencies also share a single objective—to promote abroad U.S. goods and services and the industries that produce and provide them. What the current trade and environment debate has illustrated, environmentalists maintain, is that USTR does not and cannot ensure that environmental protection will be woven into the fabric of trade policy.

EPA: A TRADITION OF PUBLIC PARTICIPATION

As the trade and environment conflict emerged within the government among and between agency policy makers, one of the grittiest fights erupted over transparency and public participation in the process. The issue of transparency and public participation illustrates one of the classic differences between the trade and environment communities. To the environmental community, transparency refers to the ability of the external, nongovernmental public to observe and influence the development of public policy. To the trade community, transparency refers to the degree to which regulations affecting trade are discernible to importers.

The role of public participation within EPA mirrors U.S. environmental decision making, which historically has been conducted in an open and democratic process. Government response to environmental concerns has been quickened by such events as the publication of Rachel Carson's *Silent Spring* or the public outcry over Love Canal and Three Mile Island. In the United States, public participation is an essential feature of the system by which environmental statutes become law, and then are implemented and enforced.

The most significant U.S. environmental law containing public participation provisions is the National Environmental Policy Act of 1969 (NEPA). NEPA, one of the oldest federal environmental statutes, requires federal agencies to prepare Environmental Impact Statements for proposed major federal actions that may significantly affect the quality of the human environment. The NEPA regulations set forth an extensive process guaranteeing opportunities for public participation and dialogue during the planning stage of these actions. Another prime example of the commitment to the principle of public participation was the adoption of the Emergency Planning and Community Right to Know Act in 1986. In essence, this act embodies the concept that communities must be able to ascertain the amounts and kinds of hazardous chemicals used in their midst. It also established the Toxics Release Inventory (TRI) to provide accurate information to the public about potentially hazardous chemicals. The act is credited with reducing pollutant emissions and is viewed as one of the more effective environmental policy tools.

While Congress mandated the EPA's public participation mechanisms, many have now seeped into the souls of agency bureaucrats who have experienced the anger of a public, uninvolved in the rule-making process, destroying months or years of work. These bureaucrats have become advocates for the right of the public to participate in the development of policy because of the faster acceptance of the rules resulting from that process.

Legislative, administrative, and judicial processes provide opportunities for input in the making and implementation of environmental laws. These avenues include providing information to legislators and a requirement under the Administrative Procedures Act (APA) that applies generally to all agencies, including environmental agencies. The APA requires that agencies allow for public notice and comment during the rulemaking process.

Other U.S. laws and mechanisms include the Freedom of Information Act, which gives the public the right to obtain, by request information that is in the possession of government agencies, with certain statutory exceptions, including those for trade secrets and certain records or files compiled for law enforcement purposes. Another example is the Sunshine Act, which mandates that agency meetings be open to public observation, again with certain exceptions.

EPA's experience with citizen participation through NEPA and TRI, among others, has led EPA to focus on a more open, flexible approach to creating environmental policies. EPA is required to work more closely with business, industry, consumer, and environmental organizations to develop mutually acceptable programs. Environmentalists maintain that this approach has demonstrated that an open, transparent process in which government works with all relevant sectors can lead to a better-informed public, a less adversarial relationship between the business and environmental communities, and better policy as a result.

In 1991 then EPA Administrator William Reilly requested that the National Advisory Council for Environmental Policy and Technology (NACEPT) establish a federal advisory committee to address the relationship between trade and environment to assist the agency in clarifying its position on the issue.

NACEPT's Trade and Environment Committee, comprised of experts from the trade, environment, public policy, international affairs, and business communities, provided a unique forum within the government to create a dialogue on trade and environment. At the time, no other forum existed within the government that allowed such an open, transparent debate involving these issues.

PUBLIC PARTICIPATION AND
THE ROLE OF FEDERAL ADVISORY COMMITTEES

Public participation is also vital to the Federal Advisory Committee Act (FACA). FACA provides a significant mechanism for reaching more substantive and far-reaching policy and scientific advice. Enacted in

1972, FACA formally recognizes the merits of seeking the advice and assistance of the public on a broad range of issues affecting federal policies and programs.

There are over one thousand federal advisory committees in existence addressing an extremely diverse range of issues relevant to the government. Theoretically, President Clinton's economic summit held in Little Rock in December 1992 served the purpose of a federal advisory committee. Any such advisory function or forum is required to be managed under FACA and balanced in representation in order to ensure that equitable advice is given.

The first recorded use of an outside advisory committee in the United States was by President George Washington, who appointed a commission to investigate the causes of the Whiskey Rebellion, a revolt against a 1791 excise tax on spirits. The commission is purported to have been asked not only to advise, but to mediate a solution. Bruce L.R. Smith, in his 1992 book *The Advisors,* notes that:

> The President applauded the commission's firmness: and averred that its report proved "that the means of conciliation have been exhausted." He proceeded to suppress the rebellion by force . . . suggesting that in creating the commission he may have had motives beyond the search for neutral advice from distinguished citizens. Yet the symbolism of appointing a commission before he acted is instructive. In a grave challenge to the authority of the national government, the president felt it necessary to legitimize his actions by first investigating the problem, searching for practical advice from disinterested citizens, and acting on the basis of the facts presented to him.[2]

The Whiskey Rebellion was not the last time the government sought advice from its citizens to legitimize a preconceived conclusion. Within the government, advice is utilized in an extremely ad hoc manner; its usefulness depends entirely on the agency soliciting the advice. It is patently easy to appear to be seeking advice while only paying lip service to the concept. Among the range of options are the following:

- Identify groups with competitive positions, put them in competing advisory groups, thus allowing the agency to decide what advice to accept or reject;
- Fail to brief or educate the advisory committee members adequately, either because of a lack of effective, timely staff work or because

of "security" requirements that preclude the members from seeing relevant information;

- Craft a mission statement for the advisory committee that is narrow and self-serving and really only promotes a parochial interest for which bureaucrats already have designed a solution (known as the "rubber stamp" advisory approach);
- Identify an advisory function for the members that plays to their individual or industry's economic self-interest; and
- Do not ask for policy advice on areas where the agency has already reached a decision.

THE ROLE OF PUBLIC PARTICIPATION

Both trade and environmental groups claim to advocate the inclusion of public participation in their policy making. Interestingly, the U.S. trade community views itself as having an extremely open public advisory process, wherein nongovernmental individuals advise USTR and the Department of Commerce on trade policy. In 1974 Congress established the Private Sector Advisory Committee System. Chaired by USTR, it has almost forty committees with a total membership of approximately one thousand advisors and is arranged in three tiers: the President's Advisory Committee on Trade Policy and Negotiations; seven policy advisory committees; and more than thirty technical, sectoral, and functional advisory committees. All of these advisory bodies are composed of people from industry, and are appointed and staffed by USTR and cabinet agencies. These individuals, however, represent the interests of their companies, not a wider public constituency.

There is one significant difference between the advisory process used by EPA and that of USTR. Because world trade is competitive in nature, the trade process, as frequently argued by trade specialists, requires confidentiality if not secrecy. It is commonly felt that much of what is negotiated is proprietary information. Business and industry are put at a disadvantage if competitors—especially foreign competitors—know the details of the technical issues under discussion. Moreover, trade negotiators maintain that any requirements allowing public participation could undermine their effectiveness as negotiators because their trade adversaries would take advantage of information presented at such fora. Environmentalists, used to a more open process, often refer to the "black box" of trade policy making.

Thus while EPA's advisors represent a broad spectrum of public involvement, USTR's advisors are selected from the business and industry sectors most affected by or involved in international trade. Therefore, only narrow, limited "public" input is solicited.

Improved transparency in domestic and international trade decision making is significant to EPA. It shares the belief that environmentally neutral trade decisions are rare; trade must internalize environmental protection as a part of the trade equation to ensure the health of the environment, as well as the long-term health of the global economy. One goal of increased public participation is to develop a more democratic balance in the trade and environment equation.

When trade and environment intersect, the environmental community often finds itself unable to participate in the decision making, unable to have its views heard. As the trade and environment debate intensified around GATT and NAFTA, a clash of cultures was inevitable. The U.S. environmental community began to focus not only on the lack of public participation in domestic trade policy making, but also on the lack of public participation in GATT and its dispute resolution mechanisms, on the OECD, and on other international institutions responsible for developing and interpreting trade policies and rules.

International institutions such as GATT and OECD have not traditionally evaluated or addressed the environmental impacts of trade policy. However, Washington (at the urging of EPA) has recently taken initiatives to increase transparency and public participation in the trade decision-making process of these institutions. EPA, for example, was responsible for urging the participation of representatives from both the environment and business communities as observers at recent OECD meetings on trade and environment.

Finally, and most significantly, the fundamental dilemma for the environmental community, as compared with the trade community, is that it does not represent a product or service, but rather a wide range of resource, product, and process change objectives. This does not create an easy constituency. In 1992, for example, under pressure from the public and environmental organizations, USTR appointed five representatives from environmental NGOs to its top level NAFTA advisory committees. Questions were raised about the effectiveness of only five individuals representing the diverse environmental NGO community. Such small representation could never cover the wide range of environmental concerns.

TRADE TRUMPS ENVIRONMENT

Within the U.S. government, many view environmental protection as a domestic issue. This point of view leads to a number of problems in ensuring that trade policy adequately internalizes U.S. policy objectives with respect to environment.

The agencies or departments responsible for foreign policy have clear priorities that supersede environmental objectives, according to environmentalists. If environmental agencies are not "at the table" in international, multinational or bilateral trade negotiations, or economic summits, the priority of foreign policy agencies—diplomatic relations, balance of trade, or the promotion of U.S. goods and services—will always compete with and win over environmental objectives.

To avoid this problem, environmental policy objectives must be effectively internalized within the U.S. policy-making process. This requires that environmental protection—which includes natural resource protection and pollution issues—is effectively represented at the highest levels of the federal government. A recent *New York Times* editorial suggested that a separate cabinet level agency be created to oversee resource issues. Under the Clinton administration, EPA may attain cabinet status, leaving its scope and oversight much as it is now. However, for EPA truly to be a player in the trade and environment arena, it needs to be a member of the Trade Policy Review Group and the Trade Policy Staff Committee. The Trade Policy Review Group and the Trade Policy Staff Committee are the principal trade policy-making bodies in Washington.

In Congress, the committee structure must be revamped to ensure that economic, foreign policy, and other committees considered central to the government have environmental protection and natural resource issues in their mandate. The current government structure almost guarantees that oversight responsibility is narrow and perpetuates agencies that continue to compete over turf, not policy.

This issue recalls the question of when in the policy-making process is public advice solicited and where is it internalized. As long as the environment is "trumped" by trade, commerce, foreign policy, and economics, there is limited opportunity to implement the advice given to environmental agencies by the public. As one senior official said, "We have both industry and the environmental community begging Washington to reach a compromise policy position on trade and environment. They are willing to negotiate, it just doesn't seem as though the government, itself, is willing to."

GUERRILLA WARFARE

It began with the posters papering Washington, D.C., and escalated through the first year of NAFTA negotiations. The environmental community provided rational thought pieces and irrational, emotional speeches to shore up their side of the debate. Environmental organizations and public interest groups, used to a more open process in policy development, quickly became frustrated in their attempt to influence the trade community. Frustrations led to accusations aimed at USTR, the State Department, EPA, and even at other environmental organizations who were thought to be caving in.

The trade community threw out a broad net in seeking advice. USTR proved itself, intentionally or unintentionally, capable of a divide-and-conquer strategy. It is clear that the environmental community views the cultural differences between trade and environment as difficult to bridge. As an environmental NGO staffer recently stated, "For the foreseeable future we are going to have to be in their (USTR's) face, making sure our issues are on the table and dealt with."

Perhaps environmentalists have taken the idea of guerrilla warfare too seriously. One conclusion we have reached during the last two years, with respect to the attempt to address this issue constructively, is that both environmental and natural resource agencies in the government and environmental NGOs compete with each other to the ultimate detriment of their policy objective.

It is easy to accuse the trade community and USTR of selecting out those issues that serve their own purposes. Environmental organizations cannot even agree among themselves about what they want to accomplish vis-a-vis trade and environment, and often provide competing advice to Washington. As long as the primary fabric of trade policy is economics, and environmental policy remains an ornamental thread, agencies will be unlikely to reach an effective compromise.

THE NEED FOR PUBLIC PARTICIPATION
IN POLICY FORMULATION

The environmental community's experience biases it in favor of public participation and transparency in the policy development process. However, public participation is more than a cultural or traditional experience. Transparency in the trade policy development process is necessary because of the number and diversity of constituencies represented by environmental objectives. The environment cannot be the ornamental thread in the economic fabric; it must be an essential part of the fabric itself. Only through public participation can this weave be crafted.

At the same time, U.S. policy makers will need to decide if the cultural or traditional experience of trade policy truly requires that it be developed and negotiated in secrecy. Does openness destroy the competitiveness of business and industry? We believe that to be much less true than currently expressed by trade policy experts. There is a great deal of room for broad participation by the environmentally concerned sectors in trade policy development and, at times, even in the negotiation phase. Competitiveness may be threatened more fundamentally if environmental objectives are left out of the equation than if they are included.

Environmental NGOs and federal agencies will need to analyze what they gain or lose by protecting traditional areas of turf and constituencies. Coming to grips with the intersection between two extremely complex policy areas will require unprecedented cooperation and strategy.

It is also essential that economic policy decisions internalize environmental protection objectives effectively. This again requires that the environmental concerns are "at the table" both in the policy development phase with the general public, and at the top levels of government decision making. In the trade and environment debate, it is essential that environment be represented on the Trade Policy Review Group and in the Trade Policy Staff Committee, ideally by a cabinet-level EPA.

Finally, it is imperative that the U.S. environmental regulatory framework and policy tools be, at the very least, compatible with global or regional approaches, if not ideally the backbone of those approaches. This will permit U.S. environmental objectives to be met more easily here and abroad, as well as position U.S. goods and services in an advantageous, competitive position. Weaving this new sustainably competitive fabric requires the involvement of the public and private sectors, business, industry, and environment. Without transparency, this complex change will not occur and both trade and environment will lose.

NOTES

1. This article was written by Jan McAlpine and Pat LeDonne in their private capacities. No official support or endorsement by the U.S. Environmental Protection Agency is intended or should be inferred.

2. Bruce L.R. Smith, *The Advisors*, World Resources Institute (Washington: 1992).

PART IV

Reconciling
Trade and the Environment

16

World Trade Rules and Environmental Policies: Congruence or Conflict?

John H. Jackson

INTRODUCTION

P roposition 1: Protection of the environment has become exceedingly important and promises to be more important for future generations. An important part of protecting the environment involves rules of international cooperation and/or sanction so that some government actions to enhance environmental protection will not be undermined by actions of other governments. Sometimes such rules involve trade-restricting measures.

Proposition 2: Trade liberalization is important for enhancing world economic welfare and providing greater opportunity for satisfying lives for billions of individuals. Any measures that restrict trade often will decrease the achievement of this goal.

These two propositions state the opposing policy objectives that currently pose important and difficult dilemmas for governments. This type of "policy discord" is not unique. There are many similar policy discords, on both the national and the international scene, that governments must confront. Indeed, with respect to environmental policy and its relation to trade policy, there is at least some evidence that they are complementary, in the sense that increasing world welfare can lead to citizen demands and governmental actions to improve protection for the environment. The poorest in the world cannot afford such protection; but when welfare increases, this protection can be more affordable.[1]

An unfortunate development in public and interest group attention to trade and environment is the hostility between proponents of the different propositions stated above. The hostility is misplaced because both groups, for their respective policy objectives, will need the assistance and cooperation of the other group. Of course, some of this tension is typical of political systems. Often political participants seek to achieve opposing objectives and goals. Each side may endorse legitimate goals, but when the goals clash, accommodation becomes necessary.

To some extent, the conflicts derive from a certain "difference in cultures" between the trade policy experts and the environmental policy experts. Oddly enough, even when operating within the framework of the same society, these different "policy cultures" have developed different attitudes and perceptions of the political and policy processes—which creates misunderstandings and conflicts.[2]

These problems are part of a broader trend of international economic relations that is posing a number of perplexing and troublesome situations for statesmen and policy leaders. Part of this situation is inevitable in the light of growing international economic interdependence. Such interdependence brings many benefits from increased trade in both products and services across national borders, resulting in efficiencies and economies of scale that can raise world welfare (but not necessarily *everyone's* welfare, because some groups will be required to adjust in the face of such increased competition.)[3] These trends require a different sort of attitude toward government regulation. Within a nation, government regulation such as consumer protection, antitrust/competition policy, control of banking and financial institutions, measures protecting health and welfare (for example, alcohol and abortion control), and human rights (for example, prohibiting discrimination) are all designed by governments to promote worthy policies that sometimes clash with market-oriented economic policies. When economic interdependence moves a number of these issues to the international scene, they become much more difficult to manage in today's defective international system.

The broader context of the international system can create a series of problems and questions, including:

- General questions of effectiveness of national "sovereignty" in the face of a need to cooperate with other countries;
- Perplexing questions of how new international rules should be made— questions that often involve voting procedures;

- General questions of the appropriateness and degree to which national sovereignty will submit to international dispute settlement procedures to resolve differences;
- Problems of a single national sovereign using extraterritorial reach of its regulation (sometimes termed *unilateralism*); and
- Significant legitimate differences of view between nations as to economic structure, level of economic development, different forms of government, and different views of the appropriate role of government in economic activities.

All these circumstances and arguments occur in the context of a relatively chaotic and unstructured international system. Developing countries, for example, will have different views from those of rich countries on many "trade-off" matters, arguing that environmental regulations can unfairly restrain their economic development. They note that rich countries have benefitted from decades or centuries of freedom from environmental protection rules and even today are responsible for most of the world's pollution. To impose such rules on poor countries threatens starvation and stagnation for their populations.

This chapter is intended to probe the more specific issues of the relationship of international trade policy rules to environmental policies and rules, primarily in the context of the General Agreement on Tariffs and Trade (GATT), the most important set of international trade policy rules.

When speaking of "environmental" policies, this chapter will use that term very broadly, including, for example, measures relating to health or health risks. The phrases *trade policies* and *trade liberalization* also are used broadly to relate not only to trade in goods, but also to trade in services.

OBJECTIVES OF TRADE RULES AND
RELATION TO ENVIRONMENTAL POLICY

The most significant and widespread rule system for international trade is the GATT system (which includes GATT and over two hundred ancillary treaties plus a number of other related arrangements, decisions, etc.). GATT may soon be modified by the Uruguay Round, so this chapter will refer to the GATT/Multilateral Trade Organization (MTO) system to broadly embrace the system as it is now and may emerge within a year or two. Of course, a number of other treaties or arrangements, including regional blocs like the proposed North American Free Trade Agreement (NAFTA), are relevant to this discussion of "trade-environment policy discord," but most of the essential principles of this discord can be discussed in the context of GATT.

The basic policy underlying GATT and the broader Bretton Woods System established from 1944 to 1948 is well known. The policy objective is to liberalize trade that crosses national boundaries, and to pursue the benefits described in the economic theory known as "comparative advantage," which relates partly to the theories of the economies of scale. Comparative advantage provides that when nations specialize, they become more efficient in producing a product (and possibly also a service), and thus if they can trade for their other needs, they and the world will benefit. The international rules are designed to restrain governmental interference with that beneficial trade.

These policies recognize certain exceptions, including the problem of "externalities," which is an important part of the problem of environmental protection. For example, if a producer pollutes a stream in the manufacturing process and there are no laws against that, the producer has imposed an "externality cost" on the world, which is not recouped from the producer or the consumers of the product. This appears to be one of the most important core dilemmas or policy problems of the relationship of trade and environmental policies. Thus, much of this relationship is concerned with how environmental protection costs can be "internalized," to follow what is sometimes termed the Polluter Pays Principle.

To illustrate, a few "hypothetical" cases will demonstrate some of the possible policy clashes. In the cases below I use the initials "ENV" to indicate the environmentally "correct" country that imports (or exports) and the initials "EXP" to indicate the exporting country.

- ENV establishes a rule that requires a special deposit or tax on packaging that is not biodegradable, arguing that such packages are a danger for the environment. It so happens that ENV producers use a different package that is not so taxed. Only the packages from EXP are effected. (In some cases it can be established that the tax imposed is in excess of that needed for the environmental protection.)
- ENV establishes a border tax (countervailable duty) on any product of electronics that is imported from a country that does not have an environmental rule required by ENV, arguing that the lack of such

rule is in effect a "subsidy" when measured by economic principles of internalization and "polluter pays" and that the subsidy should be offset by a countervailable duty. EXP argues that its own method of pollution control is different but fully adequate, more efficient, and therefore cheaper, so its products should not incur the clean-up duty. Alternatively, EXP argues that its environment can better withstand pollution activity.

- ENV prohibits the importation of tropical hardwoods on the grounds that imports of tropical hardwood products tend to induce deforestation in important tropical forest areas, and such deforestation damages the world environment. ENV is a temperate zone nation with temperate forests, but does not apply any rule against temperate forest products, domestic or imported.

NATIONAL TREATMENT AND PRODUCT STANDARDS

One of the core principles of the GATT/MTO system of trade liberalization is the rule known as "national treatment," found in GATT Article III. The national treatment clause can be traced far back into treaties of centuries ago, and is applied to a number of different governmental activities.[4] It obligates governments to treat foreign products or persons the same as they treat domestic products or persons, for purposes of a variety of governmental actions.

One example of the operation of national treatment would be a regulation that imposed a higher tax on automobiles with greater horsepower and speed. If the importing country knew that its own automobile production tended to concentrate heavily in automobiles with lesser horsepower and speed, it may be violating the national treatment rule. Thus there are some delicate decisions that have to be made in interpreting GATT Article III. These issues arise in a number of "environmental" type cases. The key issue then is who should decide whether the regulation is appropriate.

Even if a regulation is nondiscriminatory both in language and in practice, some important issues about a "minimum standard" arise. A current significant case between the United States and the EC raises this issue, namely the *Beef Hormone* case. In this case the EC prohibits the sale of beef that has been grown with the assistance of artificial hormone infusions. The United States argues that it applies hormones by a method that is totally safe for human ingestion and that the EC has no scientific basis for its regulation, which incidentally happened to hurt U.S. exports of beef products to the EC. The EC replied that it had no obligation to provide a scientific justification.

This dispute has festered on. The United States pointed to a clause in the Tokyo Round Standards Code, which might have given some opportunity to require scientific justification for a product regulation. However, negotiators in the Uruguay Round have developed a draft phytosanitary text designed to provide some minimum standards for government regulation requiring "scientific principles" as justification. This draft text has raised some serious concerns on the part of environmental policy experts in the United States and elsewhere who worry that this text would inhibit national governments or sub-federal governmental units from enacting and implementing regulations that go beyond some minimum international standard. The draft language itself does not seem to call for this, but the implication that there will be an opportunity by exporting countries to challenge regulations of importing countries and to require the importing country to justify the regulation on the basis of "sound science" raises substantial fears that GATT panels will tend to rule against regulations that go beyond a lowest common denominator of national environmental regulations in the GATT/MTO system. This pushes the discourse into the question of institutions.

GENERAL EXCEPTIONS IN ARTICLE XX: HEALTH AND CONSERVATION

GATT contains Article XX entitled "General Exceptions," which includes important provisions that override other obligations of GATT, in certain circumstances defined in the Article. Although it is not practical or appropriate in this chapter to deal with all of Article XX, there are certain key measures that we can address. Quite often, concern for environmental matters focuses on paragraphs (b) and (g) of Article XX, which relate to measures:

(b) necessary to protect human, animal or plant life or health . . .; and

(g) relating to the conservation of exhaustible natural resources if such measures are made effective in conjunction with restrictions on domestic production or consumption . . .

The exceptions of Article XX are subject to some important qualifications in the opening paragraph of Article XX. To a large degree, these provisions provide a softened measure of "national treatment" and most favored nation obligations. They require governments that take measures that arguably qualify for the exceptions of Article XX to do so in such a way as to minimize the impacts mentioned in the opening paragraph. This has led some panel reports to interpret Article XX so as to require a nation to use the "least restrictive alternative" reasonably available to it in taking measures designed to support the goals of the exceptions of Article XX.

There are a number of important interpretive problems with respect to Article XX, some of which are key to the environment-trade liberalization clash. Two interpretive questions in particular stand out, namely the interpretation of the word *necessary* and the question of *whose health,* or *which exhaustible natural resources* can be the object of an acceptable national government regulation.

With respect to *necessary*, clearly this word is one that needs interpretive attention. It is partly interpreted by the "least restrictive alternative" jurisprudence mentioned above. Thus, if there are two or more alternatives that a government could use to protect human life or health, it is not *necessary* to choose the one that has more restrictions on trade when an alternative exists that is equally efficient to protect human life or health. This will obviously impose some restraint on the latitude that nations or sub-federal governments have to impose regulations for environmental purposes. On the other hand, this restraint is considered important to prevent Article XX from becoming a large loophole that governments could use to justify almost any measures motivated by protectionist considerations. This slippery slope problem worries many in connection with Article XX. The problem arises in a number of cases, including those of packaging or fish, as outlined in the introduction.

The other interpretive problem is conceptually more difficult. When GATT Article XX provides an exception for measures necessary to protect human, animal, or plant life or health, should it be interpreted to mean life or health only within the importing country, or anywhere in the world? Article XX has not been interpreted to allow a government to impose regulations necessary to protect life or health of humans, animals, or plants existing outside its own territorial borders. This issue arose in the tuna-dolphin case. The problem is the typical slippery slope danger, combined with the worry that powerful (and wealthy) countries will impose their own views regarding environmental, social, or welfare standards on other parts of the world where such views may not be entirely appropriate. The term *eco-imperialism* has been coined for this problem.

If an importing nation can prohibit goods from a poor third world country in which the production occurs in a manner that is moderately dangerous to humans, could a nation prohibit the importation of goods produced in an environment that differs in many social or cultural attributes from its own society? Why should one country be able to use its trade laws to depart from the general liberal trade rules of the GATT/MTO system to enforce its own view of how plant or animal life in the oceans beyond its jurisdictional limits of the territorial sea are treated, or how tropical hardwoods are harvested?

Other countries may have a somewhat different view of the tradeoff between economic and welfare values of production, and human life or health. Even in the industrial countries, there is tolerance of certain kinds of economic activity that almost inevitably will result in human deaths or injury, such as major construction projects for dams or bridges. These are difficult issues and ones that will require a lot of close and careful attention, presumably in the context not only of new rule making (or treaty drafting), but also in the processes of interpretation through the dispute settlement mechanisms. Thus, once again, institutional questions become significant.

PROCESS-PRODUCT PROBLEM: THE TUNA-DOLPHIN CASE AND GLOBAL COMMONS QUESTIONS

An important conceptual "difficulty" of GATT is the so-called product characteristic problem, which relates closely to the Article XX exceptions and also to the national treatment obligations and other provisions of GATT. This issue is central to the tuna-dolphin case and needs to be explained.

Suppose an importing country wishes to prohibit the sale of domestic or imported automobiles that emit a higher than specified standard of pollutants in their exhaust. Subject to our discussion above, there seems to be little difficulty with this regulation. It relates to the characteristics of the product itself. If the product itself is polluting, then on a nondiscriminatory basis the government may prohibit its sale or also prohibit its importation, as a measure to prohibit its sale.

Suppose on the other hand, the government feels that an automobile plant in a foreign country is operated in such a way as to pose substantial hazards to human health, either through dangers of accidents from the machinery, pollutants, or unduly high temperatures in the factory. On an apparently nondiscriminatory basis, the government may wish to impose a prohibition on the sale of domestic or imported automobiles that are produced in factories with certain characteristics. However, note in this case that the imported automobiles themselves are perfectly appropriate and do not have dangerous or polluting characteristics. Thus, the target of the importing country's regulation is the "process" of producing the product. The key question under the GATT/MTO system is whether the importing country is justified in taking a process-related measure either under national treatment rules of nondiscrimination, or exceptions of Article XX, which do not require strict national treatment nondiscrimination. The worry of trade policy experts is that to allow the process characteristic to be the basis for trade restrictive measures would be to open a pandora's box that could cut a swath through GATT.

The tuna-dolphin case relates to these issues. Although the GATT panel report is not entirely clear on this matter, it seems fair to say that there were two important objections to the U.S. embargo on the importation of tuna because of its objection to the way the tuna were fished, which caused danger to dolphins. First, the question of eco-imperialism arises, where one nation unilaterally imposes its fishing standards (albeit for environmental purposes) on other nations in the world without their consent or participation in the development of the standard. Second, the problem of the inconsistency of the import embargo with GATT rules emerges. Unless there is some GATT exception that would permit the embargo, which relates to the "process-product" interpretation problem and therefore to the national treatment rule and the general exceptions of GATT, the inconsistency remains between Articles III and XX.

The approach in the GATT system so far has given great weight to this slippery slope concern, interpreting both the Article III (including some Article XI questions) and the Article XX exceptions to apply to the product standards and to life and health within the importing country, but not to extend these concepts and exceptions to "processes" outside the territorial limits of jurisdiction. The alternative threatens to create a great GATT loophole and is a serious worry.

The theory of comparative advantage, which drives the policy of liberal trade, suggests that an important reason for trade is differences among nations. These can be differences of natural resources, but also of cultural and population characteristics such as education, training, investment, and environment. To allow an exception to GATT to permit some governments to impose unilateral standards on production processes as a condition of importation would substantially undermine these policy objectives of trade liberalization. On the other hand, trade sanctions that include embargoes are a very attractive and potentially useful means of providing enforcement of international cooperatively developed standards, including environmental standards.

Thus, there is an important tradeoff that GATT must face. It is not adequate for GATT simply to say that trade should never be used as a sanction for environmental, or human rights, or anti-prison labor purposes. A number of situations already exist in which GATT has at least tolerated, if not explicitly accepted, trade sanction type activity for what is perceived to be valid overriding international objectives. For example, trade sanctions on South Africa have acceptable international objectives.

The implications of this problem are that specific and significant attention must be addressed by the GATT/MTO system to provide for exceptions for environmental purposes, in a way that will establish boundaries to these exceptions to prevent them from being used as excuses for a variety of protectionist devices or unilateral social welfare concerns. Possibly these should be limited to situations where governments are protecting matters that occur within their territorial jurisdiction.

It may be feasible to develop an explicit exception in the GATT/MTO system, possibly by the reasonably efficient waiver process for a certain list of specified broad-based multilateral treaties. One of the concerns expressed about the tuna-dolphin case in GATT is the implications that it might have for the Montreal Protocol on Substances that Deplete the Ozone Layer (Montreal Protocol) and the danger to the earth's ozone layer. The Montreal Protocol provides a potential future authorization of trade sanction measures against even nonsignatories for processes, not product characteristics, which violate the norms of the treaty. If the current rules of GATT are interpreted to exclude exceptions for the process situation, the Montreal Protocol measures would be contrary to GATT obligations, except as among the signatories to it.

Although it may take some time and study to develop the precise wording of an appropriate amendment or treaty exception for the GATT/MTO system for these environmental treaty cases in the short run, it could be efficient to use a GATT waiver to clarify the issue as to specifically named treaties. (Some language used in the NAFTA text suggests the possibility of a GATT waiver along the same lines.) In all likelihood, there are sufficient signatories to the Montreal Protocol who are also GATT members to adopt rather easily a GATT waiver (requiring a two-thirds vote of the GATT Contracting Parties) to authorize the trade measures contemplated in the Montreal Protocol. But at the same time, it might be wise to go a few steps further and include in such a waiver several other specified treaties, such as the Basel Convention on the Control of Transboundary Movements of Hazardous Wastes and their Disposal, and the Convention on International Trade in Endangered Species of Wild Fauna and Flora. Obviously, the waiver can also be amended in the future to add more specifically named treaties.

Even under such a waiver approach, there are still some important policy and treaty drafting questions that must be faced. For example, should the exception to GATT be worded to apply only to the mandatory trade measures required by the specified environmental treaties? Or should they also be extended to those measures that are deemed discretionary but "authorized" by the environmental treaties? Or would the GATT waiver even authorize GATT members to apply trade measures unilaterally to help enforce the substantive environmental norms contained in the environmental treaties, even when such treaties do not have trade measures/sanctions indicated in their text?

SUBSIDIES

The problem of subsidies in international trade policy is perhaps the single most perplexing issue of the current world trading system. Some of the major controversies and negotiation impasses, such as the question of agriculture, relate to this problem. GATT rules have become increasingly elaborate and contain several different dimensions. Not only are there provisions in GATT Articles VI and XVI, but there is also the Tokyo Round "code" on subsidies and countervailing duties that provides obligations to the signatories of that code. The following hypothetical cases can illustrate some of the problems that could occur:

- Suppose an exporting country establishes a subsidy for certain of its manufacturing companies to allow them grants or tax privileges to assist them in establishing environmental enhancement measures (such as machinery to clean up smoke or water emissions, or other capital goods for environmental or safety/health purposes). When those producers export their goods, the goods could be vulnerable to foreign nations imposing countervailing duties. Is this appropriate or should a special exception for environmental measures be carved out?

- Can an importing country argue that the lack of environmental rules in the exporting country is the equivalent of a "subsidy" and impose a countervailing duty?
- Similarly, suppose a nation lacks environmental rules such that its domestic producers can produce cheaper and thus compete to keep out goods that are imported from other countries that have substantial environmental rules. Thus the lack of environmental rules becomes an effective protectionist device.

Obviously these hypotheticals are not so "hypothetical." A lot of the discourse about NAFTA expresses the worry that if Mexico lacks environmental rules, this will give Mexico a competitive advantage, vis-à-vis American (or Canadian) producers. Consequentially, these problems illustrate the need for careful examination of the subsidy rules to design appropriate environmental exceptions or rules without destroying the advantages of the subsidy rules.

THE INSTITUTIONAL PROBLEMS: DISPUTE SETTLEMENT, TRANSPARENCY, AND JURISPRUDENCE

GATT is a rather strange and troubled institution. Since it was never intended to be an organization itself, it was born with several birth defects. Initially, it was intended that an International Trade Organization Charter (ITO) would come into effect that would provide the institutional framework in which GATT would be one part. However, the ITO never came into being. Because of this troubled background, GATT has always been deficient in the institutional clauses normally found in a treaty establishing an international organization.

These problems have become increasingly troublesome as world economic developments have gone beyond the rules provided by the GATT system. Some of these problems are being addressed in the current Uruguay Round GATT negotiation, which may help improve the institutional situation. Other GATT problems include acceptance of new members, particularly those with different economic structures; the problem of assisting developing countries; the difficulty of facing up to some of the more newly appreciated issues that are affecting international trade flows such as cultural and economic structural differences; questions of competition policy (antitrust); and of course environmental policies.

More broadly, GATT suffers generally from institutional deficiencies in the two essential ingredients for an effective international organization: provisions for making new rules, and for making those rules effective through dispute settlement procedures.

What are the implications of this for environmental policy? First, many of the policy clashes between environmental policy and trade policy point toward institutional questions. This is most importantly the case for the dispute settlement processes of GATT. In those processes, some of the interstitial decisions involving interpretation of current or future GATT/MTO treaties will be fought out. The panel hearing the tuna-dolphin case noted that it was the inappropriate authority to make the requested interpretation of the GATT general exceptions of Article XX. It stated that such decisions should be made by the negotiators or the appropriate GATT bodies as a matter of treaty law alteration, rather than simply an interpretation of a panel.

Nevertheless, environmentalists, apart from the question of precedent, have several legitimate complaints about GATT dispute settlement, among other procedures. First, they note appropriately that GATT lacks a certain amount of transparency. GATT tends too often to try to operate in secrecy, attempting to avoid public and news media accounts of its actions. In recent years, this has become almost a charade, because many of the key documents, most importantly the early results of a GATT dispute settlement panel report, leak out almost immediately to the press. For purposes of gaining a broader constituency among the various policy-interested communities in the world, gaining the trust of those constituencies, enhancing public understanding, as well as avoiding the "charade" of ineffective attempts to maintain secrecy, GATT could go much further in providing "transparency" of its processes.

Second, the dispute settlement process is heavily criticized. GATT lacks the kind of expertise that would help it to make better decisions. In particular, it lacks expertise in environmental issues. Again, there is considerable room for improvement in this regard, perhaps with procedures that would give dispute resolution panels certain technical assistance.

Finally, there is criticism of the GATT panel processes; while operating in secret, they do not make provision for the transmittal of arguments, information, and evidence from a variety of interested groups, including environmental nongovernmental organizations (NGOs). Once again, there should be ways that GATT can correct this problem.

Apart from the dispute settlement procedures, the overall institutional set up of a GATT and a possible MTO could likewise be improved. In particular, transparency could be enhanced, perhaps by NGOs as well as by intergovernmental organizations gaining some share of participation in the GATT processes, perhaps through an annual open meeting. Furthermore, as GATT or the MTO continue to evolve, procedures already established, such as the Trade Policy Review Mechanism, might build in provisions for explicit attention to environmental concerns. Again, some of the GATT rules need to be changed.

SOME CONCLUSIONS

In the light of this discussion, what can we say about the relationship between two policy sets and whether they are congruent or conflicting? The answer obviously is a bit of both.

In broader long-term perspective, there would seem to be a great deal of congruence. Some of that congruence derives from the economic and welfare enhancement of trade liberalization policies. Such welfare enhancement can in turn lead to enhancement of environmental policy objectives, as mentioned at the outset of this chapter.

On the other hand, world trade policies and environmental policies do provide a certain amount of conflict. This conflict is not substantially different from a number of other areas where governmental policies have to accommodate conflicting aims and goals of the policy makers and their constituents. Thus, to some degree, it is a question of where the line will be drawn or how the compromises will be made. In that sense, institutions obviously become very important because the decision-making process can tilt the decision results. If world trade rules are pushed to their limit so that free trade will be unhindered by conflicts with environmental policies or actions affecting the environment, clearly the trade rules will cause damage to environmental objectives. Likewise, if environmental policies are pushed to their limit, so that governments will find it convenient and easy to set up a variety of restrictive trade measures, world trade will suffer under the excuse of environmental policies.

Furthermore, the "cultures" of the two policy communities, one of trade, the other of environment, differ in important ways. Historically, trade policy experts have tended to operate more under the practices of international diplomacy, which often means secrecy, negotiation, compromise, and to some extent behind the scenes catering to a variety of special economic interests. In addition, at the international level, the processes are slow, faltering, and lend themselves to lowest common denominator results, or diplomatic negotiations that agree to language without real agreement on substance.

On the other hand, environmental policy groups, perhaps partly because they primarily operate on the national scene, have become used to using the processes of publicity and lobbying pressure on Congress or Parliaments, to which they have considerable access. As a result, domestic processes have a much broader sense of "participation" that international processes have yet to accommodate. Furthermore, the environmental policy groups, like many other groups working on the domestic level, have a sense of power achieved through successes in the legislative and public discussion processes. The international processes have frustrated these groups because of the various obstacles delaying achievement of their environmental goals.

This difference in culture is not inevitably permanent, and indeed the international processes need to accommodate more transparency and participation, not only in the environmental case, but also increasingly in the broader way that international economic interdependence is managed. As more and more decisions that affect firms, citizens, and other groups are made at the international level, it will be necessary for the international decisionmaking process to accommodate goals of transparency, adequate expertise, and participation in the advocacy and rule-making procedures.

The notion that the United States, for example, can, or should unilaterally impose its environmental views and standards on other parts of the world, without any constraint from international rules or international dispute settlement procedures, is not likely to be a viable approach in the longer run. In some cases, when the United States submits to international dispute settlement procedures (as it must, partly to induce other countries to reciprocate), it will sometimes lose and find itself obliged to alter its own domestic policy preferences. The United States has a mixed record of compliance with the GATT rulings, although for a large powerful nation its record is not too bad.

Apart from these longer run and institutional issues, there are matters that can be undertaken jointly by the trade and environmental policy communities, in the context of the GATT/MTO system. These short term actions should include:

- Greater transparency both in the rule making and in the dispute settlement procedures of the world trading system. This would call for more participation, opportunity for policy advocacy inputs, and openness in terms of publication of the relevant documents faster and in a way more accessible to interested parties;
- Greater access to participation in the processes;
- Clarification about the degree to which the international process will be allowed to intrude upon the scope of decision making of national and sub-national governments. For example, the "scope of review" of international GATT/MTO panels over national government regulatory decisions concerning environment needs to be better defined; and
- Finally, some near-term rule adjustments or changes in those rules through one or another of the techniques for changing GATT rules (probably focusing on the waiver procedure) to establish a reasonably clear set of exceptions for certain multilateral environmental treaty provisions that call for trade action that would otherwise be inconsistent with the GATT/MTO rules.

Longer term action:

- The subsidies area will need substantial study;
- A more permanent exception will be needed either as an amendment/ waiver embellishment of the Article XX exceptions of the GATT system, or possibly in the context of the national treatment rules. This can build upon the short term rule alterations as in the waiver, with particular reference to the process-product characteristic question, to accommodate the broadly agreed-upon international environmental policy provisions, such as those now contained in some treaties; and
- Additionally, the GATT/MTO dispute settlement procedure will continue to evolve in practice, with further adjustments in that procedure over time.

NOTES

1. Gene Grossman & Alan Krueger, "Environmental Impacts of a North American Free Trade Agreement," Discussion Paper No. 158, Woodrow Wilson School, Princeton University (Princeton, New Jersey: Nov. 1991).
2. This "culture of difference" is well described in an article by Robert W. Jerome, "Traders and Environmentalists," *Journal of Commerce,* p. 4A (Dec. 27, 1991).
3. *See,* e.g., Peter B. Kenen, *The International Economy,* particularly ch. 8 (New York: Prentice Hall, 1985).
4. John Jackson, *World Trade and the Law of GATT,* ch. 12 (New York: Bobbs-Merrill Co., 1969); Jackson & Davey, *Legal Problems of International Economic Relations,* 2d ed., ch. 8 (Minneapolis, Minnesota: West Publishing Co., 1986).

17

Complementarities between Trade and Environment Policies

Robert Repetto

INTRODUCTION

Although interest in trade and environment issues has been generated by potential conflicts between these two domains, they are complementary in many respects and could be made more so. Both trade liberalization and environmental regulation have as their goal the more efficient use of available resources. Trade liberalization seeks to achieve this goal by allowing countries to specialize more fully in producing goods and services in which they have a comparative advantage, and by allowing consumers to purchase goods and services from countries that produce them most efficiently. Environmental regulation seeks to achieve the same efficiency goal by ensuring that the full incremental costs of production and consumption, including costs imposed on other parties through environmental impacts, are reflected in the decisions that producers and consumers face. Therefore, although many free trade advocates and environmental advocates ascribe moral virtues to the causes they promote, from the economic perspective both agendas are means to the same end.

It is true that environmental controls can be used to construct hidden or open barriers to trade. Conversely, trade liberalization (or trade restriction, for that matter) can exacerbate environmental pressures and ecological damages. However, if environmental protection allows markets to function more efficiently, taking environmental costs more accurately into account, while trade liberalization allows markets greater scope, then these adverse results are by no means necessary. Bearing this in mind, strategies for international negotiations could be developed to benefit both environmentalists and those interested in promoting international trade. Policies that promote economic growth and environmental quality, both in the North and the South, provide a stable base for international cooperation.

From an economic perspective, neither trade liberalization nor environmental protection are inherently or inevitably more important. The measurable efficiency gains from trade liberalization have usually been estimated to be in the range of 1 to 2 percent of GDP. Similarly, the costs of environmental controls and the residual economic losses from environmental damages are both typically 1 to 2 percent of GDP in countries with strong environmental policies, and 3 to 5 percent in countries with weaker policies. Therefore, there is no strong economic case that trade policy should take precedence over environmental policy, or vice versa.

Thus, for example, trade agreements have been written or interpreted (by trade specialists) to mean that environmental regulations with trade impacts should be constructed in a way that accomplishes the environmental objective in the least trade-restrictive manner. If that principle is accepted, it makes equal policy sense to require that trade agreements that have environmental impacts should be constructed in the least environmentally damaging manner possible. Potential complementarities between the two should be identified and acted on.

This chapter provides specific examples of trade policy changes that would benefit the environment, and of environmental policy changes that would help secure the benefits of liberalized trade. These examples are not exhaustive, but neither are they trivial. Implementing just these changes would produce significant economic and environmental benefits.

TRADE POLICY CHANGES
THAT WOULD BENEFIT THE ENVIRONMENT

REDUCING AGRICULTURAL PROTECTIONISM
AND DOMESTIC AGRICULTURAL POLICY DISTORTIONS

Agricultural protectionism in Europe, the United States, and Japan leads to much more intensive farming in these regions than is environmentally or economically justified. By inflating prices and per acre revenues while, in some cases, limiting the acreage that can be planted, agricultural policies induce farmers to use more inputs on each acre planted than they otherwise would. Farmers are driven to adopt chemical-intensive monoculture production methods that lead to more soil erosion, chemical runoff, loss of biological diversity, and conversion of natural ecosystems to cultivation than would otherwise take place.

These domestic agricultural policies are supported by barriers to imports and subsidies to exports—trade distorting measures that impose heavy costs on domestic consumers and taxpayers, and third-country producers. Within the Organization for Economic Cooperation and Development (OECD) countries, annual costs of agricultural protectionism to consumers and taxpayers are around $150 billion per year, more than twice the amount these policies increase farmers' incomes in these countries. In addition, lower world prices depress returns to developing country and other exporting country producers, inhibit badly needed investments in agriculture in those countries, and result in needlessly extensive methods of farming that are responsible for ecologically disastrous tropical deforestation. Current policies grossly distort world agricultural trade patterns, sacrificing static gains from trade of roughly $70 billion annually in the OECD countries alone.

Protectionism in the United States against sugar imports is an egregious example. U.S. sugar prices are typically three to five times world levels, costing American consumers several billion dollars per year. Markets for low-income foreign producers, such as the Dominican Republic and the Philippines, have been severely restricted, crippling the sugar industries in those countries and sending millions of poverty-stricken workers into upper watersheds to become slash-and-burn farmers. Moreover, water and chemical uses by Florida sugarcane growers south of Lake Okeechobee have been devastating to the unique Everglades ecosystem. Cattails have replaced the native sawgrass. The diversity of algal, plant, and other ecological communities has decreased as dissolved oxygen in marsh waters have disappeared. Attempted solutions have focused on complex water and nutrient management systems, rather than the fundamental problem of highly uneconomic sugarcane production by large, heavily protected corporations. (Two companies produce over half of the Florida sugar crop.)

Liberalizing agricultural trade and decoupling farm income support payments from production decisions would result in significant gains in farm productivity and consumer welfare, reductions in fiscal burdens, expansion of international trade, and improvements in environmental quality. This exemplifies the principle of complementarity.

Reducing Trade Barriers to Exports of Labor-Intensive Manufactures from Developing Countries

The Multi-Fibre Agreement and other trade barriers impose serious quantitative restrictions on exports from developing countries of labor-intensive manufactures. Such barriers affect not only textiles and apparel, but also other relatively labor-intensive sectors such as footwear. By impeding the access of low-cost producers with comparative advantage in these manufactures to industrial country markets, these restrictions substantially lower incomes in developing countries and raise consumer prices in industrial countries. For example, in the 1980s American consumers paid about $18 billion per year in excess costs for clothing and textiles alone. These costs of protection, while reducing potential employment in developing countries, have done little to save jobs in industrialized countries, where producers have rapidly adopted more automated technologies to raise productivity.

At the same time, these trade barriers intensify environmental pressures in developing countries by forcing them to intensify exports of natural resource-based commodities. By and large, developing countries have a comparative advantage in the production and export of labor-intensive or resource-intensive commodities. In the late 1980s, about half the exports of developing countries still comprised fuels, minerals, and other primary commodities. Few are able to compete in high technology or capital-intensive industries. By impeding exports of labor-intensive products, especially when developing countries are under pressure from high debt-servicing requirements, these trade barriers virtually force developing countries to raise exports of natural resource-based commodities. For example, Indonesia, despite ecological concerns, deliberately raised production of tropical forest timber products for export during the 1980s.

Eliminating these trade barriers would have significant economic and environmental benefits. Output would expand in labor-intensive processing industries, enabling developing countries to add more value to their exported primary materials and draw off labor from rural areas into higher-productivity manufacturing employment at a faster rate. Faster employment growth would mitigate poverty and poverty-related environmental problems. Reduction of rural population growth would reduce pressures on fragile ecosystems. The growth of alternative sources of foreign exchange earnings would mitigate the overexploitation of natural resources for export.

USING TRADE AND INVESTMENT INCENTIVES TO INDUCE COOPERATION IN INTERNATIONAL ENVIRONMENTAL PROTECTION ACTIVITIES

There has been much discussion of the use of trade sanctions, either unilaterally or multilaterally, to discourage non-cooperation in international environmental protection activities. The use of trade sanctions in the Montreal Protocol on Substances that Deplete the Ozone Layer to ban imports of chlorofluorocarbons (CFCs) and products containing CFCs from signatory and (eventually) from non-signatory countries is a prime example. There is concern that, if challenged, such bans could be regarded as inconsistent with the General Agreement on Tariffs and Trade (GATT) restrictions on the use of quantitative restrictions and with other GATT obligations. Even if legal under international trade rules, these policies are problematic because they rely on one welfare-reducing measure (trade restrictions) to discourage another (non-cooperation in environmental protection). There is no guarantee that the result will be a net improvement in global welfare. Moreover, there is considerable concern that such measures will be used to improve the welfare of large and powerful countries at the expense of small and weaker ones.

The use of trade concessions to elicit international environmental cooperation is an approach much more likely to generate economic and environmental gains and an overall improvement in welfare. A possible example, although not yet approved by the U.S. Congress, might be the North American Free Trade Agreement (NAFTA). The prospect of substantial gains from trade and investment has apparently been sufficient enough to induce the Mexican government to upgrade the capabilities of its environmental protection agency and to improve enforcement of its own environmental regulations. The potential gains have also been sufficient enough to induce both governments to agree to devote badly needed additional resources to environmental protection in the border area.

If successful, this approach could be applied to a broader round of negotiations over a hemisphere-wide Free Trade Agreement, and/or incorporated into subsequent negotiating rounds in the framework of GATT. The GATT Uruguay Round has demonstrated the possibility of linking agreements on trade liberalization to negotiations over other issues, such as intellectual property rights. There is no reason why agreements on trade liberalization cannot also be linked to negotiations over environmental protection.

In a world still riddled with economically burdensome restrictions on international trade and investment, it is possible to devise "win-win" strategies that would satisfy developing country growth aspirations and industrial country concerns for the global environment. The "win-win" strategy is one of the strongest rationales for contemplating a "green round" of GATT negotiations to address global environmental concerns.

This approach is also a strong argument for incorporating environmental considerations into structural adjustment programs financed by the World Bank and the International Monetary Fund. While such programs are essential throughout the world to establish sound market-based economic systems and policies, they can lead to heightened environmental pressures in specific sectors. International financial cooperation and technical assistance can enable adjusting countries to anticipate and avert environmental damages emanating from adjustment programs.

CHANGES IN ENVIRONMENTAL POLICIES THAT WOULD BENEFIT INTERNATIONAL TRADE

EFFECTIVE REGULATION OF UNPRICED ENVIRONMENTAL EXTERNALITIES

A fundamental principle of international trade is that market processes will generate patterns of production and trade that surely conform to "comparative advantage" only if all production costs are reflected in product prices. This principle is the basis of long-standing disciplines in trade agreements against trade-relevant subsidies and dumping practices. By obscuring true production costs, such practices can distort trade patterns.

An equally long-standing principle of environmental economics is that the costs of environmental damages will not be borne by the party that causes them unless there are effective legal, regulatory, or economic policies that substitute for the lack of markets in environmental quality. Such policies might take the form of legal liability for damages, effluent charges, or regulatory emissions standards. All these policies can be structured to impose on the polluter the potential costs his activities create for other parties.

It follows that governments that institute such environmental policies will improve the conditions for international trade while protecting the environment. Creating capabilities to enforce environmental regulations in Mexico, or instituting environmental regulations in Eastern Europe, are examples of these beneficial changes. Such changes enable international as well as domestic transactions to be based on actual production costs.

This assertion, however, by no means implies that all countries should implement the same environmental standards or place the same value on environmental damages. However, the cost of environmental damage is rarely zero, and many developing and formerly socialist countries have imposed virtually no effective environmental requirements on producers. This has resulted in excessive health and ecological damages and has failed to induce producers to make even low-cost changes that would use only well-known technologies and techniques. For example, before enforcement action on the Mexican-U.S. border was initiated, few *maquiladora* enterprises were managing the hazardous wastes they generated in a safe or approved manner. This led to serious problems of land and water pollution.

UNIVERSAL ADHERENCE TO THE POLLUTER PAYS PRINCIPLE

OECD governments agreed to the Polluter Pays Principle twenty years ago to avoid trade displacements and distortions that might result if some governments subsidized industries' costs of compliance with environmental standards, while others placed the onus of compliance on polluters. This principle has been applied only spottily within OECD. Agriculture, for example, has largely been exempted from it, which is another source of distortion in agricultural trade. Non-OECD countries have not universally adopted even the principle, let alone the practice.

In combination with the adoption of reasonable environmental standards, adherence to the Polluter Pays Principle would ensure that environmental costs are internalized into enterprise costs and product prices. Trade disputes over hidden environmental subsidies and "eco-dumping" would thereby be largely eliminated. Concerns over the environmental consequences of trade liberalization would also be muted, because environmental controls and costs would be adequately reflected in market costs.

Wider adherence to the Polluter Pays Principle also provides an additional economic benefit to developing countries. If the prices of their exports, especially to the northern hemisphere, included the cost of environmental compliance, then northern consumers would be paying a larger share of the environmental costs associated with their consumption patterns. For example, if environmental control costs averaged roughly 2 percent of production costs, as they do in the United States, then the $500 billion in annual exports from a developing country would include payments of about $10 billion by importers, mostly in the northern hemisphere, to help defray the costs of environmental controls. This sum is far greater than the current annual flows of development assistance to the southern hemisphere for environmental programs. For example, the pilot phase of the Global Environmental Facility involved annual commitments of roughly $500 million per year to support environmental protection in developing countries.

ELIMINATION OF DIRECT OR INDIRECT UNDERPRICING OF NATURAL RESOURCES

Natural resources, such as water and energy, are very often underpriced in both industrialized and developing countries. Water supplied by public agencies for irrigation in the United States, for example, is subsidized on average by 85 to 90 percent. Timber production in national forests in the United States is also subsidized, in that many of the costs are financed through congressional appropriations. Other countries do the same; Canada, for example, subsidizes production of hydroelectricity and timber, and Germany subsidizes the production of coal.

Whether the subsidized resource is directly exported or used as an input in the production of exported commodities, these policies distort international trade. For example, timber subsidies expand the export supply of temperate softwoods from the United States and Canada. At the same time, such natural resource subsidies result in extensive environmental damage by encouraging the oversupply and overuse of the natural resource in question. Additional coal use increases carbon dioxide emissions and other environmental impacts. Water subsidies in the western United States have led to severe environmental damages, including salinization of soils, contamination of wetlands, and reduction of fisheries and bird populations. While in the United States, because of the division of responsibility between the Environmental Protection Agency and the Department of Interior, resource subsidies of this kind are often not considered to be "environmental policies;" they significantly affect the use and management of natural resources and, in most of the world, fall within this category. Eliminating them yields trade and environmental benefits.

HARMONIZATION OF PROCEDURAL STANDARDS GOVERNING TESTING AND RISK ASSESSMENT

While countries may understandably and legitimately adopt different levels of product quality or environmental risks, without necessarily burdening international trade unduly, there are many economic and environmental gains to be obtained if the procedures for risk assessment are harmonized internationally. The following issues can be agreed upon internationally without impinging on each country's authority to decide for itself the level of acceptable risk:

- How should risks be assessed?
- What data are relevant, and how should they be collected?
- What tests and testing procedures are acceptable?

Agreeing on these important procedural matters would reduce the regulatory costs of international investment and trade. Such an agreement also would reduce the scope of trade disputes over the legitimacy and scientific basis for product standards.

There would also be environmental gains. Uncertainty regarding the actual quality of products entering the country from abroad would be reduced. The workload on environmental agencies would be reduced. And, since the United States is among the countries with the most advanced and transparent procedural standards, harmonization would probably lead to an overall improvement in practices internationally.

CONCLUSION

In summary, fears over the impacts of environmental concerns on trade expansion have been exaggerated. The two goals are potentially complementary, and good environmental policies can help secure the gains from trade and avert trade conflicts. Further, trade liberalization can lead to better environmental quality. What is needed to promote both is a consistent vision of sustainable development and a coherent set of domestic and international policies.

18

Environmental Strategies for Agricultural Trade

Justin R. Ward

INTRODUCTION

On December 1, 1992 tens of thousands of European farmers massed in angry and sometimes violent protest in the French city of Strasbourg. The demonstrators burned effigies of the European Community (EC) farm commissioner and the American trade minister, who had earlier struck a compromise on agricultural subsidies. The U.S.-EC agreement prompting the demonstrations (and for the moment averting a trans-Atlantic trade war) resolved a somewhat narrow and arcane dispute over oilseed crops such as soybeans. More fundamentally, the events of late 1992 served as a reminder that international trade and agriculture can no longer be viewed as separate domains. Government farm programs have become as much instruments of trade as of domestic food policy, while agricultural conflicts have stymied the perennial Uruguay Round negotiations under the General Agreement on Tariffs and Trade (GATT). Regardless of the outcome of the round—whose completion hinges, among other factors, upon French acceptance of the U.S.-EC farm compromise—agricultural issues will continue to challenge the world trading system.

The Uruguay Round talks have tended to focus one-dimensionally on reduced price supports and market protection for producers and agribusiness. This approach has precluded serious attention to alternative measures specifically tailored to benefit family farmers, consumers, and environmental quality.

247

It is the contention of this chapter that greater emphasis on environmental protection could help defuse agricultural trade tensions and protect natural resources internationally. The discussion briefly assesses the
environmental consequences of current U.S. and European farm policies,
and outlines broad elements of a reform agenda.

ENVIRONMENTAL IMPACTS OF EXISTING FARM POLICIES

On both sides of the Atlantic, agriculture policy has fostered production
systems that exceed environmental limits and cause social and economic
dislocation. Marty Strange, Director of the Nebraska-based Center for
Rural Affairs, has described the U.S. federal programs' substantial contribution as "a steady erosion of diversified crop and livestock farming
and a growth of large-scale, specialized grain farming," especially in the
American Midwest.

In its landmark 1989 report, *Alternative Agriculture,* the National
Research Council documented how U.S. farm programs have rewarded
intensive production of a few commodity crops (for example, corn,
wheat, cotton, rice), while discouraging sound conservation practices and
low chemical inputs. Production of the defined "program" commodities
accounts for the largest volumes of water, pesticides, and fertilizers
applied in U.S. agriculture.

Environmental impacts from conventional agriculture result in serious
economic consequences for farmers and the general public. Studies have
estimated that several billions of dollars are lost annually in water pollution and related damages from cropland soil erosion nationwide. Remarkably, expenditures on agrichemicals account for roughly one-third
of U.S. farmers' variable costs for production of wheat, cotton, and soybeans,
and approximately one-half of variable costs for corn and grain sorghum.

Moreover, pesticides and fertilizer nutrients threaten surface water
and ground water in agricultural regions throughout the United States. A
1991 U.S. Geological Survey (USGS) study conducted throughout the
Mississippi River Basin detected atrazine, one of the most widely used
herbicides in American agriculture, in every stream sample collected.
One-fourth of the samples exceeded federal health levels for this chemical, which the U.S. Environmental Protection Agency (EPA) has classified as a possible human carcinogen. Most municipal drinking water

systems, including some supplied by Midwestern rivers and streams in the USGS analysis, lack pesticide-removal technology to treat water that reaches household taps. The USGS findings thus raise troubling prospects of human consumption of pesticides in both rural and urban areas throughout America's heartland.

Similarly, the EC's Common Agricultural Policy (CAP), which, like the U.S. programs, supports specialized production of a few commodities, has caused extensive natural resource degradation. The Council for the Protection of Rural England, a British conservation organization, says the CAP has "fueled agricultural intensification, subsidizing the removal of landscape features and wildlife habitats from the countryside and encouraging an excessive use of inputs."

Just how intensive is European agriculture? Consider the Netherlands, which, despite being one of the world's smallest and most densely populated countries, ranks among its largest agricultural exporters. A major reason for the Netherlands' prominence in farm trade is the extraordinary volume of fertilizer applied by Dutch farmers to boost crop yields. The environmental price is high, as nutrient contamination from fertilizer applications and concentrated livestock production threatens drinking water supplies in the Netherlands and other European countries.

Government intervention in agriculture has come at enormous cost to U.S. and European treasuries. Direct federal farm payments in the United States approached a total of $150 billion during the 1980s, with tens of billions of dollars in additional subsidies for credit, insurance, and irrigation water. Various tax preferences and import restrictions also subsidize the U.S. agriculture industry.

Europe likewise channels massive subsidies to agriculture. The CAP accounts for more than half the budget of the twelve nation EC. In recent years, annual CAP expenditures on agriculture have exceeded $40 billion. The policy also imposes huge implicit taxes on consumers.

Government agricultural spending has not prevented, and in some respects has actually promoted, steady attrition in the number of people engaged in farming. Over the last three decades, the portion of the French population working or living on farms dropped from nearly 25 percent to 6 percent. The United States has experienced a similar (albeit less precipitous) downward trend, with farmers currently representing less than 3 percent of the nation's population, as opposed to approximately 9 percent in 1960.

In their drive to capture export markets, the European and American farm programs impose heavy social and environmental costs in the developing world. According to the European Ecumenical Organization for Development, "surplus food dumping, whether through direct export subsidies or the systematic underpricing of producers, has been a major source of Third World food dependency, and has exacerbated the debt crisis in many developing countries by driving down prices for agricultural exports."

Echoing these themes, former World Resources Institute Vice President Jessica Tuchman Mathews has observed that current agricultural subsidies:

> . . . encourage farmers in the developed countries to overproduce at unnecessary environmental cost. Governments then dump the surpluses on the international market, forcing down prices. This in turn reduces production by farmers in developing countries whose crops are taxed, not subsidized, by their governments. To partially make up for low prices, these governments heavily subsidize irrigation, pesticides, and fertilizer, causing their overuse and consequent water pollution, health problems, and land degradation.[1]

Southern hemisphere countries raised similar points at a recent international conference on sustainable agriculture and rural development, sponsored by the United Nations Food and Agriculture Organization.

ELEMENTS OF A REFORM AGENDA

Comprehensive policy reform for sustainable agriculture will be difficult to obtain through unilateral action alone. The U.S. Congress has demonstrated scant willingness to amend subsidy programs—however inequitable or inefficient those programs may be—without parallel measures by the EC. Likewise, European reluctance to "disarm" in the face of American competition has thwarted beneficial changes to the CAP.

The world's agricultural superpowers should work cooperatively to craft farm policies for conservation and environmental protection. For example, sustainable agriculture objectives should be pursued in any "Green Round" of GATT. The following are some steps by which countries can promote open trade, world food security, and a healthy global environment.

ENCOURAGE DIVERSIFIED CROP ROTATIONS

The environment would benefit greatly from removal of farm program barriers to crop rotations. For instance, farmers who shift to a crop rotation from continuous corn production (the practice of raising corn on the same land year after year) can forgo insecticide applications. In the U.S. Corn Belt alone, some 14 million acres of cropland are now devoted to chemical-intensive, continuous corn production.

Particularly beneficial are rotations that include "resource conserving" crops such as forage legumes (e.g., clover, alfalfa), pasture grasses, or small grains. Resource-conserving rotations can improve soil productivity and crop yields, while mitigating erosion and runoff pollution. The economic and environmental gains can be significant, according to a growing number of producers who have successfully implemented resource-conserving rotations. Government program rules should be tailored to reward, not penalize, farmers who make the transition to alternative cropping systems and reduced chemical inputs.

The Integrated Farm Management Program Option (IFMPO), which Congress enacted as part of the 1990 farm bill, moves in this direction. What distinguishes this measure from conventional programs are its requirements for resource-conserving crop rotations and related practices to prevent water pollution and soil degradation. Participating farmers retain full support payments, and the right to sell alternative crops grown on portions of fields idled from surplus commodity production.

Unfortunately, the farm statute limits the IFMPO to the status of a pilot program, and the U.S. Department of Agriculture (USDA) has dragged its feet on implementation. Farmer enrollment has thus been low throughout rural America, and the program's environmental potential has not been achieved. Nevertheless, the IFMPO portends an encouraging shift away from subsidies that reward chemical-intensive production of a few surplus commodities.

REDUCE FARM PAYMENTS TO WEALTHY INVESTORS

Agricultural subsidies in the United States are heavily skewed toward upper-income recipients. More than 40 percent of direct farm payments flow to the very small fraction of producers with annual net incomes averaging close to $100,000 and net worths averaging nearly $750,000. Many of these beneficiaries are investors with little connection to actual farming operations. Clearly, the distribution of USDA program payments has deviated from the original objective to provide reasonable support to family farmers.

Compounding the inequity, recent agricultural spending cuts have fallen hardest on small- and medium-scale producers. Provisions of the farm bill and related budget legislation reduce many family farmers' incomes significantly, but have no impact on producers with very large acreages devoted to subsidized commodities.

Entrenched farm lobbies have frustrated payment limitation proposals. During the 1990 farm bill debate, Congress rejected an amendment to withhold subsidies from persons with annual net incomes above $100,000, a level three times the national average. This provision could have saved taxpayers more than half a billion dollars each year, and possibly averted the across-the-board cuts incurred mainly by family farmers. Congress also voted against tightening loopholes that have made a mockery of the $50,000 per-farmer ceiling in commodity program payments.

Europe has similarly resisted proposals to limit farm support payments. Changes to the CAP announced in early 1992 did not include graduated compensation provisions to reduce subsidies to the largest farms, which contribute disproportionately to massive surpluses.

A more targeted approach to farm payments would help alleviate government waste of taxpayer monies. More importantly, savings from rational payment limitations could be redirected to conservation and environmental programs that, as discussed in the following section, have received short shrift in agricultural budgets.

SUPPORT CONSERVATION STEWARDSHIP

There is a worldwide trend toward integrating conservation objectives into agriculture policies. The EC, for instance, has recently designed special farm programs to protect environmentally sensitive lands. Examples include financial assistance for farmers who reduce agrichemical applications, and compensation to producers who idle cropland for ecological purposes. An initiative to promote organic food production has been established in the Netherlands. These programs respond partially to sound recommendations by organizations like the World Wildlife Fund, the Royal Society for the Protection of Birds, and the Council for the Protection of Rural England, which have advocated replacing production-oriented subsidies with environmental management payments.

In the United States, the 1985 and 1990 farm bills contained landmark conservation provisions. For instance, the conservation reserve program has enrolled more than 35 million acres of severely eroding cropland in protective pasture or tree cover. The reserve has yielded major environmental gains through water pollution control and other benefits.

Related farm bill programs include: "sodbuster" and "swampbuster" measures to withhold farm subsidies from the indiscriminate cultivation of erodible fields and natural wetlands; a "conservation compliance" mandate for erosion-control planning on fragile cropland soils; incentives for conservation easements on endangered wetlands; and federal assistance for pesticide use reduction and other farm management changes to protect water quality. Taken together, these initiatives reflect growing public sentiment that the large federal investment in agriculture must be tied to good land stewardship.

The farm bill conservation programs also reduce trade-distorting surplus production. These programs are a marked departure from the policies of the early 1970s, when former Agriculture Secretary Earl Butz exhorted American producers to plant "fencerow to fencerow" to achieve maximum production for world markets.

Unfortunately, signs of weak implementation are apparent across the rural landscape. A recent study from the Soil and Water Conservation Society reported that, contrary to USDA assertions of near-total compliance, more than 40 percent of farms sampled were failing to implement required conservation compliance measures. The Society's assessment found inadequate erosion control treatment on many newly plowed grassland fields subject to sodbuster requirements, contrary to the nondegradation standard for such lands. Similarly, lax USDA enforcement of swampbuster requirements continues to allow wetland drainage for subsidized agricultural production.

While production-oriented subsidies have flowed unchecked to wealthy investors, low funding levels have compromised the farm bill conservation measures. In particular, Congress has devoted only token appropriations to incentive payments for wetland conservation easements and for water pollution prevention. Senate Agriculture Committee Chairman Patrick Leahy (D-Vermont) summed up environmentalists' frustration when he said, "We cannot talk about a green farm bill when we are unwilling to put our money where our mouths are."

Wes Jackson, director of The Land Institute in eastern Kansas, has astutely criticized farm policies that are based on "exporting topsoil." With Jackson's observations in mind, we must work toward better implementation and funding of existing conservation programs. Countries must also resist future impulses to expand trade-distorting surplus production in ways that reverse recent conservation gains.

Finally, we must develop additional strategies to reduce trade distortions and environmental damage. For example, farmers who participate in the federal commodity programs now must idle portions of their fields each year. These annual "set-aside" requirements have been ineffective in controlling crop surplus and in protecting natural resources. Another option would be to allow farmers to satisfy their supply—control obligations through reduced fertilizer applications, diversified crop rotations, or other alternatives to annual set-asides.

REDUCE EXPORT SUBSIDIES

As noted, export subsidies encourage environmentally destructive over-production and international dumping of agricultural commodities. These subsidies, which primarily benefit exporting companies, come at substantial cost to the taxpayer. For instance, the U.S. Government spends approximately $1 billion annually on the Export Enhancement Program (EEP), which pays grain traders to liquidate American crop surpluses on world markets. In mid-1992 President Bush raised EEP outlays by an additional $1 billion under special legislative authority triggered by failure to complete the Uruguay Round negotiations.

Largely due to European resistance on the issue, the parties to the round appear prepared to settle for relatively modest disciplines on export subsidies. For example, the proposal offered by the former GATT Director General Arthur Dunkel in December 1991 prescribed reduction commitments of 36 percent in export subsidy outlays, and 24 percent in quantities exported through the end of this decade. The United States-EC compromise of late 1992 is even less ambitious, and although headed in the right direction with respect to export subsidies, will provide only a partial remedy to surplus dumping. This is particularly true given that the reductions would be calculated from a historical baseline period when export subsidies were high.

The time has come for an international truce to end the predatory use of export subsidies in agriculture. Continued reliance on these trade war weapons cannot be justified for lack of good alternatives. There are far better ways for governments to intervene in support of profitable farming operations and a high quality rural environment.

TAX PESTICIDES AND FERTILIZERS

In some circumstances, excessive pesticide and fertilizer applications contribute to trade-distorting surplus production. The market does not capture these applications' externalities, or their true environmental cost. Farm policy skews the economics through direct and indirect subsidies for high chemical inputs.

Taxes on pesticides and fertilizers would help reflect the true environmental costs of high-production agriculture, and create a level playing field for producers who reduce chemical use on their farms. A 1990 study from the World Resources Institute found that a 25 percent tax on agrichemical inputs "could encourage lower levels of input use, and where economically viable alternatives exist, could cause a shift to alternative agricultural practices." A tax along these lines would reflect the internationally accepted Polluter Pays Principle, which has been applied too rarely in agricultural contexts.

Benefits could be achieved through even a modest excise tax on agrichemicals, with revenues dedicated to promotion of environmentally sound farming alternatives. For example, a 1 percent tax on pesticide sales would raise over $50 million annually in the United States, enough to fund the statutory authorization for USDA's main research program for sustainable agriculture. Since its inception in 1985, that valuable program has suffered from chronically low congressional appropriations and has accounted for less than 1 percent of federal spending on agricultural research.

Useful precedents can be found for the excise tax approach. Domestically, under its state groundwater protection law, Iowa dedicates pesticide and fertilizer tax receipts to research projects on alternative crop systems, non-chemical pest control, and other aspects of sustainable agriculture. Internationally, Denmark taxes pesticides to provide revenues for research and extension programs toward a national objective of reducing pesticide use by one-fourth. The countries of Austria, Finland, and Sweden have instituted agrichemical input taxes, although Sweden apparently allocates a portion of these revenues to environmentally dubious export subsidies.

Pesticide and fertilizer taxes would fit with the growing use of economic instruments to advance environmental goals. Such taxes would also reduce the trade-distorting effects of current agricultural programs.

CONCLUSION

More than ever before, agricultural policy choices are being framed within trade negotiations. As the Uruguay Round process has demonstrated, this presents both risks and opportunities for the global environment. There is no simple fix that will remove all international conflicts surrounding agricultural markets and trade. Environmental strategies can lead to some creative solutions, however, if countries can exercise good judgment in domestic politics and world diplomacy.

NOTES

1. Jessica Tuchman Mathews, "A Retreat on Trade?" *Washington Post,* p. A21 (January 17, 1992).

19

Environmental Policy and Trade Agreements: The New Nexus

Senator Max Baucus

T he official title of the Earth Summit held in Rio de Janeiro last June was the United Nations Conference on Environment and Development (UNCED). The name is significant; it demonstrates a new, worldwide recognition that environmental concerns are directly tied to economic growth and international relations. Trade agreements, as the primary mechanism governing international economic relations, are emerging as significant policy tools in the struggle to repair and protect the global environment.

Environmentalists and the U.S. Congress have begun to study trade agreements in this new light, and there is a growing understanding of the effects that these treaties can have on the environment, as well as their potential to promote environmentally sound development worldwide. For the past year, the environmental community has been watching carefully as two important trade negotiations draw to a close. Both the Uruguay Round of the General Agreement on Tariffs and Trade (GATT) and the North American Free Trade Agreement (NAFTA) could be completed by the Clinton administration in the upcoming year.

The Uruguay Round of GATT, which has been underway since 1986, received much attention during the closing days of the Bush administration when an unsuccessful attempt was made to conclude the talks. NAFTA, which was signed by President Bush on December 17, 1992, will still require the conclusion of ongoing supplemental negotiations before Congress will vote on the pact. The negotiations on the side agreements resulted from Congressional insistence that NAFTA address environmental and labor concerns raised by the prospect of free trade between countries at such disparate levels of development.

In his State of the Union Address and in subsequent speeches, President Clinton has expressed his support for both NAFTA and GATT; it now falls to the Clinton administration to complete these agreements. Congress will continue to raise environmental and labor issues as we work with the administration to conclude the side agreements and the enacting legislation for NAFTA. We will also push for inclusion of environmental concerns in the GATT, both in the present Uruguay Round text and in future negotiations.

TRADE AND ENVIRONMENT: A BRIEF BACKGROUND

Economists tout the benefits of trade, insisting that economic growth for all participants is produced by unhampered exchange of goods. However, environmental degradation is a significant consequence of the economic development that accompanies increased trade, and it affects trading partners and nonpartners alike on both a local and global level.

Pollution does not recognize national boundaries. Pesticides, emissions and general waste created in one country do not obediently stay within that country's borders. More and more, ecosystems that span or define national boundaries, like the Danube River in Europe or the Rio Grande in North America, are being desecrated. In many cases, those who cause the pollution are beyond the regulatory reach of those who suffer from it. On a broader scale, human activities have changed the very composition of the earth's atmosphere, with potentially disastrous consequences for all its inhabitants.

The environmental effects and costs of production, classified in economic theory as externalities, can create unintentional third-party losers. A striking aspect of transnational environmental externalities is that when each nation adheres to a certain environmental standard, all nations benefit, but that if any subset of the nations concerned does not adhere, all may lose. These environmental externalities create a potential for conflict among nations and require international agreements to resolve them.

The relationship between trade and the environment also extends to the international competitiveness of a country's industries. Inconsistencies in environmental standards between nations can create an unfair playing field for trade. Countries like the United States, with strict environmental standards, have two major concerns on this score. First, strict environmental laws may influence a company's decision to relocate its production facilities abroad. This business flight may translate into a substantial loss of jobs for those countries intent on protecting the environment. Second, environmental regulations may affect a product's competitiveness in the international marketplace, because the costs of adhering to the regulations are included in production costs.

Our challenge in negotiating trade agreements is to protect our right to maintain rigorous environmental regulations within the United States and to promote environmentally sound development worldwide, without drastically inhibiting trade, harming American business competitiveness, or appearing to impose unilaterally our values outside our own country.

THE NORTH AMERICAN FREE TRADE AGREEMENT

NAFTA was the result of an amendment to the 1979 Trade Act that called upon the administration to study a North American Free Trade Area. Such an area is as good an idea today as it was in 1979, for free trade normally promotes U.S. national interests. Securing unrestricted access for American firms to the $6 trillion North American market of 360 million consumers is in the best interest of the United States. Such a secure market could give U.S. industry a tremendous economy of scale advantage vis-a-vis competitors in Japan and Germany. At a time when the world may be withdrawing into trading blocs, the United States is well advised to work on building trade ties with its closest neighbors.

However, NAFTA raises questions not present in previous trade agreements. The existing Free Trade Agreement between Canada and the United States links nations with similar wage rates and roughly equivalent commitments to environmental protection. The European Community has slowly and carefully expanded to include nations at disparate levels of development, but even there no nations with such wide development gaps have opened their borders to free movement of goods and services.

NAFTA is ground breaking in that it is both the first post Cold War trade agreement and the first trade agreement negotiated between developed countries and a developing country. Wage rates in Mexico are extremely low. In three key sectors—steel, autos, and textiles—wages in

Mexico are only about one-tenth of levels in the United States. Though the Salinas administration has made recent improvements in environmental enforcement, Mexico continues to lag behind Canada and the United States in industrial pollution control. Many Americans and Canadians are legitimately concerned that such sharp differences could lead to job flight to Mexico.

Mexico has good environmental laws on the books and is making a renewed effort to enforce environmental standards. Recently, more than one hundred Mexican plants have been shut down due to environmental violations. But Mexico's commitment to enforcing environmental regulations remains questionable. Until a few months ago, Mexico had only about 60 officers devoted to enforcing environmental regulations. The United States, by comparison, employs almost five thousand.

There have been understandable concerns voiced from the beginning of the NAFTA negotiations that wage and environment issues be addressed in any free trade agreement with Mexico. Beginning in his campaign and continuing to the present, President Clinton has hinged his support for NAFTA on his pledge to negotiate strong side agreements on labor and environment. Congress has also made it clear that adequate treatment of these issues is necessary if NAFTA is to be approved. The president and Congress hope to change the "Bush NAFTA" into the first trade agreement appropriate for the 21st Century.

What must a forward-looking trade agreement include? Commercial provisions, of course, which for the most part are addressed appropriately in the NAFTA text. But it must also consider some nontraditional issues such as ensuring progress in preserving the environment and protecting labor rights. Here NAFTA lags, and the supplemental agreements offer opportunities.

At a minimum, there are three environmental issues that must be addressed in NAFTA or its side agreements and implementing legislation. First, U.S. environmental laws and regulations must be insulated from challenge under NAFTA. NAFTA does include some provisions aimed at addressing this concern, but Congress requires assurance that NAFTA will not become a back door for lowering U.S. environmental standards.

Second, sufficient resources must be devoted to enforcing environmental regulations in the border area. The Salinas administration has devoted more than $400 million to this task, but neither the United States nor Mexico has secured an adequate, long-term funding source for environmental requirements at the border. The price tag for this could be in the billions of dollars. Those opposing environmental provisions in NAFTA often note that the House and Senate Appropriations Committees have denied requests for funds aimed at cleaning up the border region with Mexico. However, the Committees have denied this request because the Bush administration proposed paying for the border program by effectively cutting similar cleanup programs in other parts of the United States. It is not hard to understand why many members opposed such a request. This approach robbed Peter to pay Paul.

The lack of success in the appropriation process simply demonstrates why the problems at the border must be addressed during the NAFTA debate. The amounts of money involved are staggering, and the problems require careful, creative consideration now, while our attention is focused.

Third, we must have guarantees that all three countries will enforce strong environmental laws. A recent study by the Office of Technology Assessment noted that lax enforcement of environmental laws can confer a significant subsidy on those industries that avoid regulation. Without some mechanism for bringing environmental compliance into line, NAFTA could result in significant job losses in the United States and Canada, as well as increased pollution. If Mexico does not have sufficient enforcement resources, whether technical, financial, or political, then one of the side agreements must deal with helping it acquire those resources.

The most immediate of the unaddressed issues is an assured source of funds for environmental protection. These funds are unlikely to come from the current budget in these tight budgetary times. A dedicated source of funds should therefore be established. I favor a Free Trade Trust Fund built upon tariff revenues. Opponents claim that new tariffs could block trade and have no place in NAFTA, which has as its goal a reduction of impediments to trade. However, there is no need to fund the Free Trade Trust Fund with a new tariff. Dedicating to the trust fund a portion of current tariff collection on goods moving between NAFTA nations would provide ample funds for worker adjustment in the United States and environmental enforcement in Mexico. Alternatively, a new fee, capped at less than one percent, could be applied to trade between NAFTA partners, and phased out over five to ten years. Such a small fee would have no significant negative effect on trade, but it could go a long way toward addressing the concerns many have regarding NAFTA.

Ensuring enforcement of Mexico's environmental regulations presents perhaps an even thornier problem than funding. Sidebar negotiations to

NAFTA have so far produced an agreement in principle to create a North American Commission on the Environment (NACE), a trinational body to address environmental issues. The membership, duties, and enforcement powers of the Commission are poorly defined, however, and the effectiveness of the environmental provisions of NAFTA hangs in the balance.

The NACE has been conceived as everything from a yearly meeting of environmental ministers to an enforcement organization with the power to close down polluting industries. Neither extreme is desirable. A yearly assessment of environmental conditions and progress, even when accompanied by recommendations and pledges for action, goes nowhere near far enough in addressing the real problems of industrial pollution. On the other hand, none of the three nations is likely to, or should, cede full enforcement authority to an appointive body beyond national control.

Congress will work to create a NACE that serves as a positive force for improving environmental practice throughout the continent, particularly in Mexico. Rather than serving as just a watchdog or advisory agency, NACE should be proactive. Duties should include receiving and investigating complaints against alleged violators of environmental laws, and working with polluters to obtain technology and funding to bring their operations into compliance. NACE must not become just another expensive, report-writing organization, generating informed recommendations that sit unheeded on bureaucrats' shelves.

The side agreement must also address the largest gap in NAFTA as presently constructed: the lack of any penalty for the failure to enforce environmental laws and regulations. A NACE of whatever form will be more effective if it has teeth. No trade agreement before has included restrictions that depend on the process by which a good is made. However, all the environmental aspects of NAFTA are unprecedented. If we are able to craft an acceptable environmental enforcement process, then we will have taken a great step toward our goal of making trade agreements into forces for positive environmental change.

I have proposed that a country be authorized to use trade measures in cases where NACE investigations show that one signatory has engaged in a pattern of non-enforcement of environmental laws. Because the goal of the side agreements is environmental compliance, and not the creation of a mechanism for disguised protectionism, the enforcement process must provide for both consultations and technical cooperation. We hope by these means to avoid the use of trade measures by resolving disputes through assistance in enforcement of environmental laws. Similarly, because our goal is not to infringe on the discretion of domestic enforcement officials, but to eliminate abuses, NACE enforcement procedures should provide guidelines for distinguishing between prosecutorial discretion and prosecutorial misconduct.

Naysayers argue that providing "teeth" to the NACE risks causing NAFTA to collapse under the weight of the environmental burden. Nothing could be farther from the truth. While we must endeavor to ensure that the commercial benefits of NAFTA go forward, a NACE that encourages each party to enforce its own environmental laws will not overburden NAFTA. Instead it will work in concert with NAFTA's goal of providing a level playing field upon which increasingly liberalized trade can go forward.

GENERAL AGREEMENT ON TARIFFS AND TRADE

GATT has been very successful at promoting trade, but it was not crafted to be environmentally sensitive. U.S. environmental organizations recently recognized that GATT may pose a threat to hard-won legislative battles. Their attention was focused on the issue in 1991, when a GATT dispute resolution panel ruled that tuna import restrictions mandated by the U.S. Marine Mammal Protection Act (MMPA) were an unacceptable restriction of trade. This ruling outraged environmentalists and underscored a fundamental problem with GATT. The pact threatens our ability to pass and enforce environmental protection measures. Furthermore, GATT currently is a tool for promoting economic development and thus far has not sought to promote environmentally sound development worldwide.

The Uruguay Round is nearing completion, but there is still time to make changes. We in Congress and a number of environmental organizations are urging the Clinton administration to offer the environmental provisions in NAFTA as a starting point for GATT. These provisions are scattered throughout NAFTA, in its treatment of standards, sanitary and phytosanitary measures, investments, and dispute settlements. The addition of these provisions would make a difference in the protection of U.S. laws and agreements, and could help protect U.S. businesses from the subsidies conferred by lax environmental standards in other nations.

The preamble to GATT, like that of NAFTA, should state explicitly the general goals of environmentally sensitive investment and sustainable development. Although it is merely a symbolic gesture, it is an important acknowledgment of the importance of these issues. On a more concrete level, GATT must be made compatible with international environmental agreements, such as the Montreal Protocol on Substances that Deplete the Ozone Layer and the Basel Convention on the Control of Transboundary Movements of Hazardous Wastes and their Dispolal.

Finally, we must require a commitment from the GATT parties to schedule a GATT negotiating session focused on environmental issues. This "Green Round" would draw on the experience gained from the NAFTA agreement, and would address, among other things, the questions of enforcement and international standards.

THE ROLE OF CONGRESS IN TRADE AND ENVIRONMENT

Under the U.S. Constitution, the power to enter into trade agreements is shared by both the executive and legislative branches of government. Although some members of Congress have exercised leadership on trade issues, the post-World War II Congress generally has given the executive branch wide latitude to set U.S. trade policies. This was due primarily to the 1930 Smoot-Hawley tariff fiasco, which convinced many people that congressional involvement in trade policy leads to rampant protectionism.

As the NAFTA process demonstrates, however, this perception is changing, and environmental issues have helped to catalyze that change. In the past twenty years, Congress has passed numerous environmental laws, some of which have either direct or indirect trade impacts. The MMPA, with its restrictions on imports of tuna, is an example of a direct link between environmental laws and trade. Indirect effects of trade on environmental regulations come primarily from the possibility of challenge to environmental standards as indirect barriers to trade. Numerous environmental groups and members of Congress have expressed alarm that hard-won battles leading to, for example, California's pesticide residue restrictions, could be challenged under trade agreements as not "scientifically based" or as "more trade-restrictive than necessary to fulfill a legitimate objective." Both are restricted in proposed GATT language.

With the progressive globalization of economic activity, Congress increasingly serves as a watchdog to ensure that trade decisions do not endanger America's environmental protections. Congress has worked closely with the Clinton administration during the negotiations of NAF-TA's supplemental environmental agreement to ensure that the final NAFTA package protects our regional and global environment. This congressional-executive branch interplay demonstrates how Congress can both cooperate and lead in developing forward-thinking trade policies and agreements.

Congress is likely to continue to play a hands-on role in trade policy making, working with the executive branch to ensure that our trade agenda advances our economic, social, and environmental interests. I expect continued evolution in the rules for congressional consideration of trade agreements, currently called "fast-track," with the aim of preserving the benefits of stability and speed in negotiating trade agreements, but also expanding the role of both Congress and the public in crafting these agreements. And as debate continues on congressionally mandated action to retaliate for unfair trade practices (the so-called 301 provisions, named for the section of trade law under which they occur) environmental practices and their economic effects will be a central concern.

THE FUTURE OF TRADE

Addressing the environment through trade agreements is revolutionary. Historically, trade has been an esoteric realm—the province of lawyers and economists and business people. The trade community too often cries foul when outsiders try to influence the rules governing trade and mutters about distortions of the marketplace and imposition of cultural values by one country on another. The same arguments arise whether the restriction on trade is founded on politics (as with Cuba's Communist regime), or human rights (as with China's prison labor), or even trade irregularities (as with Japan's dumping of goods). Using trade restrictions for these purposes may or may not be correct, but environmental issues are different for two philosophical reasons beyond the practical issues of subsidies and competitiveness.

First, environmental degradation is a direct result of the economic growth that trade pacts promote. In fashioning trade agreements, we must recognize this fact. It is of course important to respect matters of internal sovereignty with regard to environmental laws and regulations, but it is likewise imperative to make it possible to raise living standards without poisoning the air and water. Only when an enforceable, global standard is in place for the production of tradeable goods, will the comparative advantage of environmentally damaging production be removed.

Second, the environment has become a global problem. The flow of water and air carries pollutants beyond their areas of origin. As we learn more and more about the interactions between our atmosphere, oceans, and ecosystems, we find that the chemicals we introduce and the land use we change may irreparably alter fundamental characteristics of the earth we inhabit. In light of this knowledge, we cannot afford to continue our economic development and remain oblivious to its consequences. The rules governing trade are the only global controls on economic development, and we must find ways to use them to promote development that will not destroy the earth.

The task is not easy or uncontroversial. Perhaps it is not possible, though I believe that it is. The progress on NAFTA is a beginning. If we are successful in fashioning an agreement that proves to be good for North American economies and for North America's environment, it will serve as a model for the world. In following this path, the United States will be moving beyond the speeches and promises made at UNCED. We will offer genuine change in the institutions that affect the patterns of economic development, and we will see how deep those promises actually reach.

20

Environmental Harmonization and Trade Policy

Steve Charnovitz [1]

INTRODUCTION

T his chapter presents an overview of environmental harmonization. The first section will discuss the theory of harmonization and present the main arguments for and against it. The second section will explain how harmonization works within the world trading system. In particular, I will cover the General Agreement on Tariffs and Trade (GATT), the European Community (EC), the United States, and the North American Free Trade Agreement (NAFTA). The concluding section will consider the future of environmental harmonization.

Before proceeding, it will be useful to clarify some terminology. The word *harmonization* means a movement toward equivalent standards (and regulations) by different countries. Two types of standards will be discussed. Product standards relate to the characteristics of a good—for example, its design or performance. Process standards relate to the way in which a good is manufactured, transported, and used—for example, the pollution emitted during production. Governments can also harmonize their degree of economic control (for example, the regulation-deregulation spectrum) and their tax policies, but these issues—which can have important ecological implications—will not be directly addressed here.

The chapter reaches four main conclusions. First, although the concept of social policy harmonization goes back over a century, the idea remains controversial. Because achieving uniformity in standards is unlikely (and is often not desirable), it may be more fruitful to refocus the debate toward policy convergence as the desired goal. Second, a review of existing systems shows that there is no obvious or best way to harmonize. Harmonization is difficult even for a government that has the legal authority to undertake this task. Yet harmonization would be immeasurably more difficult for a supranational institution with limited authority and public accountability. Third, one way to achieve greater policy convergence is to set minimum standards for goods in international commerce. Such standards might be attained through negotiations of like-minded countries. Fourth, an international organization could aid the development and enforcement of such standards. The chapter proposes the creation of a new organization using a tripartite structure.

THEORY OF HARMONIZATION

Although the issue of harmonizing environmental standards had its initial wave of importance in the early 1970s, the concept of international harmonization of government regulation harks back to the mid-19th Century. There were academic socialists, liberal manufacturers, and other visionaries who, for different reasons, put forward proposals for a "uniformity" in national factory laws. As one German theorist explained: "Factory legislation, particularly the stabilization of the normal workday, must be international; its place is in commercial treaties, and its end should be the common good of all nations."[2] These ideas led to a number of intergovernmental and trade union conferences around the turn of the century which culminated in the establishment of the International Labor Organization (ILO) under the League of Nations. The ILO, now part of the United Nations system, has a unique tripartite structure of government, employer, and worker representatives from 162 member countries. The ILO writes and promulgates treaties establishing minimum international labor standards.

The need for labor and environmental process standards (or taxes) for domestic production is generally accepted. But the application of such standards to foreign production is fraught with contention. When presented with the question of whether the United States can have mutually beneficial trade with a country that mistreats its workers and degrades the environment, many traditional economists would answer affirmatively. Indeed, some go so far as to argue that such differences in domestic social policies are the fuel that drives the piston of "comparative advantage." In other words, far from undermining free trade, the existence of different regulatory regimes (which leads to different costs) is viewed as enhancing the benefits of voluntary exchange.

This classical approach can be criticized on three counts. First, this viewpoint might be correct if trading nations were closed societies (except for the trade) or, clearer yet, were located on different planets. We probably would not care about global warming on Mars or about the working conditions of droids. But if the issue is, say, commerce between the United States and Mexico, it is hard to accept eyes-closed trade if such commerce seduces investors to go south to a polluter haven (an economic spillover) or fouls the water in Texas (a physical spillover). In response, skeptics of harmonization deny that differences in regulation have any significant impact on trade flows or investment location—arguing either that the differentials are very small or that they are compensated for by adjustments in the exchange rate. But even these skeptics acknowledge that physical spillovers can potentially negate the value of unfettered trade.

Second, the fact that countries have different values, preferences, and endowments is not solely an argument against common rules. Indeed, the opposite argument can be made. Rules are needed expressly because countries follow dissimilar policies. If all countries were clones, most rules would be superfluous.

Third, although economists often argue that world environmental rules could undermine the gains from trade, other rules—for example, against injurious dumping or financial subsidies—tend to be viewed as making trade more beneficial. Leaving aside the practical necessity of accommodating environmentalists if one is to gain their political support for trade liberalization, there is a basic issue as to whether the rules of fair trade need to encompass ecological concerns. Actually, the case for responding to many environmental externalities may be stronger than the case for responding to dumping or subsidies, since these traditional concerns usually involve only small price distortions rather than irreversible damage to the ecosystem.

It is not inconsistent with the wisdom of comparative advantage to admit that there are limits below which competition is undesirable. Even GATT recognizes that countries have a right to forbid imports made using prison labor. Nearly everyone agrees that a tolerance for chlorofluorocarbons (CFCs) should not qualify as a comparative advantage. So the issue is not whether process standards are acceptable as trade rules.

That was settled many decades ago. The issue is what specific process standards are appropriate.

Distinguishing good systems of production from bad ones is often difficult. One approach is to distinguish between virtuous and vicious circles. In a virtuous circle, the more everyone does it, the better. For example, adding new technology to a production process in order to reduce costs is probably always socially beneficial (even though it may cause unemployment). In a vicious circle, the more everyone does it, the worse off we all become. For example, exposing workers to toxic chemicals in order to reduce costs is probably always socially destructive. But for borderline issues, distinguishing between beneficial and destructive practices with any degree of precision or consistency would be very difficult.

Another approach for figuring out when environmental competition is "bad" is to examine spillovers of production. There are four types. An *economic* spillover is the financial loss to a high-standard country from competition with a country having lower environmental standards. For example, jobs and investment can migrate to the country with lower standards. A *political* spillover is the negative repercussion on the regulatory regime of the high-standard country. This might be called a "Quayle Effect"—that is, international competition can serve as a pretext for lowering domestic standards. A *physical* spillover is the environmental harm that the trade causes directly (like hazardous waste spills) or indirectly, that is, by allowing one's own consumer market to propagate the environmental harm (like killing rare tortoises to make eyeglass frames). A *psychological* spillover is the moral cost associated with participating in environmentally unfriendly commerce. For instance, knowing that the tuna is not dolphin-safe could lower a consumer's utility from eating it. Although such spillovers can be identified, it is difficult to take the next step of measuring them in a neutral way.

Of course, these same difficulties occur in domestic rulemaking too. But for domestic regulations, there is a national authority empowered to delineate fair competition. The problem one faces with international rulemaking is that there is no supranational authority to do the same.

HARMONIZATION VERSUS CONVERGENCE

Given that countries do have their own internal regimes of process standards, how should these regimes be applied to international commerce? One answer is that process standards should stop at the water's edge. That stance was taken by GATT's notorious tuna-dolphin panel. Yet this is an untenable solution for several reasons.

A nation needs to be able to impose its standards on goods from foreign countries in order to maintain the integrity of its domestic rules. This principle has always been recognized with respect to product standards—for instance, health regulations. But in trying to draw a line between products and processes, the tuna-dolphin panel enmeshes GATT in inconsistency. The proposed Uruguay Round agreement acknowledges that processing and production methods may need to be considered in ascertaining a product's safety. For example, process standards regarding quick-freezing, heat treatment, and irradiation can be imposed on exporters when visual inspections at the border would be insufficient or impractical. In addition, the Uruguay Round agreement would require nations to consider whether imports were produced in a manner that safeguards intellectual property. Without process standards related to copyrights and trademarks, absolutely unfettered trade would be viewed as debasing domestic commerce and infringing upon legal rights.

It is inconsistent for GATT to maintain that process standards are acceptable for certain causes (like copyrights) and forbidden for others (like marine mammals). Countries need to be able to impose process standards in order to encourage international cooperation where nations cannot achieve their goals in isolation. For example, no country can safeguard migratory birds and many other endangered species by its own endeavor. While trade controls are not essential to collective action, they are a readily available and reliable tool to encourage cooperation and discourage free riding.

Since mandating that process standards be "for internal use only" is not a realistic option, the world trade regime must find another way to deal with dissimilar process standards that reduce efficiency and lead to trade conflict. One potential solution is harmonization. The economic case for harmonization is that it facilitates trade by reducing market fragmentation. Harmonization lowers design and information costs, and generates greater economies of scale. The political case for harmonization is that it facilitates trade liberalization by obviating complaints about the lack of a "level playing field." In addition, international agreements can give nations cover to take actions that might otherwise be impeded by domestic opposition. In a few areas, there is also a public health advantage to harmonization. For example, all countries would probably benefit from common rules on transportation and disposal of high level hazardous waste.

Just as there is a need for domestic regulation, there is a corresponding need for international regulation. But it is not clear how to "internationalize" domestic regimes. A country's domestic regulations are an outgrowth of the political system, local conditions, and social preferences within that country. How does one blend an international standard from the choices of each country? Harmonizing up to the maximum (for example, the most risk-averse) would be one possibility. Harmonizing down to the minimum (for example, the lowest common denominator) would be another. But these procrustean solutions are almost always unacceptable. Any rigid standard will generally be too high for some countries and too low for others.

Because standard setting is both art and science, countries should retain the right to establish their own standards and to compete on the basis of how wise their standards are. For example, it would not be useful to have only one approved way to harvest tuna or one approved type of fishnet. Yet it would be desirable to have an agreement among all fishing nations that dolphin safety should be a key concern in determining the legitimacy of commerce in tuna.

Given the impracticality of full harmonization, what other solutions are available? One is to shift the goal from harmonization to policy convergence. Policy convergence means a lessening of the gap, not uniformity. In determining how much convergence is desirable, an important factor is the extent of spillover involved from one country to another. For instance, when dealing with high physical spillover problems such as the spread of disease, a consistency in quarantines, testing, and disinfecting techniques may be highly advantageous.

Whatever standards are developed, however, should not serve as unintended or inflexible ceilings. As Kenneth W. Dam has noted, consumers will demand steadily higher standards and, therefore, international agreements should not frustrate such an increase.[3] It is also important not to let glacially paced international negotiations serve as an excuse for national inaction.

At the core of policy convergence is the presumption that gravitational relationships exist between the environmental policies of each country. This is the main way in which environmental harmonization differs from labor harmonization. The labor policies of one country have no direct impact on the labor policies of another because there are no physical spillovers (refugees aside) beyond borders. (On the other hand, labor harmonization may be easier to prescribe because there are more international norms on labor than on the environment.)

HARMONIZATION RULES

This section discusses the harmonization rules in several major trade agreements or common markets.

GENERAL AGREEMENT ON TARIFFS AND TRADE

Although GATT is sometimes described as a world trade constitution, it is important to understand what GATT does and does not do. It has no rules regarding the content or composition of traded goods. For example, it neither permits nor prohibits trade in babies, pollution permits, ivory, or plutonium. What GATT regulates is trade restrictions and distortions by governments. Thus, all product and process standards potentially fall under GATT rules.

GATT has three basic disciplines: most-favored-nation; national treatment; and non-protection (of domestic production). While adherence to these rules could have the result of reducing dissimilarities among national regulatory regimes, GATT does not impose any explicit harmonization. But one of GATT's duties, found in Article XXXVIII(2)(e), is to seek feasible methods "to expand trade for the purpose of economic development, through international harmonization and adjustment of national policies and regulations, through technical and commercial standards affecting production, transportation and marketing, and through export promotion."

GATT STANDARDS CODE

Because these GATT disciplines were deemed too weak, a standards code was developed as part of the Tokyo Round of trade negotiations during the 1970s. The GATT Standards Code (Standards Code), officially the "Agreement on Technical Barriers to Trade," provides tighter rules for the thirty-eight nations that currently subscribe to it. Thus, the Standards Code supplements, but does not modify, GATT.

The Standards Code has two main disciplines. First, Contracting Parties must ensure that standards are not prepared or applied with a view to or the effect of creating "unnecessary obstacles" to international trade. It should be noted that this is a substantive constraint, requiring a judgment as to whether the standard is unnecessary. The second discipline is that Contracting Parties must use international standards as a basis for national standards except where such international standards are "inappropriate" for reasons such as the protection of the environment or human health or safety. By creating a presumption in favor of multilaterally written standards, the code facilitates the "harmonizing" of national regulations. International standards are preferred over national standards not because international standards are technically better, but because they are less susceptible to protectionist manipulation.

URUGUAY ROUND

The current Uruguay Round of trade negotiations has continued the quest for harmonization. Domestic standards are proposed to be covered by two codes: the Sanitary and Phytosanitary Code (S&P), and a revised Standards Code. Unlike all of the Tokyo Round codes, including the Standards Code, the new agreements are anticipated to become obligations of all GATT members.

The new S&P agreement includes an entire section on harmonization. It requires parties to base their national standards on the international standards established by organizations such as the Codex Alimentarius Commission. But countries may adopt a level of protection higher than the international one if a series of hurdles is met. Specifically, each Contracting Party must consider cost-effectiveness, use measures which are "the least restrictive to trade," and avoid arbitrary or unjustifiable distinctions in the levels it considers appropriate in different situations. While these hurdles are not insurmountable, they could have the effect of prodding national standards toward international levels, which might be lower for some countries. The requirement for avoiding arbitrary or unjustifiable distinctions could be especially difficult for a country like the United States with inconsistent health standards administered by different agencies. For example, cheese pizza is regulated by the U.S. Food and Drug Administration, while pepperoni pizza is regulated by the U.S. Department of Agriculture.

The proposed Standards Code builds on the existing code by establishing criteria for when a standard becomes an unnecessary obstacle to trade. Specifically, standards may not be more trade-restrictive than necessary to fulfill environmental and health objectives. Although the proposed Standards Code does not mandate downward harmonization, it would (like the S&P) make it more difficult for countries to set their own standards. How much more difficult depends upon the range of alternatives to regulation (e.g., labeling) that must be tried first under a least trade restrictive test.

EUROPEAN COMMUNITY

The EC has a number of different and sometimes conflicting rules regarding environmental harmonization. In general, powers not conferred on the EC by treaty continue to reside in Member States. The Treaty of Rome has an entire chapter on the approximation of laws. Under these rules (as amended in 1987), the Council of Ministers may, by a qualified majority, adopt regulations or directives regarding the internal market (for example, automobile emissions, use of asbestos, and product labeling). In proposing harmonization measures relating to health, safety, or environmental protection, the EC Commission must take "as a base a high level of protection." While the high level language in the treaty was left ambiguous, it apparently does not mean only upward harmonization—that is, using the highest base among the member countries.

Because harmonization can be imposed by a qualified majority (as opposed to requiring unanimity), the treaty provides for opting out by member nations with health or environmental standards higher than the EC level. In such cases, the higher national standards are subject to review by the EC Commission using the disciplines provided for in Article 36 of the Treaty of Rome. Although the language in Article 36 is based on GATT's Article XX, Article 36 has been interpreted more narrowly. Specifically, national environmental measures must: (1) not be arbitrary discrimination, (2) not have negative effects disproportionate to the objectives pursued, (3) be necessary to achieve environmental objectives, and (4) use the means that least restrict the free movement of goods.

The authority of an EC member state to enact its own standards depends upon the extent to which the EC has acted on that subject. Nations are free to adopt their own standards in the absence of EC action.

But under the doctrine of mutual recognition, nations must accept the standards of another EC member unless there is some overriding environmental or health reason for insisting on adherence to their national laws. When the EC Commission issues directives that concern "essential requirements" of health, safety, environmental protection, or consumer protection, there is less flexibility for a Member State to maintain its own standards.

In addition to these rules on harmonization, the treaty also includes authority to enact regulations specifically on the environment (e.g., water quality or use of CFCs). The Council must approve such actions (under Articles 130r and 130s) by unanimous consent. The treaty calls for environmental legislation when the EC's environmental objectives can be better obtained at the European level than at the national level. By taking community-wide actions, the Council of Ministers is able to adopt strict measures that will have the same competitive impact on all EC members. The Maastricht Treaty on European Union would change the current voting requirement to provide for Council decisions on the environment (with some exceptions) by a qualified majority. It would also provide for a safeguard clause allowing Member States to take provisional measures for non-economic reasons, but subject to review by the Commission.

Under Article 130t of the current treaty, Member States have the right to introduce and maintain more stringent protective measures than EC levels, but only if such measures are compatible with the treaty (Articles 30 and 36). Because the rules for compatibility are strict, Article 130t does not establish a minimum level above which countries may freely go. Yet there is not rigid harmonization either. The right to introduce more stringent environmental measures exists, but is subject to discipline, particularly when the EC legislation at issue concerns the free circulation of goods.

UNITED STATES

Although the Commerce Clause of the U.S. Constitution confers the power to regulate commerce on the national government, this conferment does not preclude all sub-national regulatory power. Thus, states can enact their own standards, subject to the right of the U.S. Congress to establish minimum federal standards or to pre-empt state jurisdiction.

The Congress may also write a uniform national standard. But this is rarely done for environmental or health matters.

In addition to federal legislation, state laws are regulated by judicial review. Indeed, this is the most common method by which state commercial powers have been circumscribed. In some cases, state law has been subordinated to conflicting federal statutes under the Supremacy Clause. But in most cases, the binding disciplines on state law arise from constitutional interpretation of the Commerce Clause, in the form of a long line of Supreme Court decisions going back to 1827.

The general rule is that states may legislate on matters of legitimate local concern provided that the state regulation does not materially restrict the free flow of commerce or interfere with matters in which uniformity of regulation is a predominant national concern. In scrutinizing state law, the courts will determine: whether the measure is "reasonable" or "necessary" given the facts of the case; whether the measure discriminates against out-of-state products; whether the local interest can be provided for as well with a lesser impact on interstate commerce; and whether national interests are balanced against competing state interests.

The Commerce Clause disciplines are based on proportionality (although the term is not common in American jurisprudence). Indeed, the United States disciplines can be tighter than the EC rules and are considerably tighter than GATT rules. For instance, sub-national treatment— treating out-of-state products no worse than in-state products, is no defense in U.S. courts against a state standard that unduly burdens commerce.

In summary, although the states have no rights of environmental self-determination, there is little direct harmonization dictated by federal law. Certainly some state laws have been overturned and some state action has been prevented by judicial guidelines. But states continue to retain a significant degree of competence in environmental and health matters. As the Supreme Court noted in 1986, the Commerce Clause "does not elevate free trade above all other values."[4]

North American Free Trade Agreement

NAFTA was designed to be more environmentally sensitive than the proposed Uruguay Round agreement. It does this in four ways. First, although both the Uruguay Round and NAFTA call for the use of international standards, NAFTA specifies that this be done "without reducing" the level of protection of health or the environment. Thus, NAFTA precludes downward harmonization, and may even imply upward harmonization.

Second, while the Uruguay Round does not mandate downward harmonization, it does set a number of conditions for the use of nationally distinct standards such as proportionality, least trade restrictiveness, and consistency. Almost all of these conditions are left out of NAFTA. Even the term harmonization is dropped.

Third, NAFTA reverses the burden of proof in environmental disputes. In other words, it will be up to the complaining party to demonstrate the inappropriateness of an environmental standard. This is an important shift from the procedures now used in GATT, the EC, and the United States, which require member governments to show the need for their standards.

Fourth, NAFTA exhorts the three parties not to "waive or otherwise derogate" from domestic health, safety, or environmental measures in order to encourage investment. The article provides for consultation between parties if complaints are lodged, but there is no recourse to dispute settlement. Still, this provision is significant in recognizing that competition between countries to attract investment by lowering environmental standards is ultimately self-defeating.

OTHER PRINCIPLES

In addition to the harmonizing principles discussed above, a few others should be noted. One is the use of science to shape the development of standards. This principle is embodied in the Treaty of Rome, the Uruguay Round, and NAFTA. Using sound science as a guide is, obviously, better than using bad science. But it is naive to think that even full agreement on scientific evidence would result in harmonization. The main reason why environmental standards differ between countries is differences in values (e.g., attitudes toward risk). Science is unlikely to homogenize these values.

Since 1972 the Organization for Economic Cooperation and Development (OECD) has espoused the Polluter Pays Principle. (This principle was added to the Treaty of Rome in 1987 in vague terms.) While there has been a congruity in government policies toward forgoing environmental subsidies, the key factor has probably not been the persuasiveness of the OECD, but rather the fiscal binds of most governments.

Another principle is full internalization of environmental costs. This is sometimes mischaracterized as part of the Polluter Pays Principle, but the OECD addresses only who should pay, not how much should be paid. In the absence of a common policy toward internalization, the prices of environmentally sensitive goods in different countries will diverge, and may thus eventuate in trade friction. One problem with universal adoption of the internalization principle at this time is that it would seem unfair to the developing countries. They view the ensuing higher prices as a handicap that the industrial countries did not bear during their period of development.

Two main findings emerge from this review. First, environmental harmonization is always difficult, even within a polity. The strong desire of communities to have their own environmental standards should give pause to those who see worldwide harmonization as a feasible goal.

Second, one ought to be cautious about applying the disciplines used at the federal level (such as proportionality) to the international level. It is one thing for a political institution, like the United States or the EC, to balance the costs and benefits of an environmental standard. (They do not have an easy time doing it, but they do have politically accountable policymakers and legally authoritative judicial systems.) It is quite another to cede such authority to an international body, especially a single-minded one like GATT.

FUTURE OF HARMONIZATION

Harmonization is inevitable in an increasingly interdependent world; harmonization becomes less plausible as environmental consciousness and nationalism grows. Both propositions are supportable. Yet both cannot be right.

Some types of harmonization are more logical than others. One can imagine a world on the same metric system, using common electrical voltage, and driving on the same side of the road. Nevertheless, such common-sense harmonization seems unlikely (recall the ill-fated Euro-plug). Far more likely, perhaps, would be harmonization for the truly essential things, like health and the environment. Still, that would imply a worldwide uniformity of values, discount rates, and attitudes toward risk—doubtful in the foreseeable future.

At this point, it is not clear how much of a constituency there is for harmonization. In 1972, the OECD adopted the principle that: "Where valid reasons for differences do not exist, Governments should seek harmonization of environmental policies . . ."[5] In 1980, the Brandt Commission warned of the temptation for a country to set lower environmental standards in order to attract industry and create jobs; it concluded that "there is an obvious need to harmonize standards, to prevent a competitive debasement of them."[6] But in its obtuse approach to the environment, GATT has undermined support for harmonization by transforming a constructive idea into a potentially dangerous one.

Harmonization is now perceived as a two-edged sword. Environmentalists, particularly in industrial countries, are worried about downward harmonization. The elites in developing countries are worried about upward harmonization. Subnational governments want to preserve their right to diverge from national standards. Transnational corporations might benefit from common regulations, but many corporations are already acting voluntarily to carry their standards with them when building new foreign facilities. (It remains to be seen what the environmental implications of the new "relationship enterprises" will be.)

Nearly everyone claims to be against downward harmonization. Yet upward harmonization to the highest level of regulation is illogical and costly. In the absence of any theory justifying a middle-ground, optimal level of harmonization, a more practical approach would be to agree upon multilaterally set minimum standards in the short run, and to seek greater policy convergence in the long run.

PROCESS STANDARDS

It is dogma in trade policy circles that unilateral import standards should relate to products only—not processes. Defenders of this position argue that process standards are intrinsic to a country and should not be anyone else's concern. Thus, what Brazil does with biodiversity is solely its business. Whether China burns more fossil fuel is its business. But this doctrine of insularity is already obsolete from an ecological perspective, and is becoming less acceptable from the perspective of international law.

It may be true that there is a category of issues that are purely internal, where no country has a valid interest in another's process standards. Although much of the analytical writing on trade and environment has sought to use this category as a basis for deriving general principles, the important issues are the ones in which other countries believe they do have an interest. That is where the debate needs to focus.

Those who deny that process standards should be the subject of international negotiations do not have history on their side. Process standards on fishing go back to 19th Century treaties. Throughout the 20th Century, there have been plurilateral or multilateral negotiations on many environmental or health issues such as bird conservation, marine pollution, whale protection, workplace health, and disease control. The point is not that all of these negotiations resulted in international standards (yet many of them did), or that they resulted in trade controls (yet many of them did). The point is that international regulation of process standards is neither a new idea nor a radical one.

Another common argument against process standards is that they are "protectionist" and "imperialist." But process standards are not inherently protectionist. There is a clear difference between a local-content requirement and an environmental-content requirement. Furthermore, many process standards are no more imperialist than product standards are. For instance, a requirement that all tuna sold be dolphin-safe is functionally equivalent to a requirement that all soft drinks sold be in recyclable bottles. In both cases, foreign exporters have to meet certain specifications if they want to sell to the regulated market. The customer is always right.

Any unilateral standard, product or process, may seem unfair or coercive to an exporter who does not meet it. Yet convenience to exporters is not a criterion GATT utilizes to judge product standards. GATT uses criteria such as national treatment, non-discrimination, and non-protectionism.

Why should GATT not utilize these same criteria to judge process standards? Nations ought to be able to extend their domestic product and process standards to imports. This points to where the tuna-dolphin panel went wrong. If it had applied the normal GATT rules to the U.S. Marine Mammal Protection Act (MMPA), the decision would have been quite different. Instead, the panel invented new rules and new interpretations in order to erect a GATT bulwark against recent progress in environmental standards.

CARROTS, STICKS, AND STANDARDS

Conducting international negotiations is one thing. Attaining a consensus is another. How can an agreement on minimum standards be achieved among a hundred countries with different values and resources? One approach is to devise a clever mix of carrots and sticks from a diverse enough issue garden to allow a cross-fertilization of concerns. The goal is not only to obtain an agreement, but also to maintain its stability.

The carrots are the basic tool. Because countries face different economic trade-offs (for example, some countries may benefit from global warming), an assistance mechanism can be developed to enable gainers to compensate losers and rich nations to "bribe" poor ones. This assistance could be in the form of financial aid or technology transfer, as provided under the Montreal Protocol on Substances that Deplete the Ozone Layer (Montreal Protocol), or it could be trade concessions.

But carrots alone may not be sufficient. Uncooperative countries might attempt to extract more assistance or concessions than the global community is willing to provide. During the past decade, for example, American diplomats attempting to negotiate a dolphin-safe fishing agreement were frustrated by the unwillingness of countries like Mexico to undertake any responsibility for marine mammals. In such cases, sticks like trade sanctions may be needed to force free-riding countries to enter multilateral agreements.

In between carrots and sticks are environmental product and process standards applied equally to both domestic production and imports. Such standards are not carrots because they provide no additional benefit to foreign countries. Yet they are not sticks either so long as such standards are applied to all countries in an evenhanded manner. The characterization of such process standards as "sanctions" is an all too common misnomer.

By taking their own product and process standards to the bargaining table, countries will be better able to strike mutually beneficial deals. If the tuna-dolphin panel has its way in defenestrating national standard setting, all that remains are power-based combinations of carrots and sticks. But because the stick of a trade sanction is likely to be GATT-illegal, that leaves only carrots legitimately on the table. While it may be possible to achieve international agreements with carrots alone, it is hard to imagine any such agreement remaining stable as the appetite for carrots increases.

ESTABLISHING A RANGE

The first step in a negotiation would be to obtain a worldwide minimum standard that may be exceeded but not undercut. (The terminology gets a little confusing. By a minimum standard, I mean a minimum level of protection. Such a standard might operate by setting a maximum exposure level.) For example, there are no internationally recognized norms on dolphin safety while fishing for tuna. Establishing such a minimum is the first step toward delegitimizing the practices of countries like Mexico who claim that their dolphin-lethal techniques are irrelevant to the acceptability of tuna.

The second step would be a maximum standard to establish the highest level of protection. For example, the MMPA sets a dolphin-protection goal "approaching a zero mortality and serious injury rate." An international maximum might set a more reasonable level. If the United States insists upon zero, it should perhaps compensate other countries whenever the zero standard distorts tuna sales in favor of American suppliers. Ideally, this compensation would take the form of a cash transfer rather than an agreement to allow other countries to impose higher tariffs on imports from the United States.

Once the range of minimum and maximum standards is set, periodic discussions can be held on further convergence. There might be a presumption of upward convergence only, but the goal should not generally be the attainment of a single standard. Just as the world benefits from environmental cooperation (for example, the negotiated range), the world also gains from the competition made possible by a variability in standards.

Although it would not work for product standards, a two-tier approach may be possible for many process standards. For instance, the United States might establish a stringent process standard for its domestic commerce, but then accept imports produced under lower standards so long as such imports meet the international minimum. A two-tier approach is currently used in the MMPA that allows imports to have a 25 percent higher dolphin kill rate than American tuna producers have.

INTERNATIONAL ENVIRONMENT ORGANIZATION

Several analysts have suggested that GATT be broadened to address environmental harmonization.[7] GATT is certainly in need of reform. For instance, it should abandon its penchant for secrecy and assure that its dispute panels hear the environmental side of a case. Yet while a little greening would be fine, no amount of retrofitting would qualify GATT to set technical and commercial standards affecting production and transportation [Article XXXVIII(2)(e)]. Instead, a new International Environment Organization (IEO) should be established to develop ecological product and process standards for international commerce.

The IEO would be modeled after the ILO in structure and in function. It would be a tripartite organization composed of government, business, and the public (like environmentalists and consumer groups). Its function would be to develop standards, provide technical assistance to environmental agencies (such as how to conduct inspections), collect comparable environmental data, and investigate complaints. All standards would be available for adoption by each government, but need not be treaties (which ILO standards are) given the difficulty of formal ratification. The standards might instead be considered soft law. Just as international labor standards do, international environmental standards should take into account a country's level of development.

Establishing an IEO would fill the lacuna that now exists in global environmental governance. Many single-issue international negotiations have been successful (such as the Montreal Protocol), but a continuation of this ad hoc approach may be inadequate. What is needed is a permanent organization that would integrate efforts to solve different environmental problems and be prepared to deal quickly with new issues as they arise. As Lawrence E. Susskind has observed, "finding creative linkages . . . can generate economic incentives that will change the equation of acceptability for some nations. This means that several environmental treaties should always be negotiated simultaneously . . ."[8]

When new international standards are achieved, the IEO should encourage countries to convert any domestic process standards to them. For example, the United States now forbids shrimp imports from countries that do not have a turtle protection program comparable to that imposed on American producers. If an international turtle safety standard existed, then the IEO could ask the United States to adopt that standard.

What is the rationale for a tripartite organization? Why not assign this task to a government-only organization such as the new United Nations Commission on Sustainable Development? Certainly, intergovernmental institutions play an important role and should be better utilized. But more broad-based approaches may be necessary to deal with global issues of increasing complexity and consequence. An IEO needs environmentalists to remind governments of the linkages within the ecosystem and to speak for the interests of future generations. An IEO needs business leaders to remind governments that regulations have costs and that environmental righteousness can be as inimical to commerce as protectionism is. An IEO needs government officials to keep the organization relevant and to prevent it from turning into a debating society. Government involvement is also critical for assuring that industry collaboration does not become anticompetitive.

It is true that environmental groups have had formal or informal advisory roles in most of the recent environmental negotiations. What is being proposed here is that this role be upgraded from advisory to membership, from "down-the-hall" to "at-the-table." Of course, it should be noted that even "down-the-hall" status is not accorded environmentalists by GATT. A new relationship with environmentalists needs to be instituted as part of the Uruguay Round.

The President of the United States has legislative authority for negotiating new international agreements to "apply uniform standards" for pollution control.[9] This authority could be used now to begin international negotiations on establishing an IEO. Achieving such a new organization would be difficult. But the effort is worth making in view of the daunting challenges ahead. By creating an organization that makes it easy for businesses, environmentalists, and governments to work together, we can engender the cooperation and innovation needed for building a greener world.

NOTES

1. The author wishes to thank Patrick Low and J. David Richardson for their thoughtful comments.

2. J. Baron (1878) as quoted in John W. Follows, *Antecedents of the International Labor Organization*, pp. 86-87 (Oxford: Clarendon Press, 1951).

3. Kenneth W. Dam, *The GATT: Law and the International Economic Organization*, p. 195 (Chicago: The University of Chicago Press, 1970).

4. *Maine v. Taylor*, 477 U.S. Reports 131, 151 (1986).

5. "Recommendation on Guiding Principles Concerning International Economic Aspects of Environmental Policies," *International Protection of the En-*

vironment: Treaties and Related Documents, Bernard Ruster and Bruno Simma, eds., vol. 1 (Dobbs Ferry, New York: Oceana Publications, Inc., 1975).

6. Independent Commission on International Development Issues, *North-South: A Program For Survival*, p. 114 (Cambridge: MIT Press, 1980).

7. For example, see Research and Policy Committee, Committee for Economic Development, *The United States in the New Global Economy: A Rallier of Nations*, pp. 28-30 (1992).

8. Lawrence E. Susskind, "New Corporate Roles in Global Environmental Treaty-Making," *Columbia Journal of World Business*, p. 69 (Fall/Winter 1992).

9. United States Code, Public Law 92-500 §7, vol. 33, p. 1251.

Afterword

Ambassador Michael Smith

As both an unabashed free trader and a card carrying environmentalist, I was particularly troubled during the early days of the trade and environment debate. As the debate grew increasingly vicious, I found myself having two unsettling dreams. In the first dream, a long-fanged GATTzilla trampled all over the institutions of democracy, spewed toxics about the land, and eagerly devoured poor Flipper, the helpless dolphin. The second dream was equally troubling. In it a heinous looking creature that bore only the vaguest resemblance to a dolphin destroyed the Geneva home of the General Agreement on Tariffs and Trade (GATT) in the wake of its powerful tail, halted high seas trade by deep-sixing ships, and left the vast majority of the world's population cowering and impoverished in makeshift shantytowns.

My experiences with trade and the environment have given me a split personality of sorts. My trader leanings are drawn to the persuasive arguments of Professor Bhagwati. Following the theory of comparative advantage, free trade is vital to economic efficiency and raising the standards of living around the globe. Trade also serves an important role in preserving global security through interdependence.

It follows then that if every nation is free to use the trading system to impose its values, environmental or otherwise, willy nilly on other nations, the entire trading system will surely collapse under the weight of these obstacles. Today we will use trade to dictate to the rest of the world how many parts per million of benzene is permissible, tomorrow it will be how many hours in the day a worker can work, next it will be the per capita number of schools a country must have. Surely, these seemingly innocent and laudable social goals will sooner or later be hijacked by pro-

287

tectionist interests. Having served as an international trade diplomat, and knowing the adroitness with which our trading partners use trade measures, I fear that the United States will find itself on the losing end of this protectionist stick more often than not. We will have opened a Pandora's box of protectionism.

Herman Daly's argument taking on the conventional wisdom of trade thinking is, however, also compelling. Daly extends the writings of Keynes and argues that from an environmental standpoint "goods should be homespun." Daly challenges the traditional belief that trade solves environmental problems by increasing the economic resources to throw at the problem. Daly's argument hinges upon a belief that increased trade has a tendency to increase the scale of human activities. To Daly, the scale of our activities has already eclipsed the sustainable mark. He believes that the future of our society lies in sustainable development, scaling back, and increasing the environmental efficiency of resource useage, not growth. In his view, trade is a tool of the latter and not the former.

Having dedicated my career to the premise that increased liberalized trade is good both economically and socially, it is troubling to me to think that these beliefs may be not totally valid or not valid in all cases. However, I am not an unswerving ideologue and cannot dismiss Daly's arguments lightly. The blistering heat of summers in the District of Columbia provides a constant reminder of our environmental plight. Each time the mercury tops out above one hundred degrees, I can't help but wonder if the latest heat wave is somehow the product of self-induced global warming driven by worldwide consumer demand for air conditioners and refrigerators driven by fossil fuels. I then become an avid booster of nuclear fuel, no doubt alienating my ardent environmental colleagues.

If trade is part of the problem, what is the solution? The path of history already demonstrates that sealing our borders to trade most certainly is not likely to help. Unless the companies of the developed world provide the developing world with clean technologies, there will be neither growth, development, nor environmental improvement. If we allow ourselves to become protectionist trade island states, old, inefficient, pollution belching factories will meet local demands with all the homespun goods Daly wants, but that cost us all economically and environmentally. If we reject closer ties with our neighbors we will never come to grips with global environmental problems. Brazil has little reason to preserve its rainforests if our backs are turned to her.

Yet, if trade rules do indeed hamper or even slow our ability to address environmental threats such as tainted foods, ozone depletion, and the loss of biodiversity, as John Audley argues eloquently in his chapter, then the rules must be changed. There is neither a trade dog nor an environmental dog; neither policy should by rule wag the other. Herein lies the issue: how can the trade and the environmental systems be reformed so that they can be made mutually reinforcing?

In order for the trade and environment debate to move forward, we first have to move beyond our GATTzilla and Flipper phobias. My friend and colleague John Jackson begins his chapter with three sound presumptions. First, environmental protection is vital to preserving our planet and to ensuring the quality of human life over the span of generations. Second, liberalized trade is equally important to our economic well being and to the quality of human life. Third, you can't have one without the other. The logic is sound. You can't trade in trees if there are no more trees left. Similarly, you can't run an environmental protection program if there is no money to fund it.

This understanding that trade and environmental policies can be, and in many instances already are, mutually reinforcing is brought home by both Justin Ward and Robert Repetto in their chapters. Justin Ward's chapter focuses largely on the environmental effects of trade barriers in the agriculture field, an area I am all too familiar with from my years at the Office of the United States Trade Representative. For the past fifty years the United States has fought, bitterly at times, with our European friends over their domestic and community-wide agricultural policies, which have impeded liberalized trade. Justin Ward, however, does us one better in the trade field. Mr. Ward's chapter shows how these protectionist European policies, and a few of our own domestic policies as well, amount not only to bad economic policy but also to bad environmental policy. In the agricultural sector, it is evident that a healthy dose of trade liberalization is in everyone's best interest.

Bob Repetto's chapter also lays out a framework for mutually reinforcing trade and environmental policies. Mr. Repetto's chapter argues that the ill effects of trade policies on the environment are not caused by trade policies themselves, but rather by market distortions caused primarily by the failure to internalize the cost of environmental protection. Thus, if you want to know why liberalizing trade can speed the loss of tropical rainforests, look not at trade policies, but at the domestic and international policies that go into pricing the resource. Bob Repetto's point is well taken. How much would a molecule of ozone depleting substance cost if the health care costs associated with the increased numbers of skin cancer victims from ozone depletion were factored in? Assuming that some means exist for making a product reflect the full range of its environmental costs, the competiton and efficiencies provided through trade liberalization could alone be a driving force for greater environmental protection, a very important point for both traders and environmentalists to ponder, to say nothing about political leaders.

As my government expertise has taught me, however, developing sweeping visions is easier than translating those visions into workable policies. For example, traders and environmentalists alike generally support effective international agreements as the most constructive way of dealing with global and transboundary environmental threats. But, absent trade measures (such as the threat of sanctions) in multilateral environmental agreements, how can an international environmental threat be addressed? Paraphrasing Thomas Hobbes, men will agree to limits on their actions only if others agree to be bound by similar constraints on their actions, and only if the benefits of these limits are shared by only those constrained. Take the example of China and the Montreal Protocol on Substances that Deplete the Ozone Layer (Montreal Protocol). Until recently, China had refused to sign the Montreal Protocol or commit to meeting the letter or intent of its terms and obligations. China has also made a political commitment to its people to ensure a "refrigerator in every home." Most refrigerators still rely on ozone-depleting chemicals as their coolants, and alternative "ozone-friendly" coolants tend to be more expensive. Given China's population, a refrigerator in every home would constitute a substantial fraction of the world's refrigerators, and would account for a large part of the ozone-depleting coolants in use worldwide. These factors served to make the success of the Montreal Protocol in great measure contingent upon China's actions. Even if every nation in the world except China had agreed to the Montreal Protocol's provisions, the effect of China's increased useage of ozone-depleting chemicals would have negated virtually all benefits of the Montreal Protocol. China could have undermined the Montreal Protocol and in so doing also gained a competitive advantage for its industries that rely on coolants. In this situation, what incentive would exist for other countries to abide by a failed Montreal Protocol that would place them at an economic disadvantage vis-à-vis China? The Montreal Protocol, however, sought to address this "free rider" situation through incentives and trade sanctions aimed at encouraging other nations to join and comply with the terms of the agreement. This combination of carrots and sticks has induced China recently to agree to an ambitious program for stemming ozone depletion. The fact that these carrots and sticks played a major role in the success of the Montreal Protocol seems to argue for a rule of leniency in judging whether trade measures in an international environmental agreement are allowable, or even desirable.

Limiting the use of trade measures, however, to only those instances where an environmental treaty of global acceptance calls for them raises serious environmental policy issues even if it eases the consciences of the trade purists. For example, looking at this issue from a U.S. perspective, what does the American president do when confronted with a global environmental threat while the Neros of other nations sit fiddling idly by?

From a classic trade perspective, such a global embargo on unilateral environmental trade measures would advance the goal of liberalized trade. However, the party suffering the multilateral trade measure cares little that its trade rights are being denied at the behest of one hundred countries as opposed to one. If a GATT party is sanctioned for breaching an environmental accord to which it is not a member, the fact that the sanctions are multilateral has no bearing on whether the sanctions are a technical infringement of the party's GATT rights. The party being hit with the measure has reserved its GATT rights in refusing to join the environmental accord, and the parties to the accord cannot among themselves suspend the other party's reserved rights. Thus, from a classic trade perspective, such a policy embargo is not a panacea.

Moreover, what sort of precedent does agreeing to such a limitation set for the trade policies of countries, like the United States, which have steadfastly fought for their right to take trade measures unilaterally. This is not a pedantic fear. When the nations of the world agreed to a statement in the United Nations Conference on Environment and Development's (UNCED) Agenda 21, denouncing unilateral environmental trade measures, the United States took a reservation. This reservation served not only environmental policy ends, but also trade policy ends. As to environmental policy, the United States was, and is still today, developing its position on unilateral environmental trade measures; agreeing to the UNCED statement would have undercut this effort. As to trade policy, the United States feared that such a statement might come back to haunt it during the ongoing Uruguay Round negotiations.

While a recognition of environmental trade measures contained in multilateral agreements is not a panacea, it is a major and necessary first step. Trade rules should, where appropriate, provide greater leeway for trade measures taken under the explicit terms and obligations of a multilateral environmental agreement, particularly where the agreement has support from a range of nations with diverse interests. (For example, a treaty with membership of both producer and consumer, developed and developing nations in its membership appears to be more environmentally motivated and less like a trade cartel.) In providing such leeway, rules must be crafted to differentiate between legitimate measures adopted in the good faith belief that they are required under some multilateral environmental accord, and measures taken to deliberately restrict trade under the misappropriated cover of an environmental accord. Given the reluctance of the international community to react before the lion is out of the cage, the GATT parties must also address the need for a certain degree of leeway for unilateral measures in the face of compelling threats. To be realistic, however, this is likely to be a more protracted process with no easy solution at hand.

This question of what gives a party the right to adopt measures unilaterally comes to the forefront in the debate over a party's ability to adopt standards. Standards set the terms for what products can and cannot be brought into a country. Different types of standards range from the amount of pesticide residue that may remain on a grape to the number of miles a car must be able to travel on a gallon of gas. While standards seem innocuous at first glance, they are perhaps the most fertile field of actual and potential trade protectionism alive today. Any intelligent person can find enough of a difference between two products, say an imported grape and a domestic grape, to craft a standard that by "some strange coincidence" just happens to disproportionately effect imported grapes. Standards can be ill used for unscrupulous ends; they are also the cornerstone for many of the valid protections we in the U.S., for example, enjoy. Note the difference between being protective and being protectionist. Without these standards we would have no ability to ensure that the food we eat, and the products we rely on, are safe regardless of their origin. Here again we cannot afford porridge that is either too hot or too cold; it must be just right. We need the right to adopt legitimate, non-discriminatory environmental, health, and safety standards. In the world of standards, too many countries march to their own drummer; and to mix analogies, the opportunites for trade mischief are real. Hence, we also need the ability to differentiate such standards from disguised protectionism—at times no easy task.

As Dan Esty points out in his chapter, NAFTA may provide a step in this direction. While some in the environmental community remain dissatisfied with certain aspects of the NAFTA standards provisions, there can be no doubt that these provisions are a substantial step in the right direction for trade and environment thinking. For example, NAFTA's standards provisions explicitly provide that each party retains the right to set environmental, health, and safety standards, even though an individual country may adopt a standard that well exceeds the internationally accepted level of protection. Provisions such as those in the NAFTA standards sections that establish workable and equitable balances between trade and environmental concerns are an important step toward reconciling these two vital policy spheres. The GATT parties would be well advised to explore seriously the adoption of NAFTA-esque provisions into the GATT rules.

Finally, it is important to remember that the private sector plays a vital role in this reconciliation process. As Paul Hawken of the Smith and Hawken Company has said, "[b]usiness is the only mechanism on the planet today powerful enough to reverse global environmental and social degradation." Or, as I sometimes put it in a more direct fashion, if the private sector has made money by dirtying up the planet, it should certainly be able to make money cleaning it up. Speaking now to our environmental friends, the best way to ensure that the private sector will indeed clean up the planet is to provide a profit motive, not just a punitary motive for this behavior.

Corporations large and small have realized that environmental awareness is more than a cost of doing business. Environmental awareness is a major component of business goodwill—the value of being a good neighbor. Multinational corporations today export more than just their products, they export their technologies, expertise, and most importantly their emerging environmental values. The role of business in reconciling trade and environment issues is likely to grow as it becomes increasingly clear that preserving the environment is the right thing to do from both a social and an economic standpoint. For example, the Department of Commerce estimates the environmental goods and services market alone is $370 billion worldwide. Moreover, this figure includes only products and services dedicated to environmental protection and cleanup, such as scrubbers and liners. Add in the market for manufacturing process technologies that are more environmentally sound and the $370 billion figure grows exponentially.

Although there will be obstacles from time to time, as business interests, traders, environmentalists, policy wonks, academicans, and even "faceless" bureaucrats, begin to understand each others fears and needs, the process of reconciling trade and environmental policies is not only occurring, it is somewhat inevitable. As attention to the reconciliation of trade and environmental policies increases, I find that my nightmares of evil GATTzillas and Flippers are slowly fading. I can see myself one day having a new dream in which GATTzilla and Flipper, working side by side, bring clean water, clean air, safe food, shelter and happiness to the world's population. "To sleep, perchance to dream . . ."

Selected Sources and References

American Society of International Law, "Washington Convention on Nature Protection and Wildlife Preservation in the Western Hemisphere (Convention on International Trade in Endangered Species of Wild Fauna and Flora)," In *International Legal Materials,* vol. 12. Washington, D.C.: American Society of International Law, 1973.

American Society of International Law, "United Nations Convention on the Law of the Sea," In *International Legal Materials,* vol. 21. Washington, D.C.: American Society of International Law, 1982. *[Not yet in force.]*

American Society of International Law, "Montreal Protocol on Substances that Deplete the Ozone Layer," In *International Legal Materials,* vol. 26. Washington, D.C.: American Society of International Law, 1987.

American Society of International Law, "Vienna Convention on the Protection of the Ozone Layer," In *International Legal Materials,* vol. 26. Washington, D.C.: American Society of International Law, 1987.

American Society of International Law, "Wellington Convention on the Regulation of Antarctic Mineral Resource Activities," In *International Legal Materials,* vol. 27. Washington, D.C.: American Society of International Law, 1988.

American Society of International Law, "Single European Act," In *International Legal Materials,* vol. 25. Washington, D.C.: American Society of International Law, 1989.

American Society of International Law, "Basel Convention on the Control of Transboundary Movements of Hazardous Wastes and their Disposal," In *International Legal Materials,* vol. 28. Washington, D.C.: American Society of International Law, 1989.

American Society of International Law, "United Nations Framework Convention on Climate Change," In *International Legal Materials,* vol. 31. Washington, D.C.: American Society of International Law, 1992. *[Not yet in force.]*

American Society of International Law, "Convention on Biological Diversity," In *International Legal Materials,* vol. 31. Washington, D.C.: American Society of International Law, 1992.

General Agreement on Tariffs and Trade (GATT), "General Agreement on Tariffs and Trade," In *International Protection of the Environment: Treaties and Related Documents.* Dobbs Ferry, NY: Oceana Publications, Inc., 1975.

General Agreement on Tariffs and Trade (GATT). *Draft Final Act Embodying the Results of the Uruguay Round of Multilateral Trade Negotiations,* GATT Doc. MTN.TNC/W/FA Geneva: GATT, December, 1991. This is known as the Dunkel draft text.

General Agreement on Tariffs and Trade (GATT). *Report of the GATT Panel, Canada-Measures Affecting Exports of Unprocessed Herring and Salmon,* GATT Doc. L/6268. Geneva: GATT, March 1989.

General Agreement on Tariffs and Trade (GATT), "Dispute Panel Report on United States Restrictions on Imports of Tuna," Reprinted in *International Legal Materials*, vol. 30. Washington, D.C.: American Society of International Law, 1991. This is known as the tuna-dolphin decision.

General Agreement on Tariffs and Trade (GATT), "Trade and Environment Report," In *International Trade 90-91,* vol. 1. Geneva: GATT, 1992.

Housman, Robert, and Paul Orbuch, "Enforcement of Environmental Laws Under a Supplemental Agreement to the North American Free Trade Agreement," *Georgetown International Environmental Law Review.* vol. 5, Issue 3. (1993): 593.

Housman, Robert, and Paul Orbuch, "Integrating Labor and Environmental Concerns into the North American Free Trade Agreement: A Look Back and a Look Ahead," *American University Journal of International Law and Policy. [Forthcoming.]*

Housman, Robert, "A Kantian Approach to Trade and the Environment," *Washington and Lee Law Review* 49 (1992): 1373.

U.S.-Canada Binational Panel, "In re Canada's Landing Requirements for Salmon and Herring," Panel No. CDA 98-1087-01 (1989), In *International Trade Reporter Decisions*, vol. 12. Washington, D.C.: Bureau of National Affairs, 1989.

McAlpine, Jan C., Patricia LeDonne, and Charles Gnaedinger, eds. *The Greening of World Trade.* Washington, D.C.: Environmental Protection Agency, 1993.

Organization for Economic Cooperation and Development (OECD), "Recommendation on Guiding Principles Concerning Environmental Policies," In *International Protection of the Environment: Treaties and Related Documents,* vol. 1, edited by Bernard Ruster and Bruno Simma. Dobbs Ferry, NY: Oceana Publications, Inc., 1975.

United Nations. *Treaty Establishing the European Economic Community,* United Nations Treaty Series, vol. 11. New York: March, 1957.

United States Trade Representative. *North American Free Trade Agreement Between the Government of the United States of America, the Government of Canada, and the Government of the United Mexican States.* Washington, D.C.: United States Government Printing Office, 1992.

World Commission on Environment and Development, *Our Common Future.* New York: Oxford University Press, 1987.

Zaelke, Durwood, and Robert Housman, "The Collision of the Environment and Trade: The GATT Tuna/Dolphin Decision," *Environmental Law Review* 22 (1992): 10268.

Zaelke, Durwood, and Robert Housman, "Making Trade and Environmental Policies Mutually Reinforcing: Forging Competitive Sustainability," *Environmental Law* 23 (1993): 545.

Index

A

Adams, John, 48

Administrative Procedures Act (APA), 208

Advisors, The (Bruce L.R. Smith), 209

Advisory Committee on Trade Policy and Negotiations, 48, 210

African Elephant Conservation Act, 15

Agenda 21. *See* United Nations Conference on Environment and Development, Agenda 21

agricultural policies
  and conservation, 252–54
  farm bills, 253

agricultural protectionism, 238–40

agricultural subsidies, 247, 250, 251–52

aid
  vs. world trade figures, 72

air quality management
  in Europe, 98–99

Alaska, 8

Alternative Agriculture, 248

Amazon, 119

Andean Pact, 113

Antarctica, 39

APA. *See* Administrative Procedures Act

Argentina, 8, 9, 113

Association of Southeast Asian Nations (ASEAN), 9

Audubon Society, 48

Australia, 7, 35, 83

Austria, 18, 93, 102, 255
  and environmental codes, 19

automobiles
  Japanese exports, 164
  life-cycle management of, 88–89

B

Basel, Switzerland, 106

Basel Convention on the Control of Transboundary Movements of Hazardous Wastes and their Disposal, 46, 86, 99, 118, 229

Beef Hormone case, 26, 181, 182, 223–24

Belgium, 7

Benchmark Corporate Environmental Survey (U.N. Center on Transnational Corporations), 136

Berle, Peter, 48

Bhopal case, 139

Bi-National Statement of Environmental Safeguards that Should be Included in NAFTA, 195

BIAC. *See* Business and Industry Advisory Committee

Biodiversity Convention. *See* United Nations Convention on Biological Diversity

Bolivia, 8

Boren, Senator David, 166

boycotts, 173

Brandt Commission, 280

Brazil, 9, 113, 119
  population trends, 112

Bretton Woods System, 222

Brundtland Commission, 30, 192

Bush administration, 8, 110, 113, 254, 261
  and "fast track" authorization, 13
  and free trade, 8
  and NAFTA, 192, 193, 194, 197, 198
business
  and environmental management, 123, 128, 132
  and environmental standards, 129
  rules for, 121–22,124–27
Business and Industry Advisory Committee (BIAC), 122, 123, 126, 132
Business Charter for Sustainable Development, 125

C
cadmium
  ban on the use of, 101
Canada, 7, 8, 83, 110. *See also* North American Free Trade Agreement
  beer can tax, 178
  and transnational pollution, 29
CAP. *See* Common Agricultural Policy
capital
  manmade vs. natural, 153
carbon taxes
  in Europe, 101
Caribbean Basin Initiative, 21
Caribbean Economic Community, 113
Caribbean nations
  and trade with U.S., 8
Carson, Rachel, 207
Center for International Environmental Law (CIEL), 195
Center for Rural Affairs, 248
Central Europe
  and environmental management, 106
CFC. *See* chlorofluorocarbon
Charnovitz, Steve, 172, 174, 175
Chile, 8, 113, 114
China
  and Montreal Protocol, 290
chlorofluorocarbon (CFC)
  damage limitation of, 29–30
  environmental-trade restriction of, 38
CIEL. *See* Center for International Environmental Law

CITES. *See* United Nations Convention on International Trade in Endangered Species of Wild Fauna and Flora
Clinton administration, 8, 160
  and environmental policy, 199–202
  and GATT, 257–58
  and NAFTA, 192, 199–202, 257–58, 265
Club of Rome, 31
CMEA. *See* Council for Mutual Economic Assistance
coal, 95, 163
Codex Alimentarius Commission, 26, 204, 274
Colombia, 113
COMECON. *See* Council for Mutual Economic Assistance
Commerce Clause, U.S. Constitution, 276, 277
Commission of the European Communities, 103
commodity processing industries, 80
Common Agricultural Policy (CAP), 107, 249
Common Market of the Southern Cone (MERCOSUR), 9, 113
comparative advantage argument, 149–50, 227–28
competition, standards-lowering, 148–49
Competitiveness Council, 168
conservation
  and agricultural policies, 252–54
Convention on the Regulation of Antarctic Mineral Resource Activities, 35
cost internalization, 31, 41–42. *See also* pollution control measures
Council for Mutual Economic Assistance (CMEA), 102–3
Council for the Protection of Rural England, 249, 253
Council of Ministers, European Community (EC), 95
Council of the European Communities, 34
countervailing duties, 131–32, 166

D

Daly, Herman, 288
Dam, Kenneth W., 272
Dartmouth College, 49
de la Madrid, Miguel, 114
Dean, Judith M., 135
deforestation
   in Latin America, 119
Delaney Clause, Food and Drug Act, 16
Denmark, 7, 93, 96, 102, 180
   agriculture, 249
   and ban on cadmium, 101–2
   ban on nonreturnable bottles, 117
   and pesticides, 255
developing countries
   and environmental regulations, 10
   and foreign investment, 134, 135–36,
      141–43
   and internalization of costs, 79–80
   and Polluter Pays Principle, 244
   and pollution, 25, 136–41
   reducing trade barriers to, 240–41
   and technology transfer, 142
   and trade reform, 80, 81
diplomacy
   and environmental management, 94
discrimination, of like products, 76. *See
      also* non-discrimination
dispute panels
   and enforcement of environmental
      standards, 39–40
   GATT, 12–13, 20
dispute resolution process, 35, 125
   business perspective on, 129–30
   GATT, 54, 179, 231–32
   NAFTA, 54, 196
   OECD, 27
   for trade-environment issues, ideal, 78,
      116–17
dolphins, 15, 170. *See also* tuna-dolphin
      panel
   dolphin-safe tuna, 173
   and MMPA, 3
domestic protection (or production?),
      147, 148–49
Down to Earth, 171
"dumping," 47, 166

Dunkel, Arthur, 13, 254
Dunkel draft, 13, 15–16, 19

E

Eastern Europe, 45, 93, 123
   and environmental management, 106
   and pollution, 25
EC. *See* European Community
ECE. *See* Economic Commission for
      Europe
eco-imperialism, 30, 226, 227
eco-labeling, 87, 88, 89
eco-packaging, 87, 88, 89
Economic Commission for Europe
      (ECE), 36, 98
economic-environment relationships, 58
economic management
   traditional vs. modern, 57
economic tools, 57–58
economies
   growth vs. development, 155
   integrating, 28–29
   isolated system, 154
   open subsystem of ecosystem, 153,
      154
   open vs. closed, 152
Economist, The, 13
Ecuador, 113
EEP. *See* Export Enhancement Program
EFTA. *See* European Free Trade
      Association
Emergency Planning and Community
      Right to Know Act (1986), 207
emissions, in Europe, 98–99
Endangered Species Act, 15
energy policy
   European Community, 98
energy taxes, in Europe, 101
Enterprise for the Americas Initiative, 88,
      113, 114, 120
environmental agreements
   history of, 111–13
environmental costs
   internalization of, 66, 67, 76–77, 79–
      80, 80–81, 222. *See also* Polluter
      Pays Principle (1972); sustainable
      development

environmental costs, internalization of,
Continued
  and developing countries, 79–80, 81
  and GATT, 76–77
  regulation of, 242–43
  and subsidies, 80
  and protectionism, 65–67
environmental impact studies, 59
environmental management
  business rules for, 125–27
  and economic development, 121
  in Europe, 94, 95, 96–103, 102, 103,
    104–8
  extraterritorial problems, 126
  international rules for, 125–27
  priority of prevention, 116
Environmental Measures and International Trade working group, 77
environmental policy, 36–39
  changes in, 87–89
  to benefit trade, 242–45
  integrating trade policy, 92
  international authority, 39–40
  and life-cycle management, 87–89
  and mutually supportive trade policy,
    74–75, 273
  and protectionism, 46
  publication participation in, 206–7
  and trade agreements, international
    organizations, 36–39
  as trade barriers, 87–88
  U.S., 212
  vs. trade policy, 47, 233
environmental problems
  change in, 84–86
  domestic
    ethical preferences, 165, 170–76
    objectives, constraining, 165–66,
      176–83
    standards lowering, 165, 168–70
    unfair trade, 165, 166–68
    vs. international, 164
  global vs. transboundary, 84–85
Environmental Protection Agency (EPA),
  206
  advisory process, 211
  cabinet status of, 212

National Advisory Committee on
  Environmental Policy and Technology, 49
  procedural advances, 49–50
  publication participation in, 206–7
  role in NAFTA negotiations, 50
  Trade and Environment Commit-
    tee, 49
environmental regulations
  domestic vs. international standards,
    195–96
  enforcement of, 195
  harmonization of, 19
  and multilateralism, 14
  and non-discrimination, 14. *See also*
    non-discrimination
  and specialization, 11
  state and local, overruling, 17
*Environmental Safeguards for the North
  American Free Trade Agreement*, 195
environmental standards, 15–16. *See also*
  harmonization
  domestic vs. international standards,
    195–96
  enforcing, 39–40
  and free trade, 90–92
  harmonization of, 19, 128–29
  and NAFTA, 293
  and protectionism, 292–93
*Environmental Standards, Industrial
  Relocation and Pollution Havens*,
  135
environmental wear
  relationship to GDP, 137–40
EPA. *See* Environmental Protection
  Agency
Euratom, 93
Europe. *See also* Central Europe; Eastern
  Europe; European Community;
  Western Europe
  carbon, energy taxes, 100–1
  environmental management, emergence
    of, 94, 95
  and foreign investment, 142
  hazardous waste management,
    99–100
  and trade negotiations, 93

European Coal and Steel Community, 93
European Common Market, 5
European Community (EC)
  agricultural policies, 252
  and air quality management, 98–99
  Beef Hormone case, 181, 182, 223–24
  description, 7, 96
  energy policy, 98
  environmental management, 95, 96,
    103, 104–8
  and European unity, 95
  and GATT, 103
  and harmonization rules, 275–76
  and OECD, 101
  Sixth Amendment, 100
  and trade agreements, 93
  and water quality management, 97
European Council, 96
European Court of Justice, 180
European Economic Zone, 93, 105
European Ecumenical Organization for
    Development, 250
European Free Trade Association
    (EFTA), 93, 102
  and environmental management, 102,
    105
  and environmental standards, 19
  and GATT, 102, 103
  goals of, 102
Export Enhancement Program (EEP), 254
exports
  and environmental regulations, 15
  subsidies, 254–55
extrajurisdictional trade measures, 86
extraterritorial enforcement
  and GATT, 15

F
FACA. *See* Federal Advisory Committee
    Act
farm policies
  crop rotation, 251
  environmental impacts of, 248–50
  pesticides, fertilizer, 255–56
  reform agenda for, 250–56
"fast track" authorization, 13, 47

FDA. *See* Food and Drug Administration
FDI. *See* foreign direct investment
Federal Advisory Committee Act
    (FACA), 208–9
Federal Insecticide, Fungicide, and
    Rodenticide Act (FIFRA), 16
Fenstra, Robert, 164
fertilizers, 255–56
FIFRA. *See* Federal Insecticide, Fungi-
    cide, and Rodenticide Act
Finland, 255
Florida, 239
Food and Drug Act, 16
foreign direct investment (FDI)
  in developing countries, 141–43
  and pollution, 136–41
forests. *See also* deforestation
  economic vs. ecological, societal
    value, 60–61
  and environmental regulations, 10
  Statement of Principles on Forests, 119
  timber subsidies, 244
Framework Convention on Climate
    Change, 34, 118
France, 7, 35, 36, 83, 93, 247
free trade
  description, 5
  effects on growth, development, 155–
    57
  and growth of per capita income, 162
  and immigration, 169–70
  and pollution, 162–63
  problems with, 151
  sustainable scale, 150–51
Free Trade Commission, 198
Free Trade Trust Fund, 261

G
GATT. *See* General Agreement on
    Tariffs and Trade
GATTzilla, 161, 203
GDP. *See* gross domestic product
GEMS. *See* Global Environmental
    Monitoring System
General Agreement on Tariffs and Trade
    (GATT), 263–64

General Agreement on Tariffs and Trade
(GATT), *Continued*
and Agenda 21 (UNCED), 73, 74
Agreement on Technical Barriers to
Trade, 87
amendment to, proposed, 117
Article III, 204, 223, 227
Article VI, 229
Article XI, 204, 227
Article XVI, 229
Article XIX, 131
Article XX, 26, 42, 51, 54, 177, 224–
26, 227
Article XX(b), 37, 176, 179, 224
Article XX(g), 38, 176, 224
Article XXV, 187
Article XXXVIII(2)(e), 273
description, 6
dispute resolution process, 20, 35, 36,
179, 231–32
panels, 12–13
vs. NAFTA process, 54
and Dunkel draft, 13
and EC, 103
and EFTA, 102, 103
enforcement of, 12–13
environmental costs, internalization of,
73, 76–77
Environmental Measures and International Trade working group, 77
and environmental regulations, 14,
133–34
environmental standards, proposed,
15–16
and extraterritorial enforcement, 15
and "fast track" authorization, 13
foundations of, 124
GATTzilla, 161, 203
and harmonization, 19, 273–75
institutional deficiencies of,
230–32
and local environmental law, 17
and Montreal Protocol, 228–29
and MTO, 14, 75, 79
"national treatment," 223
objectives of, 222
"original intent," 175–76

and Polluter Pays Principle, 41
preamble to, 263–64
and process, product standards, 176,
226–27, 280
provisions of, 11
public protest against, 203, 204
recommended actions for, 232, 234
reform of, 75–77
Sanitary and Phytosanitary (S&P)
Code, 274
Sanitary and Phytosanitary (S&P)
Decision, 179
and spillovers, suggested rules for,
187–88
Standards Code, 179, 224, 273, 274,
275
and subsidies, 107
and sustainable development, 73
and tariffs, 6
Technical Barriers to Trade, Code on,
26
Tokyo Round, 224, 229, 273
Trade and the Environment, 163–64,
171–72, 177
Trade Policy Review Mechanism,
232
tuna-dolphin case, 3, 15, 37–38, 46,
76, 204, 227
Uruguay Round, 3, 6, 11, 114, 160,
221
and agricultural subsidies, 247
description of, 36
development of, 13
dispute resolution process, 130
environmental impact of, 13–14
and environmental requirements,
192
and GATT reform, 75
and harmonization, 14, 274–75
and product standards, 26
review of, 78
and sustainable development, 78
and UNCED, 71
violations of, for environmental
reasons, 51–52
General Agreement on Tariffs and Trade
(GATT) Council, 17, 20

Generalized System of Preferences, 21
Geneva, Switzerland, 36
Gephardt, Richard, 196
Germany, 7, 93, 96
  air quality management, 98, 99
  packaging waste regulation, 107–8
  water quality management, 97
Ghandi, Mahatma, 172
Gladwin, Thomas N., 139
Global Environmental Monitoring
  System (GEMS), 137–38
Gore, Al, 159
Greece, 7, 93, 106
gross domestic product (GDP)
  and environmental policy, 238
  and environmental wear, 137–40
Grossman, Gene, 163
*Guiding Principles Concerning the
  International Economic Aspects of
  Environmental Policies,* 26, 83, 84
  and change in trade policy, 89, 90

H
Haberler, Gottfried, 178
Hair, Jay, 48, 198
harmonization, 195–96, 245. *See also*
  environmental standards
  vs. convergence, 270–73
  description, 14, 267
  and Dunkel draft, 15–16
  environmental standards, 19
  and environmental standards, 87, 128–
  29
  future of, 279–80
  and life-cycle management, 89
  rules for
    EC, 275–76
    NAFTA, 277–78
    U.S., 276–77
  theory of, 268–70
Harper's magazine, 169
Hawken, Paul, 293
hazardous waste management
  in Europe, 99–100
health care
  economic significance of, 62
Hills, Carla A., 110, 193, 198

Hobbes, Thomas, 290
Hudec, Robert, 182
Hudson, Stewart, 49
human resources
  economic vs. value, 62–65

I
IBRD. *See* International Bank for
  Reconstruction and Development
ICC. *See* International Chamber of
  Commerce
Iceland, 7
IEO. *See* International Environment
  Organization
IFMPO. *See* Integrated Farm Manage-
  ment Program Option
ILO. *See* International Labor Organiza-
  tion
IMF. *See* International Monetary Fund
immigration
  and free trade, 169–70
Immigration Act (1905), 169
*Implications for the Trade and Invest-
  ment of Developing Countries of
  United States Environmental
  Controls,* 133
imports
  and environmental regulations, 15
  and protectionism, 4–5
India, 140, 170, 171, 172
Integrated Border Environmental Plan,
  49
Integrated Farm Management Program
  Option (IFMPO), 251
intellectual property rights, 39, 75, 271
Inter-American Development Bank, 115
Intergovernmental Negotiating Commit-
  tee, 37
Intergovernmental Panel on Climate
  Change, 37
internalization of environmental costs.
  See environmental costs, internaliza-
  tion of
International Bank for Reconstruction
  and Development (IBRD), 84
International Chamber of Commerce
  (ICC), 122–23, 125, 126

International Environment Organization (IEO), 283–85
International Labor Organization (ILO), 268
International Maritime Organization, 36
International Monetary Fund (IMF), 59, 242
International Trade Organization (ITO), 230
Iowa, 255
Ireland, 7, 93, 136
Israel, 9
Italy, 7, 96
  hazardous waste management, 99
ITO. *See* International Trade Organization

J
Jackson, John, 35, 49, 175
Jackson, Wes, 254
Jamaica, 8
Japan
  automobile exports, 164
  exports, imports, 4, 9
  and foreign investment, 142
  and OECD, 7, 83
  Structural Impediments Initiative, 28

K
Kantor, Mickey, 198
Keynes, John Maynard, 151–52
Krueger, Alan, 163

L
Land Institute, The, 254
Latin America
  deforestation, 119
  economic policy, 112–13
  and environmental protection, 118
  and sustainable development, 113–15
  and trade with U.S., 8
Latin American Economic System (SELA), 113
Leahy, Patrick, 253–64
Leonard, Jeffrey, 135
life-cycle management
  and business, 128
  in environmental policy, 87–89

"like products"
  and life-cycle management, 89
  discrimination of, 76. *See also* non-discrimination
Limits to Growth (Club of Rome), 31
London, England, 36
London Guidelines for the Exchange of Information on Chemicals in International Trade, 86
Love Canal, 207
Luxembourg, 7
Luxembourg Compromise (1964), 93

M
Maastricht, Germany, 93, 105, 106
Maastricht Treaty on European Union, 276
maquiladoras, 11, 29, 63, 93
Mathews, Jessica Tuchman, 250
"May 1 Plan," 204
McClosky, Mike, 49
MERCOSUR. *See* Common Market of the Southern Cone
Mexico, 63, 113, 136. *See also* North American Free Trade Agreement; tuna-dolphin case
  and dolphin-safe tuna, 172–73, 174
  and environmental management, 115
  and environmental protection, 29, 114
  environmental regulations, 259–60, 261
  Integrated Border Environmental Plan, 49
  and NAFTA, 204, 259–60110
  "pollution haven," 48
  population trends, 112
  and the sale of tuna to the U.S., 3
  tuna-dolphin case, 46
    enforcement of, 39–40
  and U.S. border, 196–97, 201
  U.S. businesses in, 11, 114, 115
  wage rates, 259–60
MFN. *See* most-favored-nation
Migratory Bird Act, 15
MMPA. *See* U.S. Marine Mammal Protection Act
MNC. *See* multinational corporations

Montreal Protocol on Substances that
Deplete the Ozone Layer (1987), 3,
17, 46, 86, 112
and CFCs, 29, 38
and China, 290
and GATT, 20, 228–29
and product process issue, 228
most-favored-nation (MFN). *See also*
non-discrimination; non-most-
favored-nation
status, 12
tariffs, 21
most-favored-nation status. *See also* non-
discrimination
MTO. *See* Multilateral Trade Organization
Multi-Fibre Agreement, 240
Multilateral Trade Organization (MTO)
description of, 75
and GATT, 14, 79
negotiation and review of, 78–79
and sustainable development, 79
multilateralism, 14
multinational corporations (MNCs). *See
also* foreign direct investment;
transnational corporations
and environmental control regulations,
135
mutual recognition doctrine, 28
"mutually supportive." *See* United
Nations Conference on the Environment and Development, Agenda 21

N
NACE. *See* North American Commission
on the Environment
NACEPT. *See* National Advisory Council
for Environmental Policy and
Technology
NAFTA. *See* North American Free Trade
Agreement
Nairobi, Kenya, 36
National Advisory Council for Environ-
mental Policy and Technology
(NACEPT), 208
National Association of Manufacturers,
49

National Environmental Policy Act
(NEPA) (1969), 207
National Oceanic and Atmospheric
Administration, 206
"national treatment" of foreign
goods, 12
National Wildlife Federation (NWF), 48,
49, 197
National Wildlife Federation (NWF)/
Pollution Probe-Canada, 195
natural resources. *See also* sustainable
development
economic vs. ecological, societal value,
60–61
underpricing of, 244–45
Natural Resources Defense Council,
48, 195
Nature Conservancy, 48
NEPA. *See* National Environmental
Policy Act (1969)
Netherlands, 7, 96
agriculture, 249
air quality management, 99
New York Times, 204, 212
New Zealand, 83
NGO. *See* nongovernmental organizations
non-discrimination
description, 14
and GATT, 12, 77
and internalization of environmental
costs, 77
and production methods, 77
non-most-favored-nation (non-MFN)
tariffs, 21
non-tariff barriers
and GATT, 12
nongovernmental organizations (NGOs),
170–71, 206
Nordic Council, 93, 101
North American Commission on the
Environment (NACE), 195, 197, 262–
63
North American Free Trade Agreement
(NAFTA), 47, 259–63
accession clause, 115
and Bush administration, 192, 193,
194, 197, 198

North American Free Trade Agreement
(NAFTA), *Continued*
    and Clinton administration, 192, 199–
        202, 257–58, 265
    dispute resolution process, 36, 54, 196
    environmental protection, 29, 109–10,
        115
    environmental review of, 49
    environmental standards, 192, 193,
        293
    environmentalists' conditions for
        support of, 195–97
    environmentalists' strategies for, 193–
        94
    EPA role in negotiations, 50
    Free Trade Commission, 198
    and harmonization rules, 277–78
    and international environmental
        agreements, 51
    issues, 48, 54–55
    and Mexico, 204
    "minimalist" strategy, 194
    and natural resource conservation,
        29
    and "pollution haven" concern, 53
    preamble to, 50–51
    and product standards, 26
    and protectionism, 51
    sanitary, phytosanitary provisions of,
        52
    and sustainable development, 50
    and trade agreement precedence, 51
Norway, 93, 102
NRDC. *See* Natural Resources Defense
    Council
nuclear energy, 95
NWF. *See* National Wildlife Federation

O

OAS. *See* Organization of American
    States
Organization for Economic Cooperation
    and Development (OECD), 36, 122
    background on, 83–84
    and business, industry involvement,
        123–28
    and carbon, energy taxes, 101
    chemicals program, 87
    description of, 6–7
    dispute resolution process, 27
    and environmental policy, 86
    and GATT, 7, 133
    Guiding Principles, 26, 123, 130–31,
        132
    Joint Session on Trade and Environ-
        ment, 77
    and Polluter Pays Principle, 25, 278
Organization of American States (OAS),
    113
    Resolution 1114, 113
Our Common Future (Brundtland
    Commission), 30, 111, 193

P

Paraguay, 9, 113
Paris, France, 36, 83
Pearson, Charles, 133, 135, 141
pesticides, 249, 255–56
    and health risks, 16
phytosanitary measures, 52
Polluter Pays Principle (1972), 92, 127,
    222, 255. *See also* internalization of
    environmental costs
    application of, 130–31
    description of, 25, 40–41, 116
    and developing countries, 244
    and GATT, 41
    and OECD, 83, 243, 278
    renewed commitment to, 126
    and trade reform, 80
    and UNCED, 41, 73
pollution. *See also* spillovers; sustainable
    development
    in developing countries, 25
    energy sources, 95
    in Europe, 98–99
    and free trade, 162–63
    relationship to GDP, 137–40
    spillovers, 48, 49
    and subsidies, 41, 42
    transnational, 29
pollution control measures, 40–41. *See
    also* cost internalization
    and border adjustments, 41

"pollution havens," 29, 48, 53, 114, 136
   and transnational corporations, 134
population trends, 112
Portugal, 7, 93, 96, 99, 102, 106
poverty, 140, 162, 193
Precautionary Principle, 92, 116
*Preliminary Overview of Environmental
   Concerns Arising from the NAFTA,*
   195
Private Sector Advisory Committee
   System, 210
process (production) standards, 16, 176,
   267, 271, 280–81
   agreement on, 282–83
   and GATT, 226–27, 281
   and non-discrimination, 77
   virtuous vs. vicious circles, 270
product standards, 16, 267
   and EC, 28
   and GATT, 226–27
   and NAFTA, 26
   and Uruguay Round, 26
protectionism
   agricultural, 238–40
   description, 4–5
   from environmental costs, 65–67
   and environmental policy, 46
   and environmental protection, 124
   and NAFTA, 51
   and standards, 292–93
Punta del Este, Uruguay, 3

Q
Quayle, Danforth, 168

R
Radetzki, Marian
   "intensity of environmental wear"
      hypothesis, 136–40, 141
Reagan administration, 8, 112
recycling, 87, 88–89
   packaging waste regulation, 107–8
regional economic integration, 28
Reilly, William, 49, 110, 197, 208
*Report on Development and the Environ-
   ment* (World Bank), 121, 192

Report on Environment and Development
   (Brundtland Commission), 192
Resolution 1114 (OAS), 113
Rio de Janeiro, Brazil, 30, 109, 159
Rio Declaration on Environment and
   Development, 41, 118, 174
Risk assessment
   vs. risk management, 130
Romania, 136
Rome, Italy, 36
Roosevelt, Franklin Delano, 64
Royal Society for the Protection of Birds,
   253

S
Salinas de Gortari, Carlos, 114, 260
sanitary measures, 52
Sawhill, John, 48
SEDESOL. *See* Social Development
   Secretariat
SELA. *See* Latin American Economic
   System
Seveso, Italy, 99
Sierra Club, 49
Silent Spring, 207
Single European Act (1986), 93, 103, 106
Smith, Bruce L.R., 209
Smith, Michael, 49
Smoot-Hawley Tariff Act (1930), 21,
   134, 182, 264
Social Development Secretariat
   (SEDESOL), 49, 50
"sodbuster," 253
Soviet Union, 4, 25, 45
S&P. *See* General Agreement on Tariffs
   and Trade (GATT), Sanitary and
   Phytosanitary; phytosanitary
   measures; sanitary measures
Spain, 7, 93, 96, 106, 136
special tariffs, 21
specialization
   and environmental regulations, 11
Speth, James Gustave, 110
spillovers, 44, 48. *See also* pollution
   examples and solutions, 183–88
   suggested rules for, 187–88
   types, 270

standards. *See* environmental standards;
   harmonization; process standards;
   product standards
standards-lowering competition, 148–49
Statement of Principles on Forests, 119
steady-sate paradigm, 152–55
steel, 95
Stockholm, Sweden, 24, 30, 111
Stockholm conference. *See* United
   Nations Conference on the Human
   Environment
Strange, Marty, 248
Strasbourg, France, 247
structural adjustment, 59
Structural Impediments Initiative, 28
subsidies, 107, 114, 229–30, 244–45
   agricultural, 250, 251–52
   and exports, 254–55
   pollution, 41, 42
   restrictions under GATT, 17
   and trade reform, 80
Susskind, Lawrence E., 284
sustainable development, 30–31, 50, 66,
   67, 193
   definition of, 111, 120
   and GATT, 73, 76
   and Latin America, 113–15
   and MTO, 79
   and trade reform, 72
   and UNCED, 45, 119
sustainable scale, 147, 150–51
"swampbuster," 253
Sweden, 255
   and ban on cadmium, 101
Switzerland, 93, 102
   air quality management, 98

T
tariffs
   categories, U.S., 21
   and GATT, 6
   reducing, 11, 12
Technical Barriers to Trade, Code on
   (GATT), 26
technology transfer, 142
Thailand, 179
Third World. *See* developing countries

Three Mile Island, 207
Tokyo Round Code on Subsidies and
   Countervailing Duties, 229
Tokyo Round Standards Code, 224
Toxics Release Inventory (TRI), 207
trade
   approaches to, 4–6
   description of, 4, 58
   extrajurisdictional measures, 86
   international authority of, 33–35
   managed trade, 5–6
   price system of, 60–61, 62–65
   and protectionism, 4–5
   and sustainable development, 31, 66, 67
   vs. world aid figures, 72
Trade Act (1979), 259
trade agreements. *See also under names of
   agreements*
   and environmental concerns, 33, 52, 67,
      72, 118–20
   environmental criteria for, 116–18
   and environmental policy, 45–47
Trade and the Environment (GATT), 163–
   64, 171–72, 177
trade barriers
   and developing countries, 240–41
   and environmental policy, 87–88
   non-tariff, 12
   packaging waste regulation, 108
   Technical Barriers to Trade, Code on
      (GATT), 26
trade-environment issues
   categories, 23–24
   history of, 24–27
   re-emergence of, 27–31
trade institutions, international. *See
   under names of institutions*
trade legislation, "fast track," 13
trade policy
   change in, 89–92
   changes that would benefit the
      environment, 238–42
   environmental advances in, 48
   and environmental policy, 74–75, 92,
      237
   vs. environmental policy, 47, 233
Trade Policy Review Group, 212, 214

Trade Policy Staff Committee, 212, 214
trade reform
  and developing countries, 80, 81
  and environmental policy, 74–75
  national, multilateral solutions for
    environmental issues, 77–78
  subsidies, 80
trade sanctions, 241
  and environmental policy, 46
Trail Smelter case, 29
Train, Russell, 48
"transfrontier pollution," 84. *See also*
  pollution
transnational corporations
  investment and pollution, 135–36
  investments in developing countries,
    134, 135–36
transnational pollution, 29
transparency, 206–7, 234
Treaty of Rome (1987), 41, 278
  Article 36, 275, 276
TRI. *See* Toxics Release Inventory
trickle down economics, 73
Trowbridge, Sandy, 49
TSCA. *See* U.S. Toxic Substances
  Control Act
tuna-dolphin case, 15, 26, 204, 227
  enforcement of, 39
  and GATT dispute panel, 46, 161
  report, interpretation of, 37–38
Turkey, 7

U

UN. *See* United Nations
UNCED. *See* United Nations Conference
  on Environment and Development
UNCTAD. *See* United Nations Conference on Trade and Development
UNEP. *See* United Nations Environment
  Programme
unfair trade
  and environmental standards, 166–68
Union Carbide, 139, 140
United Kingdom, 7, 93, 96, 102
  air quality management, 98, 99
  water quality management, 97

United Nations (UN)
  Brundtland Commission, 30
  sustainable development, 30–31
United Nations Center on Transnational
  Corporations, 136
United Nations Commission on Latin
  America and the Caribbean, 114
United Nations Commission on Sustainable Development, 77, 79, 284
United Nations Conference on Environ-
  ment and Development (UNCED),
  20, 34
  Agenda 21,
    critique of, 71, 73–74
    description of, 119
    and GATT, 73, 74
    goals of, 74
    review of, 113
    and trade reform, 72
  agreements signed at, 118
  attendance, 159
  cost internalization, 42
  Polluter Pays Principle, 41, 42
  representation, attendance, 109
  and sustainable development, 45, 111
  and Uruguay Round, GATT, 71
  and the U.S., 291
United Nations Conference on the
  Human Environment, 24, 30–31, 111
United Nations Conference on Trade and
  Development (UNCTAD), 84, 127
  description, 7
  and technology transfer, 142
United Nations Convention on Biological
  Diversity, 34, 118
United Nations Convention on
  International Trade in Endangered
  Species of Wild Fauna and Flora
  (CITES) (1973), 17, 29, 46, 86, 229
United Nations Convention on the Law
  of the Sea (1982), 34
United Nations Environment Programme
  (UNEP), 36, 37, 77, 122, 137
  and environmental protection, 111–12
United Nations Food and Agriculture
  Organization, 87

United States
  Beef Hormone case, 181, 182, 223–24
  business in Mexico, 11, 115
  Clean Air Act, 128
  Commerce Clause, U.S. Constitution,
    276, 277
  Congress, role in trade and environ-
    ment, 264–65
  Council for Business Investment, 125
  Council for International Business, 126
  Department of Agriculture, 206, 251
    and farm bills, 253
  Department of Commerce, 206, 239
  Department of Energy, 206
  employment, 114
  environmental agencies, 206
  environmental policy making, 212
  farm bills, 253
  Food and Drug Administration (FDA),
    16, 206
  and foreign investment, 142
  and GATT dispute panels, 233–34
  harmonization rules for, 276–77
  Integrated Border Environmental Plan,
    49
  and managed trade, 6
  Marine Mammal Protection Act
    (MMPA) (1973), 46, 148, 161, 196,
    204, 263
  and Mexican border, 201
    cleanup of, 196–97
  and protectionism, 4, 239
  public participation in environmental
    policy, 207, 210–11
  Structural Impediments Initiative, 28
  Toxic Substances Control Act (TSCA),
    100
  trade law (Section 201), 131
  Trade Representative (USTR), 47, 198,
    206, 213
    Advisory Committee on Trade
      Policy and Negotiations, 48

  advisory process, 210–11
  environmental advances, 48
  and NAFTA, 50
United States-Canada Free Trade
  Agreement (1987), 28, 29, 38, 110,
  116. *See also* North American Free
  Trade Agreement
Uruguay, 9, 113
Uruguay Round. *See* General Agreement
  on Tariffs and Trade, Uruguay Round
USTR. *See* United States Trade Repre-
  sentative

V
Venezuela, 113
Vienna Convention for the Protection of
  the Ozone Layer, 112
von Moltke, Konrad, 49

W
Washington, George, 209
Washington Post, 204
water quality management
  in Europe, 97, 98
Waxman, Henry, 196
Weiner, Myron, 162
Western Europe, 83
Whiskey Rebellion, 209
WHO. *See* World Health Organization
WICEM. *See* World Industry Conference
  on Environmental Management
World Bank, 59, 115, 121, 135, 136, 192,
  242
World Commission on Environment and
  Development, 111, 193
World Health Organization (WHO), 137
World Industry Conference on Environ-
  mental Management (WICEM), 122,
  125
World Meteorological Organization, 37
World Resources Institute, 255
World Wildlife Fund, 48, 252

Contributors

Charles Arden-Clarke is a policy analyst for World Wildlife Fund International (also known as the World Wide Fund for Nature) in Switzerland, focusing on trade and environment issues, and on environmental issues concerning transnational corporations and agriculture. He has also worked as an environmental consultant with the Political Ecology Research Group in Oxford, U.K., performing scientific and policy analysis on the environmental effects of nuclear power, conservation of the Antarctic, acid rain, and other areas.

John Audley is presently teaching at the University of Maryland, Department of Government and Politics. He was the Director of the Trade and Environent Program for the Sierra Club's International Department, where he represented the Sierra Club in all negotiations regarding NAFTA, GATT, and the OECD working process. He also formerly served as Policy Analyst for Senator Dennis DeConcini, where he developed policy positions on trade and the environment during the Fast Track period. He has published several articles concerning NAFTA.

Norman A. Bailey is a consulting economist and President of Norman A. Bailey, Inc. His clients include governments, corporations, financial institutions, trade associations, and consulting and law firms on four continents. In early 1981, he served as Senior Director of National Security Planning for the National Security Council of the United States and was later named Special Assistant to President Reagan. He has published hundreds of articles and several books on international economics and politics.

Senator Max Baucus has represented Montana in the United States Congress since 1974. He served two terms in the House of Representatives before being elected to the Senate in 1978. Senator Baucus is the Chairman of the Senate Environment and Public Works Committee. He is also a senior member of the Senate Finance Committee, where he chairs the International Trade Subcommittee.

Jagdish Bhagwati is the Arthur Lehman Professor of Economics and Professor of Political Science at Columbia University. In addition, he has served as Economic Policy Advisor to the Director-General of GATT. He has published over 200 scientific papers and is the author and editor of over 30 books. His latest is *The World Trading System at Risk*, (Princeton, 1991). He writes frequently for the *New York Times*, the *Wall Street Journal,* and the *Financial Times*, and reviews occasionally for the *New Republic*.

Steve Charnovitz is Policy Director of the Competitiveness Policy Council in Washington, D.C. From 1987 to 1991, he was a Legislative Assistant on trade and tax issues for House Speaker Jim Wright and Speaker Tom Foley. Before 1987, he was an International Relations officer in the Bureau of International Affairs, U.S. Department of Labor. He has written on trade policy for a number of journals, including the *California Management Review,* the *SAIS Review*, the *World Economy*, the *Journal of World Trade,* and *International Environmental Affairs*.

Herman E. Daly is a Senior Economist in the Environment Department of the World Bank in Washington D.C. Before joining the Bank in 1988, he was Alumni Professor of Economics at Louisiana State University. Co-founder and associate editor of the journal *Ecological Economics*, Mr. Daly has written many articles and several books, including *Steady-State Economics, Economics, Ecology, Ethics* (Island Press); and, with co-author John Cobb, Jr., *For The Common Good: Redirecting The Economy Toward Community, The Environment, and a Sustainable Future*.

Daniel C. Esty is an International Affairs Fellow with the Council on Foreign Relations and a Visiting Fellow at the Institute for International Economics. He formerly served as the Deputy Assistant Administrator for Policy, Planning and Evaluation at the U.S. Environmental Protection Agency, where he headed up its trade and environment work. Mr. Esty is also a member of the Center for International Environmental Law's Trade and Environment Program Advisory Committee.

John H. Jackson is one of the foremost authorities on international trade law and GATT. He is at the University of Michigan Law School where he is Hessel E. Yntema Professor of Law. Professor Jackson also serves on the Advisory Committee to the Center for International Environmental Law's Trade and Environment Program. He formerly served as General Counsel to the United States Trade Representative's Office. Professor Jackson has written numerous articles and books on international trade.

Hal Kane researches topics of environment and economics at the Worldwatch Institute. He is author of *Time for Change: A New Approach to Environment and Development* (Island Press) and co-author of *Vital Signs: The Trends that Are Shaping Our Future*, in addition to numerous articles and essays. Previously he served as a speech writer for Gro Harlem Brundtland.

Pat LeDonne is a Program Analyst with the Global Environment and Trade staff, National Advisory Council for Environmental Policy and Technology (NACEPT), at the U.S. Environmental Protection Agency. She has worked for the states of Alaska and Washington focusing on trade issues, and for the International Trade Administration in the Department of Commerce.

Jan C. McAlpine serves as a Team Leader for the Global Environment and Trade staff in the Office of the Administrator, Office of Cooperative Environmental Management, at the Environmental Protection Agency. Ms. McAlpine is Designated Federal Official for the Trade and Environment Committee of the National Advisory Council for Environmental Policy and Technology (NACEPT). Prior to working for the Federal government, Ms. McAlpine was with the Water Environment Federation.

Robert J. Morris became the Washington Representative of the United States Council for International Business in September 1985 and was named Senior Vice-President in Washington in 1989. By agreement with the involved business organizations, Mr. Morris is currently serving as the U.S. business observer to the Organization for Economic Cooperation and Development (OECD) work on trade and environmental linkages. Mr. Morris had been a career Foreign Service Officer of the United

States, where he served as Deputy to the Under Secretary of State for Economic Affairs, and was also accorded the rank of Ambassador in connection with his work in 1983 coordinating U.S. policy on East-West economic relations.

Ambler H. Moss, Jr. is Dean of the Graduate School of International Studies and Director of the North-South Center, University of Miami. From 1978 to 1982 he served as U.S. Ambassador to Panama. In 1992 he chaired the Western Hemisphere Working Group of the Environmental Protection Agency's Trade and Environment Committee.

Charles S. Pearson, is a Professor at and Director of International Economics at the Paul H. Nitze School of Advanced International Studies, The Johns Hopkins University. He is an expert in the areas of international trade, development, and environmental economics. Professor Pearson has taught graduate level courses for over twenty years at SAIS and was named Director of International Economics in 1988.

Robert Repetto is Vice President and Director of the Program in Economics & Population at the World Resources Institute. Before joining WRI in 1983, Dr. Repetto was an Associate Professor of Economics in the School of Public Health at Harvard University and a member of the economics faculty at Harvard's Center for Population Studies.

Michael Smith is President of SJS Advanced Strategies, an international trade and consulting firm. He has also served as United States Ambassador to GATT, as well as Senior Deputy United States Trade Representative. He is the head of the Advisory Committee to the Center for International Environmental Law's Trade and Environment Program.

Candice Stevens is a Principal Administrator in the Economics Division of the Organization for Economic Cooperation and Development (OECD) Environment Directorate, where she is responsible for trade and environment issues. She previously worked in the OECD Directorate for Science, Technology and Industry on issues relating to trade and the globalization of industry. Prior to coming to the OECD, Dr. Stevens worked for the U.S. Government in the Environmental Protection Agency, the Department of the Interior, the Department of Commerce, and the Congressional Office of Technology Assessment.

Justin R. Ward is a Senior Resource Specialist in the Washington, D.C. office of the Natural Resources Defense Council (NRDC), where he currently directs the organization's agricultural project, as well as its project on international trade and the environment. Mr. Ward has also worked extensively on issues concerning national forest management. He is the author of numerous articles and reports, including *Reaping the Revenue Code*, the 1989 NRDC study of sustainable agriculture and tax policy.

Thomas A. Wathen is a lawyer currently employed as a program officer for conservation and the environment at The Pew Charitable Trusts, where he works on forest protection, marine conservation, and trade policy. He previously worked as a consultant to the Rockefeller Family Fund and the Environmental Grantmakers Association, where he wrote *A Guide to Trade and the Environment*. The author of books and articles on auto safety, solid waste, and small town democracy, Mr. Wathen has worked with consumer and environmental organizations since 1974. He also has served as the executive director of three statewide public interest groups in New York, Colorado, and Indiana.

David A. Wirth is an Assistant Professor of Law at Washington and Lee University School of Law. Mr. Wirth previously was Attorney-Advisor for the Oceans and International Environmental and Scientific Affairs in the Office of the Legal Advisor of the U.S. Department of State in Washington. He has written numerous articles on the legal aspects of trade and the environment.

Konrad von Moltke is a Senior Fellow at the World Wildlife Fund and an Adjunct Professor of Environmental Studies at Dartmouth College in Hanover, New Hampshire. He was the founding Director of the Institute for European Environmental Policy.

ABOUT THE EDITORS

Durwood Zaelke is President of the Center for International Environmental Law (CIEL) and Adjunct Professor of Law and Scholar-in-Residence at the Washington College of Law, The American University, where he also co-directs the CIEL/AU Joint International and Comparative Environmental Law Research Program. Previously he was a Senior Fellow at King's College London, Director of the Sierra Club Legal Defense Fund in Alaska and Washington, D.C., and also practiced with the U.S. Department of Justice, the Environmental Law Institute, and a private law firm.

Paul Orbuch is a staff attorney with the Center for International Environmental Law (CIEL) and an Adjunct Professor of Law at The American University's Washington College of Law. At CIEL, he has counseled government entities, international organizations, and a range of environmental groups on trade and environment issues. Previously he was an associate with Howrey & Simon (Washington, D.C.) specializing in international trade law, and a staff member on the President's Industry Policy Advisory Committee for Trade and Policy Matters.

Robert F. Housman is a staff attorney at the Center for International Environmental Law and an Adjunct Professor of Law at The American University's Washington College of Law. He serves as a consultant on trade and environment issues for the Organization for Economic Cooperation and Development, the U.S. Environmental Protection Agency, and he has counseled a range of environmental groups. Previously he was an associate with Skadden, Arps, Slate, Meager & Flom (Washington, D.C.) and an Aide to Dr. Iann Twinn, House of Commons (London, England).